CW01373210

Black & White
And Red All Over

IN THEIR WORDS

"Although I was the Fairs Cup skipper, Frank played a massive part in helping to steer the ship as our vice captain. He was invaluable to all we managed to achieve and as one of the few local lads involved, it meant the world to him."

BOB MONCUR

"It was a genius move by 'Cloughie' to sign Frank on a free transfer when some thought he was over the hill. Was there ever a more reliable footballer?"

GARRY BIRTLES

"Frank offers a football man's view of life from all angles. Quite simply, he's been there and done it all."

SAM ALLARDYCE

"There were loads of top-notch wingers in our era and not one of them got the better of Frank."

MALCOLM MACDONALD

"He was the best back-up man in the business. I always knew he was there for me."

JOHN ROBERTSON

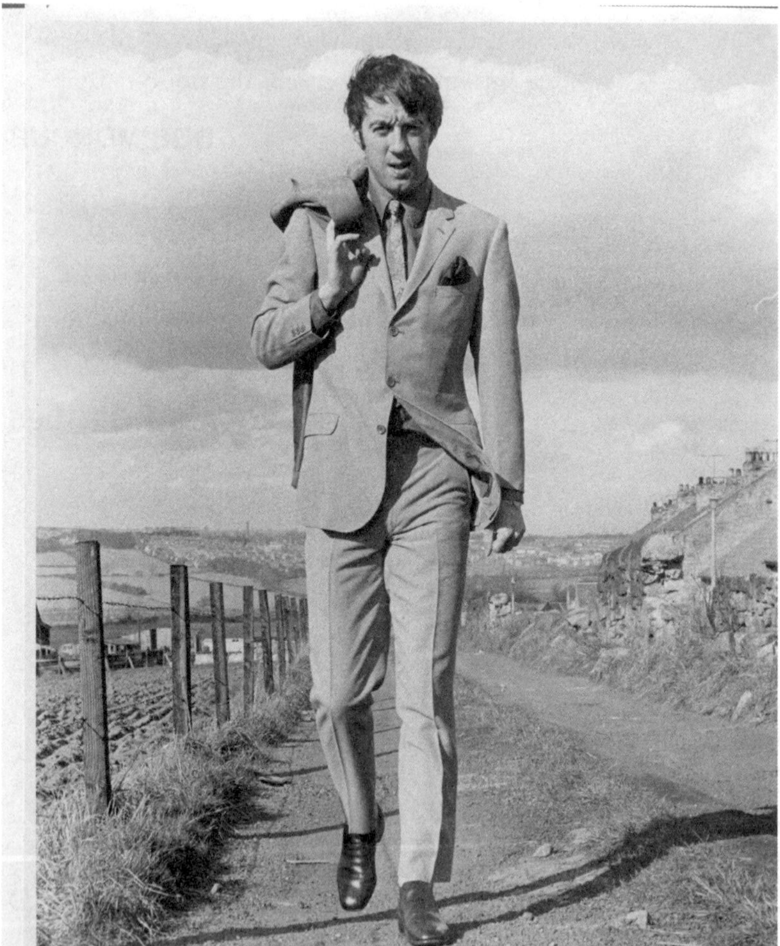

FRANK CLARK

The Autobiography

WITH **TERRY BOWLES**

www.frank-clark.co.uk

Frank Clark – The Autobiography
Black & White And Red All Over

First published in Great Britain
in 2018 by Bowles Clark

Copyright © Bowles Clark 2018

Frank Clark and Terry Bowles have asserted their rights under the Copyright, Designs and Patents Act 1988 to be identified as the authors of this work.

ISBN (HB) 978-1-78926-782-2
ISBN (PB) 978-1-78926-783-9

Printed in Great Britain by Bell & Bain Ltd, Glasgow

CONTENTS

-    Foreword by Howard Wilkinson
1. Tunnel vision en-route to Europe
2. Why would I want to be a footballer?
3. Tommy Smith's tackle nearly changed my life
4. Don't get 'Shirty' - Toon are going up
5. Pele, Best and a backdoor route into Europe
6. We were the Fairest of them all
7. On Ramsey's radar – and a bizarre goal in Europe
8. Bandy legs and bushy sideburns... a new hero has landed
9. All downhill after Cup Final shambles
10. Injury-prone? It helps when you work for a genius
11. 'Robbo' sees the light as we fly to promotion
12. Chicken 'n chips - our recipe for the Double
13. The biggest prize in Europe – what a way to sign off!
14. Roker Roar was special - pity it didn't last
15. New life as honorary Eastender
16. Sixth in line for Clough's throne
17. Miami mission sets up dream combination
18. Tipped for England... but it all fell apart
19. Poisoned chalice? It didn't have to be
20. In the hot-seat with no place to hide
-    Valued subscribers

Foreword by
HOWARD WILKINSON

Outstanding memories of sporting achievements, lodged in your psyche over the past 50 years, can often gain a lustre that grows ever brighter. Every now and again, however, a person comes along whose array of special achievements are never given quite the credit and publicity they deserve. As you wend your way through the revealing pages of this book you will quickly realise that Frank Clark is one such person. He is low on profile, high on achievement. Other rare surprises to be found within the fabric of the story are his willingness to reveal, admit and explain his mistakes and their consequences. He also speaks about, as he puts it, "his incredible luck at repeatedly falling into good teams." I know many of those who played with him and they will forcefully insist that Frank Clark made *their* team a much better side.

I vividly remember the day Frank and I first met, 57 years ago. It was a bitterly cold, bleak and misty afternoon in late December and the pitch at Doncaster was frost bound. Frank was playing left back for Durham Grammar Schools and I was on the right wing for Yorkshire Grammar Schools. We won, I scored and that was about the only kick of the ball he allowed me!

In many ways since that first encounter our careers have run in parallel. In fact we are members of the same exclusive 'club'. You can probably count on the fingers of one hand the number of people who have been a player, manager and chairman at the same professional club. Frank has filled all three roles at Nottingham Forest, I did the same with Sheffield Wednesday.

I felt honoured when I was asked to write the Foreword for his autobiography. Over the years our friendship has grown and I have developed the utmost respect for him personally and professionally. There are, however, rare occasions when friendship can be tested and that especially applies when he treats us to one of his solo guitar and singing sessions!

I cannot pay him a bigger compliment than to say that if I was managing today and he was playing, he would be near the very top of my list of wanted players. Give me 11 Frank Clarks and I'd be very confident of winning things – and sleeping soundly the night before any game. He had all the qualities you look for in a player and was seriously good at what he did. He worked hard and dedicated himself to becoming the best he could possibly be. He started as an amateur with Crook Town and finished up a two-time winner of top European competitions. His incredible record of more than 650 first-class appearances with Newcastle United and Nottingham Forest illustrates his remarkable levels of consistency.

Was he a shouter and bawler on the pitch? No. Did a manager have problems with his discipline or his relationships with other players? No. Was he quick to take responsibility? Yes he was. Frank was a natural leader and the complete footballer.

The bigger the challenge, the better he'd respond and there was no better example than when Newcastle handed him a free transfer at the age of 31. Despite the fact that he was – and still is – their most decorated player and stands fourth in their all-time list of appearance makers, clubs were not exactly queuing up to sign him. Given that situation, lesser characters might well have faded away. Frank did just the opposite. The next four years at Forest were the most successful of his career. He helped them win promotion, then the League Championship and two League Cups before rounding things off by playing in the European Cup Final against Malmö in his last appearance as a player. He is living proof that "talent always bounces back up."

Frank always had a lot more going for him than just his technical competence as a player. He was a manager's dream with his consistent high performance in matches and low maintenance in between them. Quiet and unassuming in everyday life, he was transformed on match-days. He was trustworthy, strong-minded, determined and honest. Above all, he was a leader who could always be relied upon in the toughest of battles.

His career in management lasted the best part of 20 years – including a lengthy spell as Leyton Orient's managing director – and the stand-out moment has to be when he won the LMA's 'Manager of the Year' Award in 1995. Winning the respect of peers and professional colleagues is the best possible affirmation of a person's capabilities and the award is decided by individual votes cast by each member of the association. It is presented to the manager who, irrespective of club's finishing league position, has made the most of the players, money and other attributes at his disposal. Frank took the award after his exciting Forest team finished third in their first season back in the top flight.

Although it could be said that he ended the managerial section of his career too early, it has enabled the League Managers' Association to have the benefit of his experience. When Graham Taylor, Lawrie McMenemy, John Camkin, Olaf Dixon and I got together in the autumn of 1992 to form the LMA it was the likes of Frank we had in mind as people who would join our committee, be willing to commit to our objectives and fight for the cause. He had a spell as our part-time chief executive in those early days and for many years has been our vice-chairman.

As those who really know Frank would expect, there are no great sensation-seeking passages in this book. It is, however, a fascinating insight into the life of an ordinary, humble guy who achieved extraordinary things on and off the pitch. You also get a very accurate account of the way football and footballers have changed over the past 40-plus years.

In 2019 it will be 50 years since Frank was an ever-present in the Newcastle team that won the Inter-Cities Fairs Cup and 40 years since he made his last *ever* appearance as a player in the European Cup Final. These are two giant milestones for a man who wore the No.3 shirt with great distinction.

***Howard Wilkinson** was a player with Sheffield Wednesday and Brighton & Hove Albion before his first management job at Boston United. He then went on to manage Notts County, Sheffield Wednesday and Leeds United to promotion – and was the last Englishman to guide a team to the League Championship when Leeds took the title in 1992. The long-serving chairman of the League Manager's Association, he had two spells as caretaker-manager of England during his five years as the FA Technical Director from 1997-2002.*

My Thanks

People tell me I'm a contradiction and that's difficult to dispute. Why would a naturally shy person who has never been totally comfortable in the limelight spend his entire working life doing one of the most high profile jobs imaginable? Even in my leisure time, the biggest buzz I get is to play music in front of an audience. It's strange, I know, and I don't have an explanation for it. Nor do I have an explanation for how I've managed to live such a wonderful life, continually finding myself involved with teams that won things – and enjoying all the trappings that go with it.

Maybe it all goes back to the start in life my mum and dad gave me. You could never describe us as a wealthy family but they gave me everything they possibly could, both materially and spiritually. I can never thank them enough for the upbringing they gave me. This book is dedicated to them – and to the rest of my family. My wife Pam, daughters Lisa and Nicky and my sons-in-law, Paul and Duncan, could not have been more supportive. I have three wonderful grandchildren – Grace, Jack and Noah – and one of the main reasons I wanted to produce my autobiography was to provide them with a record of what the old man did with his life.

Special thanks must go to Terry Bowles, the writer who has worked closely with me to make it happen. He has been around the Nottingham football and cricket scene for even longer than me and I've thoroughly enjoyed our regular sessions, re-living the old days. Terry has been meticulous in his research and that's just as well because my memory often plays tricks after all these years. I believe

Black & White And Red All Over to be a true and accurate record of my life inside and out of football. If anything has got skewed along the way, it certainly hasn't been intentional.

I'm very grateful to Sam Bowles from the design agency STENCIL for his skill and enthusiasm in turning the words into a visually engaging book. My good friend John Gibson has provided invaluable support as our North East 'consultant' and John Phelan and Michael Manuel were extremely helpful with our Crook Town research.

I'm grateful to Ken Jones and Mark Radford for proof-reading the copy before it went to press and thanks also go to the Newcastle Chronicle, Nottingham Post, Northern Echo, JMS Photography and Nottingham Central Library for providing us with photographs.

I would also like to express my appreciation to supporters of every club I spent time with during my near-60 years in the game. I have been stunned by the level of support I've received from those committed fans up-and-down the country. I wish you the best of luck for the coming years, chasing your respective dreams on the field.

Finally, I'd like to sign off by thanking all the players and coaches I worked with for making my whole journey such a marvellous experience. Of course some of us were better than others but we all did our best and most of the time, we did it with a smile on our faces. I still find it incredible to think that I played for 17 years and in all that time I only worked for two managers – Joe Harvey and Brian Clough. I'm indebted to them both.

I hope you enjoy the book. Our intention has been to delve into history, offer an insight into the how the game has changed throughout the generations while also providing an insight into what it takes to be a player, a manager, a managing-director and a chairman. Hopefully we have managed to achieve that.

The Player

Crook Town (1961-62 – 38 League & Cup appearances)
Newcastle United (1962-75 – 486* League & Cup appearances)
Nottingham Forest (1975-79 – 156* League & Cup appearances)
(*Totals include appearances in FA Cup, League Cup, European Cup,
Inter-Cities Fairs Cup, Anglo-Italian Cup, Anglo-Scottish Cup and Texaco Cup)

Honours
1961-62 – FA Amateur Cup winner
1964-65 – Second Division promotion winner
1968-69 – Inter-Cities Fairs Cup winner
1972-73 – Anglo-Italian Cup winner
1973-74 – FA Cup runner-up
1973-74 – Texaco Cup winner
1974-75 – Texaco Cup winner
1976-77 – Second Division promotion winner
1976-77 – Anglo-Scottish Cup winner
1977-78 – Football League Championship winner
1977-78 – Football League Cup winner
1978-79 – European Cup winner
1978-79 – Football League Cup winner
1978-79 – Football League Championship runner-up

Representative Honours
England Youth (3 appearances in 1962)
England Amateurs (1 appearance in 1962)
The Football League (1 appearance in 1969)

Chapter One
TUNNEL VISION EN-ROUTE TO EUROPE

"It's Brian Clough," said the distinctive voice at the other end of the phone line. "Would you like to come and play for me?" That call didn't just turn my life around – it did it in such a way that even the most imaginative of fiction writers would claim the story was ridiculously far-fetched.

Five months short of my 32nd birthday, I'd been tossed onto the dreaded 'soccer scrapheap' by the only club that I ever really wanted to play for. My beloved Newcastle United didn't want me any more and I found myself in the situation I'd often read or heard about but never for one minute thought I would experience first-hand.

Picture the scene at St James' Park in April 1975. We'd just lost our final game of the season – 2-1 against Birmingham City – and long after the final whistle, I was the only one left in the dressing room, apart from our coach Keith Burkinshaw. That was nothing unusual. I was always the last player to get changed and Keith and I would sit there for ages, reflecting on the highs and lows of the game. Our mood was particularly gloomy because although we'd finished 15th in the old First Division, the second half of the season had been awful, and the fans had made their feelings known. But that was nothing compared to how we felt when Joe Harvey joined us. Our long-serving manager had just paid a brief visit to the Boardroom and we knew straight away that there was something amiss as he walked through the door. Eventually, after hopping from one leg to the other, he said: "I don't quite know how to tell you this... we've all been sacked. I've been moved upstairs as general manager, you (Keith) are fired and you're (me) being given a free transfer."

In an instant, the bottom fell out of my world. I was the club captain. I'd given everything I could possibly muster to the Newcastle cause over the previous 11 years and according to the people who understand these things, I was – and still am – the most decorated player in their history. Jackie Milburn, Bobby Mitchell and Bobby Cowell might dispute that claim because they won three FA Cup winners' medals in the Fifties. But I'd helped United to win promotion from the Second Division as champions in my first full season and during the course of making 486 League and Cup appearances – more than any other player in the post-War era before Shay Given overtook me – I'd figured in the teams that won the Inter-Cities Fairs Cup, The Anglo-Italian Cup and Texaco Cup (twice), and been a runner-up in the FA Cup. I was in a complete daze as I drove away from the ground. I was hit with all sorts of emotions – and not one of them was positive. No matter how you tried to dress it up, getting a free transfer was exactly the same as being sacked. It suggested I had failed to do my job properly and inevitably, I felt ashamed and embarrassed as well as sad, and anxious about what the future might hold. Above all, it soon became clear that I would have to totally re-think the life that I loved so much. Pam and I were really happy living in Whitley Bay, some 10 miles out of Newcastle on the Northumbria coast, and just three months earlier we'd moved into a beautiful new house. When I arrived home she was in the process of putting up curtains and I remember saying: "I hope they are only temporary ones."

Looking back, I can see now that I was being staggeringly naïve but I honestly believed that I would be at Newcastle in one capacity or another for the rest of my working life. I guess that feeling was based in no small part on the dealings I'd had a couple of months earlier with our chairman Lord Westwood. I'd had an approach at that time from Wally Barnes, the former Arsenal and Wales full back, who was looking for players who might be interested in getting involved in the new 'American Dream'. Soccer was just beginning to take off on that side of the Atlantic and when Wally offered me the chance to join the newly formed San Jose Earthquakes, it really appealed to me. Pam fancied it strongly and as our daughter Lisa was only young, there would be no great upheaval involved. The financial rewards would be considerable, the lifestyle looked fantastic – and there was no telling where it might lead.

Unusually for me, I'd missed a lot of games that season because of various injuries and that had opened the door for Alan Kennedy to stake a strong claim for the left-back spot. He was clearly an emerging talent and in order to accommodate us both in the team, I often found myself playing as a left-sided central defender. Even so, there were bound to be doubts about what the future might hold for me and with such an attractive offer on the table, I was duty bound to discuss it with Joe Harvey. A lot of players, particularly in his early days, were scared of Joe because he was such a forceful character but we'd always had an excellent relationship. We trusted each other. He could see what a difficult decision I was facing and suggested I should take it to the chairman. That wasn't an easy thing to do but I explained to Lord Westwood that if he could assure me that I had a future at Newcastle, I would be perfectly happy to stay. The meeting didn't last long because the chairman insisted I was going nowhere. I went home and told Pam to forget all thoughts of making a fresh start. On the back of that, I certainly believed I would spend the remainder of my playing career at St James' Park and would probably be there long afterwards. Not so. Football can be a cruel business in all sorts of ways and what's good today, so often doesn't hold good tomorrow.

When the axe fell, I got the feeling that it wasn't a unanimous decision to give me a free because of the strange way the club handled my departure. There was no big media announcement, as you would normally expect. They tried to leak it out in a low profile way but I made sure my journalist friends were fully in the picture – not least because I needed them to advertise my availability to other clubs. "Don't worry," they said. "You'll get loads of offers". A month later, the only interest had been 'soft' inquiries from Hartlepool and Doncaster Rovers, who were managed by my former captain Stan Anderson. I didn't get beyond telephone conversations because both clubs were operating in the Fourth Division and I didn't feel ready to drop down that far. But maybe I would have to re-think that the way things were taking shape. I thought I still had at least a year or two left in me at a decent level and I was bitterly disappointed not to get more offers. Of course it started to make me doubt myself. Even old friends who had moved into management that I half-expected would call were steering clear of me and as I later discovered, the word on the grapevine was that I'd become injury-prone.

One man, fortunately, was not put off by the rumours. At least Brian Clough thought I still had something to offer and when he called, I jumped at the chance to go and meet him at Scotch Corner Hotel. Mind you, I didn't exactly give a clear impression that I was keen. I arrived 90 minutes late for our meeting after my car broke down – right in middle of the Tyne Tunnel! In those days, footballers received a loyalty bonus from their clubs after completing five and 10 years of service and I 'blew' my entire 10-year payday on a Triumph Stag. I was so proud of it. That car was my absolute pride and joy but I certainly wasn't thinking in affectionate terms when it let me down at such a crucial time. There were no such things as mobile phones in those days, of course, but I managed to get hold of Pam. I asked her to call the Hotel and explain the situation to 'Cloughie'. By the time the AA had rescued me and I eventually arrived, I had no idea whether she had actually managed to make contact. Also, I wouldn't have been in the least surprised if he was halfway back to Nottingham by that time. In fact, I was relieved to find he was still there waiting for me and I'll be forever grateful for that. People tell all sorts of stories about him being intolerant – and most of them are true – but thankfully, he was in a good mood that day.

I'd met 'Cloughie' once before because I played in his testimonial at Sunderland after a serious knee injury had wrecked his career. Roker Park was packed that night as people flocked to pay homage to a great goal-scorer. The game was between Sunderland and an All Star XI, who included the complete Newcastle back-four of David Craig, Bobby Moncur, Ollie Burton and me. Even as a player 'Cloughie' was quite opinionated and what struck you instantly was his charisma and self-confidence. He was just different and it was certainly no surprise to me that he quickly made his mark in management. Just three years before we met at Scotch Corner, he had taken Derby County to the League Championship, having transformed them from a mediocre Second Division club, and now he was trying to repeat that feat at Nottingham Forest.

It turned out that he'd been alerted to the fact that I was available by Doug Weatherall, the Daily Mail's football correspondent in the North East, but if I had any thoughts about playing hard to get, he was quick to clear the air where that was concerned. "There are two reasons why I'm interested in signing you," he said. "The first is that there's no one in our club who can play left back and the second is that you're cheap." That was fair enough. I was just delighted that someone of his status thought I was good enough to play in his team – and you didn't need to spend long in his company to get very excited about the prospect of working with him. The negotiations didn't take long. I had a figure in mind that I thought I was worth but that was instantly knocked back. "I can't afford that," he said. From then on, I pretty much nodded along with the terms that were set out. It wasn't a great offer but money was not my main motivation. I quickly realised that I wanted to work for him and after we had spent two hours chatting before heading off in different directions, I knew for sure that this was the way forward for me.

In the back of my mind, as I made my way back to Newcastle, was the thought that 'Cloughie' had history when it came to giving players a new lease of life at a stage when most people thought they had very little left in the tank. He had signed Dave Mackay for Derby when he was 33-years-old, converted him from midfielder to a central defender, and he went on to have a huge influence at the Baseball Ground. I wasn't stupid enough to think that I was in the same class as Mackay because he was a great player. Widely recognised as the driving force behind the Tottenham team that won the League and Cup double in 1960-61, he showed incredible determination in fighting his way back to fitness after twice breaking his left leg, and then making a fresh start at Derby. He had moved on before they lifted the League Championship, but 'Cloughie" never left people in any doubt about the part he played in setting the Rams' rise in motion.

Could I do something similar at the City Ground? Could I use the 11-years of know-how that I'd picked up at Newcastle to help him develop a team that would be capable of challenging for honours? The more I thought about it, the more I fancied it and by the time I arrived home, I felt confident enough to promise Pam that we'd be fine. The previous few weeks had been traumatic to say the least. Neither of us had ever really been south of the Tyne Tunnel and she was understandably upset about the thought of moving away from her family and the close circle of friends we'd made. I just had a sense that everything might fall into place if we embraced the situation. Ironically, I got a call around that time from Gordon Lee, who had been appointed as team manager of Newcastle when Joe Harvey moved upstairs, and he wanted to take me back to St James' Park. He was furious that they'd allowed me to go and was pretty persuasive. It threw me into a right quandary... but not for long. I knew it was time to move on and write a new chapter in my career, as well as my life.

The parting shot from 'Cloughie' as we shook hands before leaving

Scotch Corner was to say: "I'm not going to make you my captain, you know. I've already got one of those and he's called John McGovern. I just want you to come and play and show all your good habits, like you have done throughout your career." That suited me fine because I really didn't want any extra responsibilities. I just wanted to work at keeping myself fit and maintaining a good level of performance. When I'd sat down and tried to analyse where things had gone wrong for me at Newcastle, I was convinced that the captaincy had affected me. The club was not being very well run at that time and lots of people had issues. I took my responsibilities as captain very seriously and consequently, I constantly found myself fighting other people's battles. Not only did that affect my form, it earned me a reputation in some quarters as something of a troublemaker. I definitely didn't want to go down that road again so what 'Cloughie' said was actually music to my ears.

Incidentally, I wasn't the only one embarking on a new venture. Keith Burkinshaw and I went to the annual Football Writers' Dinner, which was always a glamorous end-of-season affair in London, and I looked forward to being invited as a guest of one of our local journalists. Keith was a blunt Yorkshireman who had initially joined Newcastle as reserve-team coach and we had a great relationship. I felt really sorry for him when he was sacked in such a ruthless fashion but his life also turned around while we were at that dinner. Terry Neill, who was Tottenham's manager at the time, came across to our table to talk to Malcolm Macdonald and by the end of that conversation, after we'd given Keith a glowing reference, he'd been offered the chance to join their coaching team.

That was the start of something big for him because a few years later, by which time he was Tottenham's manager, he caused an incredible stir throughout world football by signing Argentina's World Cup winning pair of Ossie Ardiles and Ricky Villa. With a little help from some friends, Keith and I had managed to reverse our fortunes after that traumatic afternoon at St James' Park. Even so, I couldn't possibly have imagined what was in store for me over the next four and a half years. By the time I left the City Ground, I had figured in a Second Division promotion success and helped to win the League Championship, the League Cup and the European Cup.

That League Cup success came in a replay against Liverpool after we had drawn 0-0 at Wembley. A John Robertson penalty won us the second game at Old Trafford and what a sweet moment it was when I stepped up to collect my winners' medal from Lord Westwood, who was President of the Football League. I was very tempted to make some sarcastic comment but when it came to the crunch, we just smiled knowingly at each other.

Chapter Two
WHY WOULD I WANT TO BE A FOOTBALLER?
1960-62

Tears get shed on a very regular basis at Wembley Stadium. Winners are overcome by emotion as a Cup Final victory takes them to a peak that many didn't believe possible while losers are left completely crestfallen. Even drawn games can sometimes get the old 'waterworks' going... I can vouch for that.

My career was just starting to take off in 1962 and at the age of 18, I was in demand. I'd been selected to go with England Youth to take part in the UEFA Youth Tournament in Romania after making a good impression in the squad for games in this country against Wales and West Germany. But the problem was that the follow-up trip to Romania just happened to overlap with the FA Amateur Cup Final – and I'd been named in Crook Town's team to take on Hounslow at Wembley. Amateur Cup Finals were a really big deal in those days, not something you walked away from lightly, but I wanted the best of both worlds. In the end, a compromise was reached that suited all parties and I set off for London with my case full to the brim. As soon as the final was over, I would be whisked away to join up with the England lads.

Best laid plans and all that... Crook ended up drawing 1-1 after a pretty ordinary game. We thought we had done enough to sneak it after edging in front midway through the second half but Jack Taylor, who was destined to go on and referee the World Cup Final in 1974, controversially allowed Hounslow a late equaliser. Our goalkeeper Ray Snowball safely collected a corner as it swung into the six-yard box but seconds later, he was sent flying by a fierce challenge. No way was the contact shoulder-to-shoulder, which was allowed in those days, but a goal was given when the ball finished in the back of our net and 30 minutes of extra time couldn't settle it.

Of course it was great to play at Wembley, especially for an impressionable youngster who was still at school, and I was proud of the fact that I'd played in every round on the way to the final. I vividly recall shaking hands before the start with Princess Alexandra, the Guest of Honour. I also remember the lush grass being very tiring on the legs and I was absolutely shattered at the finish. I was certainly in no fit state to face up to what came next. The replay was to take place the following Saturday but if I decided to play in that, I'd have to pull out of the England Youth trip. My dad was adamant that he wanted me to stick to my plans with England but our coach George Wardle, a powerful man within the Crook set-up, was equally firm in his view that I should play in the replay at Middlesbrough. He argued there would be other opportunities for me to play for England but I might never get another chance to claim an Amateur Cup winner's medal. They marched me around the famous track that surrounded the Wembley pitch to try and resolve the situation – and they pulled no punches. It was incredibly traumatic. I knew I'd have to upset one of them and I was in floods of tears as I struggled to make my decision. In the end, I chose to turn out in the replay at Ayresome Park, where three goals in the space of nine first half minutes set us up for a 4-1 win.

It was the biggest day so far of a life that had begun on 9th September 1943, when I was born at Highfield in County Durham. It wasn't a mining village, as many were in that area, but you could never describe it as picturesque. We lived there mainly because my mother's family did, and we were very close knit. The War was still on, of course, and we had our share of grief because two of my uncles were killed in action. Dad was a Bevin Boy, which meant he was conscripted to work in the pits throughout the War, and we were incredibly fortunate because it also meant that he could continue to live at home. Looking back, I had an idyllic childhood. I attended the local primary school, just up the road, and I'll never forget the day when they matter-of-factly revealed the results of our 11-Plus exams in the middle of the school assembly. I won a place at Hookergate Grammar School and the next seven years really shaped my life. I had a wonderful education in an environment that suited me perfectly. Academically I did well and I was also given every encouragement to make my mark across a variety of sports.

Bart Harwood was the teacher who had set me on my way in football, picking me to play in the newly formed Highfield Primary School team, alongside lads who were three years older than me. Our kit used to be handed out the day before the game and we were then responsible for looking after it. I was so proud as I made my way home on that first occasion, holding my shirt of green & black quarters.

Football quickly became my obsession. I couldn't get enough of it. Every spare minute I was out on the ash pitch at the local recreation ground and no matter how many turned up to play, I usually got a game because I was one of the few who had a ball. Sometimes we played a game called 'gates' outside our home and I still have a guilty conscience about Mrs Moon, an elderly neighbour. We were not looking to cause problems but we must have made her life a misery. One day, when the ball flew into her garden, she refused to give it back. Dad eventually went to retrieve it and when he gave Mrs Moon a piece of his mind she called the Police. He ended up getting a very stern ticking off.

The whole experience when I got to Grammar School was fantastic. After earning an A stream place, I loved the work, loved the sport and became part of a group who have been my friends for life. I was a fixture in the school football team rising through the age groups and by the time I represented the Derwent Valley district team and Durham County under-15s, scouts from League clubs were regularly banging on our front door. West Brom, who had two scouts based in the North East, were particularly keen and I did agree to go there and play in a trial game. They wanted to sign me but with no motorways at that time it felt as if it had taken two days to get there. I couldn't see any future in that. In the end, I signed as an amateur with Sunderland and part of the reason for doing so was to ward off the scouts. Once I'd committed myself to them, it technically meant that no other club could approach me. I used to dash straight from school to train there two nights a week and it was a right performance. It involved catching two buses and a train each way but it was certainly good for my game. I was working alongside some senior part-timers like Len Ashurst and Dickie Rooks and I couldn't fail to learn from the experience. At around this time, my mother stepped in. She could tell that all the travelling and late nights was taking its toll and rightly insisted that I had to keep the correct balance between school and football – especially as I was coming up to my 'O' level exams. Sunderland were brilliant about it. They could have made life difficult but when we went to see the manager, Alan Brown, he understood the situation and agreed to release me.

It wasn't a case of having to twist my arm because schoolwork was really important to me. Although many people seemed to take it for granted that I was heading for a career in football, my sights were firmly set on going to university and gaining a chemistry degree. My 'O' level exams went well. I got nine passes – including numerous distinctions – and opted to stay at school and do chemistry, physics and maths at 'A' level. I was still loving my football though, and I knew I was getting better all the time.

Leaving Sunderland meant I was back on the 'open market' and it wasn't long before scouts started banging on our door again. One of them, Newcastle's chief scout Temple Lisle, was particularly persistent and it actually reached the stage where my parents automatically set an extra place for Sunday breakfast because they knew he'd be round. Even so, I wasn't about to be easily won over. I wasn't at all convinced that I wanted to be a professional footballer. It just seemed to be a very hazardous occupation and there were definitely no guarantees about the future. The maximum wage was still in force for players so there were no big financial attractions and virtually every week you heard stories about players having their careers ended prematurely by injury. Most people couldn't understand it – not least my dad – but I was very reluctant to commit to that way of life. University was my No. 1 goal and anyway, I was very happy with my life the way it was.

It was around this time that I discovered cricket. The game had never really interested me but a couple of friends persuaded me to join Lintz CC, who were just about the best club in the region. They were run by John Cromarty, the captain of the 1st XI, and his brother and they instilled strong values. They always wanted to win and play the game properly and that fitted with the way in which I always approached my sport. I soon won a place as an opening batsman in the junior team, then got into the first-team at the age of 16. Concentration and intensity were always key to my batting and as a comparatively late starter, I was very much a 'coached' player. I discovered how to play through attending coaching sessions and worked hard to develop my skills the way I was taught them. I played for the county under-16s and although I was never good enough to step up, I really enjoyed it. I turned out for Lintz until about the age of 26 and playing three times a week was a good way to help me keep fit. But it became difficult when the football seasons got increasingly longer and I decided to end my cricket career after being told by Newcastle that the only cure for a niggling groin strain was to rest it completely throughout the whole summer.

Incidentally, it was through the cricket club that I got to know Joe Jacques, and he became my best mate. He was a year behind me and after leaving school at 15, he went to play football for Preston.

They were a major force at that time and it was quite something that a year later, he was the regular centre-forward in their reserves. It was Joe who talked me into signing as an amateur for Preston – much to the annoyance of Newcastle. I liked the Preston scout, who often used to bang on our door, so I agreed to join them. But it was mainly because it meant I'd be able to spend my school holidays with Joe. On one occasion while I was there I was picked to play alongside Howard Kendall in an FA Youth Cup tie. On another, I played at centre-half in a practice match against Alex Dawson. He was a beast of a man and that unforgettable experience could easily have put me off football for life! Somewhere along the line things went awry for Joe because he changed from being a striker with a great career in front of him into a 'nasty' central defender. I often used to go and watch him play for Darlington and when he married during that period, I was his best man. He also had spells with Southend and Gillingham and the last contact I had with him was when he sent me letter when I was at Not-

Third from the left on the back row of Highfield School Under-11s.

tingham Forest and we were preparing to play Malmö in the European Cup Final. He was coaching in Sweden at that time and wondered if I might appreciate some information about how they played. I thought long and hard about whether I should hand the letter on to Brian Clough because he didn't take kindly to being told how he should do things. In the end, I did. It wasn't too long afterwards that I got a call from Bob Jackson, a former team mate at the cricket club, telling me that Joe had died. Why is it that life delivers a good 'hand' to some people and a dreadful one to others? I thank my lucky stars every day for the way things turned out for me but Joe came from exactly the opposite extreme. His life and family were touched by tragedy. As a youngster he was so much more talented than me but he never managed to fulfil that potential as a knee injury ended his career. Then he died of a heart attack at the ridiculously young age of 36.

I didn't spend too long with Preston. As with Sunderland, they agreed to release me when it became evident that the travelling distance from the North East to Deepdale meant we'd have very little contact. That didn't stand in the way of progress. At the age of 17, while playing for Highfield in the Northern Alliance, I was involved in a huge upset when we knocked Crook Town out of the Durham Senior Cup. They were one of the giants of the amateur game and I must have made a good impression because a few months later, I was invited to join them. Bert Steward, the club captain, seriously damaged a knee in the early part of the 1961-62 season – and never played again. I was so flattered that Crook officials thought I was good enough to replace such a key man and I made my debut for them three days before my 18th birthday. We managed a 1-0 win against Shildon in that midweek fixture and a section of the Northern Echo's match report read like this: "The Crook leader Tobin again failed and this was his sixth game without a goal. Garbutt, making a first appearance at inside right after transfer from Bishop Auckland, did nothing out of the ordinary and of Crook's three newcomers the left back Clark shaped best." My career in the 'man's world' was up and running.

It's difficult to explain what a big deal top level amateur football was at that time – and many of the finest teams in the country were packed into the south-west corner of Co. Durham. Consequently, a high percentage of our Northern League games were local derbies and the standard was terrific. We regularly pulled in crowds of around 5,000 for home games and when you think that the population of the town was less than 15,000, the football club was right at the heart of the community. Many of our players – like Ray Snowball, Jimmy McMillan and Arnold Coates – were easily good enough to play League Football but because the maximum wage was still in force, they couldn't afford to leave their day jobs and turn professional. Snowball, for example, was not only a superb goalkeeper but also the headmaster at a local school. It was a huge privilege for me to be involved. Rather than being intimidated, I found that I thrived on the atmosphere and competitive nature of things. I was very much the 'baby' of the team but I lapped it up. The lads were great with me – and I never felt out of place.

It was a myth, of course, that amateur players didn't get paid and I was grateful for the £4 that appeared in my boot after every game. That was a lot of money to me and it was the first I'd ever earned. It took me a good 45 minutes to get from home to Crook so my dad was delighted when I passed my driving test. That meant he could loan me his car – a tank-like Ford Consul that drank petrol at an incredible rate – to get myself to training and back twice a week and the 'boot money' enabled me to pay my share of the costs.

I played in 28 games during that 1961-62 season. I also played in every round of the FA Amateur Cup as we fought our way past Ossett Albion, Windsor & Eton, Dagenham, Wimbledon and West Auckland to claim a place in the final. More than 43,000 people turned up at Wembley to watch us draw with Hounslow before we completed the job in the replay at Middlesbrough.

Still the scouts kept banging on our door and the interest intensified as international honours came my way – just as George Wardle promised they would while we were at Wembley on Cup Final day. I got a letter in the post notifying me that I'd been selected for a trial with England Amateurs. It was to take place in London. We played a Probables v Possibles match and I was grateful to Snowball for not only looking after me, but also introducing me to Hammersmith Palais on the Saturday night! I was picked in the England squad to play two matches. I didn't figure against Italy in Ascoli but did play in a goalless draw against The Netherlands in Zwolle. Pulling on that England shirt was an experience all on it's own. I cannot tell you how proud it made me feel and I was delighted when I got to taste that experience again with England Youth. I'd already made my debut at that level against West Germany, in a the team that included the likes of Sunderland goalkeeper Jim Montgomery and Arsenal winger George Armstrong, and went straight from the Amateurs' tour to play in a double-header for the youth team in Israel. We won 3-1 and then lost 2-1.

It wasn't all good news, though, because my 'A' level exams were getting ever closer and during that hectic period, I allowed football to get in the way of my schoolwork. Some fortunate types sail through exams with the minimum of effort but I was no genius. I was very aware that if I wanted to get the grades that would take me to university, I needed to work hard. That meant doing plenty of revision but although I took loads of books with me when I went on tour, I don't think I opened a single one. I paid a big price for that because when my results arrived, I'd got an A in chemistry and B in physics, but my D grade in maths was classed as a failure. You didn't get to re-take your exams in those days and there was no such thing as 'clearing'. My dream had been shattered. The university offers I'd had from Sheffield and Newcastle were withdrawn and although I had the option to go to teachers' training college, I didn't want to be a teacher. For the first time in my life, I had to contend with failure. It really hurt and I reacted very badly to it. In fact, my mum was very concerned about me as I moped around the house after leaving school. All my eggs had been put into that one basket. I had no idea what I was going to do now.

Full-time football was always an option, of course, but I was still reluctant to go down that road, even though the maximum wage for players had recently been abolished. The summer came and went and I reported back to Crook for the new season. Something had to give, however, and Newcastle's incredible persistence finally paid off. I still wasn't prepared to fully commit but we came up with a package in November 1962 that suited all of us. They helped me to get a job, working three days a week as a lab technician in the Bio-Chemistry Department at the Royal Victoria Infirmary in Newcastle. The rest of the time I spent working as a part-time professional with United, training and playing in the reserves.

I was sad to leave Crook because I owed them so much. It also really upset me that being a professional footballer meant I was no longer allowed to take part in the 20-a-side matches on the ash pitch close to my home. I suppose you can't have everything.

Turning out for the mighty Lintz Cricket Club – 'concentration and intensity' were always key to my batting.

PLAYER - MANAGER - CHAIRMAN 35

Hounslow score the equalizer as Patterson shoulder charges the ball from Ray Snowball's grasp.

I'm the big bloke on the back row of the Preston Youth team. Standing next to me is Howard Kendall and on the front row (centre) is my best mate Joe Jacques.

DREAMER OF THE SIXTH

Royal handshake for Crook players

Princess Alexandra is introduced to the Crook left back, F. Clarke, before the Amateur Cup Final at Wembley. Other pictures appear on our sports page. Princess Alexandra, it is hoped will visit Durham to present new colours to the 8th DLI.

Wembley captures his mind

SIXTH - FORMER Frank Clark sits dreaming through science class. His thoughts are 300 miles away on the twin towers of Wembley Stadium... working out the formula for Soccer success.

For on Saturday the quiet-spoken prefect who enjoys a lunchtime kick around with a tennis ball in the school yard, trots on to the lush turf of Wembley to the roar of an excited 50,000 crowd.

Cheered

At 18, left back Frank is the "babe" of Amateur Cup finalists Crook Town.

And the educated feet of the schoolboy have made him one of the most eagerly sought after young players in Britain. A dozen top professional clubs, including Newcastle United and Preston, want him.

Yesterday he was being cheered by a few hundred school pals on the windswept playing fields of Hookergate Grammar School, in the Co. Durham village of Rowlands Gill ... as centre forward for the school team in an annual "Old Boys" match.

Then, as school broke up for the Easter holidays, Frank slung his satchel over his shoulder and went home to Highfield-road to pack for his trip to London.

Hoping

Smiled 6ft., 12-stone Frank: "At the moment I cannot think of anything else but the final. I just cannot concentrate on lessons.

"I have been putting in a little extra training, and the whole team is quite certain we are going to win the Cup."

But, after Saturday, Soccer will take second place for Frank. He is studying chemistry, maths and physics for his Advanced Level G.C.E. Later this year he hopes to go on to university for a General Science Degree.

Chapter Three
TOMMY SMITH'S TACKLE NEARLY CHANGED MY LIFE
1962-64

The biggest regret of my life is that my dad didn't live long enough to see me run out for a first-team fixture at St James' Park, wearing the famous black & white stripes. I made 486 League & Cup appearances for Newcastle United, and he didn't get to see any of them because he died at the age of 55, when I was just 20. It was so unfair. All those years he had spent ferrying me around to matches and training, and then he never got to see the fruits of his labours.

Dad loved his sport and although golf was really his passion – he was an active member of Garesfield GC – Saturday afternoons were all about football. Newcastle and Gateshead were just about equidistant from our home, both about eight miles away, and we went to watch them play on alternate weekends. They were two very different experiences, of course, not least because of the size of the crowds and standard of football, but as mum normally came with us to St James', I remember those trips especially fondly. They were brilliant family occasions.

To be honest, I cannot say which of the two clubs were my favourite. I loved them both and it was one of the saddest days of my life in 1960 when Gateshead were unceremoniously kicked out of the Football League. The way things worked in those days was that, come the end of the season, the bottom four clubs in Division Four had to seek re-election. Other clubs in the lower two divisions then voted on whether they should be invited to remain or be replaced by a non-league club. Only once before in their history had Gateshead needed to apply for re-election and in 1959-60 they had finished the season third from bottom, above Oldham and Hartlepool. If there was any justice in the world, they would be fine. But when the votes were tallied, non-league Peterborough United had gained more than Gateshead, and we were banished to obscurity. I was devastated. It was the first of many football stitch-ups that I was to experience. The feeling, and I'm sure it was correct, was that clubs based in the south and midlands saw it as a great opportunity to do away with one of their trips to a northern outpost. All I had left was memories of my trips to Redheugh Park and one in particular stands out. We reached the 6th Round of the FA Cup in 1953, having beaten Liverpool along the way, and I'm proud to say that I was among the crowd of 17,692 that saw us play Bolton Wanderers. We lost to a goal from Nat Lofthouse – but it was a fantastic occasion.

Most of the time at St James' Park the crowds were massive and it was standard procedure in my early years that I would be passed down the terracing, over the heads of supporters, so I could sit on the small wall that surrounded the pitch. Health & Safety regulations definitely wouldn't let you get away with that now. There was always a fantastic buzz around the place and the pre-match anticipation was gripping. I'm sure much of that was down to the fact that you never saw the players until a couple of minutes before kick-off. Everyone stared intently at the tunnel for ages in advance, longing for the moment when the captain emerged carrying a ball... and the noise that greeted him was incredible. Impressionable youngsters needed eyes in the back of their head to take it all in. I certainly found it every bit as entertaining watching how the peanut sellers operated as I did the football. That was an art form all of it's own. Those were heady days for Newcastle fans and three times in the space of five years during the Fifties we won the FA Cup. My main memory of those successes was the 1955 Final, when we beat Manchester City 3-1, because we watched it on our very first television. Our extended family all huddled around this black & white set. It seemed to be about 10 inches wide – but we didn't mind. We were just delighted to get a taste of what was happening at Wembley. I remember us having a sweepstake on who would score the first goal and mum was disappointed when she pulled out Jackie Milburn. He was never her favourite and that was strange really, because he was very much 'the man' at that time. But it didn't take long to put a smile on her face as 'Wor' Jackie scored with a rare header after just 45 seconds to land her the jackpot.

My particular favourite from that era was Frank Brennan, an uncompromising Scotland international defender who played more than 300 games for Newcastle. How could he not be my favourite after he'd presented me with my first trophy? Frank was there when my Primary School team played in a Cup Final at High Spen. I was the captain and we won the game, so it was me who went up to collect the prize. I got the chance to re-tell that tale some eight years later when, by pure coincidence, I found myself sitting next to him at a dinner. It was an annual event, organised by Vaux Breweries, and anyone from the North East who had represented their country in the previous 12 months was given an award. I qualified by virtue of my England Amateur and Youth caps but there was a technical hitch. Dinner suits were the order of the day, complete with bow ties. I didn't have either, so I borrowed them from an uncle and the suit was far too big for me. Halfway through the dinner, my over-sized sleeve knocked over a drink that went all over the table. I'd never been so embarrassed and was really grateful to Frank when he defused the situation. I was doing my best to mop it up but he insisted I should calm down and said: "People get paid to clean this up." You don't forget situations like that and although Frank had finished playing when I joined the

Newcastle staff, I saw him around from time to time and there was always a bond between us.

It's probably true to say that I was a spoilt kid and dad took it upon himself to ensure that I had an all-round education in sport. He regularly took me to watch Durham Wasps ice hockey team, and Newcastle speedway performing at Brough Park. I also recall seeing world champion Geoff Duke in action at the TT racing in Scarborough. He even took me to a Test Match at Headingley – despite the fact that neither of us was 'into' cricket at that time. I did appreciate how fortunate I was and I was certainly grateful for the support that both my parents gave me in every way.

I'm sure there were occasions when he couldn't make it because of work commitments but it just seemed that every time I played football, dad was there to support me. I remember in primary school days how five or six of us would pile into the back of his Ford Popular and he'd transport us to the games. Sometimes he got really wound up if he thought we were having a raw deal. In fact, on one occasion when I was at Grammar School our teacher actually banned him from attending games for a spell because he nearly started a riot. The usual thing was that the teacher who ran the school team also acted as referee for home games and they went to great lengths to ensure they couldn't be accused of favouritism. Dad thought one day that had gone a bit too far and when he forcefully made his feelings known, he was told he would not be welcome at the next match. Knowing him, he was probably there anyway in one guise or another.

As the years rolled by and I signed for Crook Town, he found himself with additional responsibilities. Schools football took priority over all other and as I was still at school, I was expected to turn out in their matches on a Saturday morning. The fact that I would be playing for a crack amateur team in the afternoon didn't influence the school in any way. The onus was completely on me to find my way around it. The only concession I got was that I managed to persuade my games master to let me play centre-forward because I thought I could manage that without having to burn off too much energy. When the final whistle went, dad would be waiting with a pack of sandwiches and a flask of coffee and would whisk me away to wherever Crook Town were playing. Making it in time for kick off was often a close call and looking back, the whole situation was ludicrous.

It was soon after I began my new way of life in November 1962, combining being a part-time professional at Newcastle with my role as a lab technician at the RVI, that my dad became ill. He'd actually had a problem for some time with stomach pains but wouldn't do anything about it. When he did finally relent and went to see the doctor, he was sent straight to the RVI. One of my duties as a junior member of the Bio-Chemistry Department was to test samples taken from people who came into the hospital. And I'm never likely to forget the moment when one landed on my desk with the name 'Alf Clark' attached. Alongside it had been written 'CA'. I had no idea what that meant and when I asked one of my colleagues, they told me it was suspected cancer. Dad had left it too late. There was no way back for him and over the next few weeks, I literally watched him die. He never left the hospital and although he did undergo a couple of operations, the cancer was out of control. I used to go to the ward to spend time with him every lunch period when I was at the RVI and it was just horrible watching him go progressively downhill. It left a massive hole in my life when he died but as the only child, I was very conscious of the need for me take responsibility for looking after my mother. No longer was it all about me.

As a youngster, when I was probably about 12, my dad had done me a massive favour. He took me down the pit where he worked to have a look around and see how things were done. Then, as we travelled back to the surface, he said: "I want you to promise me that you will never come down here again." It was a horrific experience and even at that early age, I vowed there and then that I would stick to that promise. I was absolutely determined that my working life would go in a different direction. Some people didn't have a choice but I was fortunate. I did. I had other options. I really enjoyed my role at the RVI, working with some lovely people, and two days a week I was training with Newcastle and playing in the reserves. It was a weird situation. Instead of going to stand on the terraces when I arrived at St James' Park, I was walking into the dressing room and a number of people sitting there beside me had been my idols. There wasn't time to dwell on that, though, and I very quickly became aware that in football terms, I'd moved into a different world.

Joe Harvey had only been in charge for a few months when I signed but he was already regarded as a legend at the club, having captained Newcastle to FA Cup triumphs in 1951 and '52. Ironically, he had begun his managerial career with Crook Town. Then, after adding to his experience with spells at Barrow and Workington, he was handed the chance to revive the flagging fortunes at St James'. A former army sergeant major, he was always big on discipline and you definitely didn't want to get on the wrong side of him. He quickly identified that a major shake-up was required because he'd inherited a poor team – and I got tangled up in the upheaval. I found myself sharing the reserves' dressing room with some really strange characters. Most of them were good lads but because they realised they had no future with Newcastle, they were bitter and disillusioned. It certainly wasn't an ideal environment for a youngster keen to make his mark in the game. It would have been so easy to pick up bad habits – and a bad attitude – in training and in matches. My challenge was to somehow rise above that. I seemed to be making a reasonable fist of doing that and the coaches were happy with my progress... but then Tommy Smith broke my leg.

The winter of 1962-63 was one of the worst on record and we didn't play for about two months because of the snow and ice. When we finally got going again our first Central League game was against Liverpool at Anfield. That was the night when one of the game's most famous hard-men added me to his list of victims. I'm not accusing him of breaking my leg deliberately because only he knows the truth about that. But from what I do know about the situation and what others told me at the time, it was certainly a reckless challenge. My right leg was broken in two places – the fibula and tibia – and the only bit of good news was that they were both clean-breaks. I've bumped into Tommy on numerous occasions at various events over the years and these days we can share a laugh about it. At the time though, it was certainly no laughing matter and all those people who couldn't understand why I was so hesitant about committing to become a professional footballer suddenly saw things from my point of view. My career could very easily have been over almost before it had begun.

In those days it wasn't compulsory for clubs to employ trained medical people to go with the reserves or youth team when they were playing. Invariably, the coach was responsible for treating you – and the limit of their ability was pretty much how to hold a sponge and bucket of water. I remember dear old Joe Richardson running on to me when I was clattered at Anfield. He sprayed some water on my face and told me to try and run it off! I did attempt to stand but immediately fell in a heap and two burly St John's Ambulance men stretchered me off to the dressing room. After three nights in a Liverpool hospital, the club sent a private ambulance to take me back to Newcastle. Motorways didn't exist in those days so the journey took forever. Every time we went over a bump in the road, I was in agony. I spent the next six weeks confined to bed in a private nursing home in Jesmond, a suburb of Newcastle, and then had a full-length plaster on the leg for the next 16 weeks. All the while, of course, my muscles were wasting away and an added complication was that an x-ray through the plaster revealed that the leg was offset. I had to go back to hospital and have it re-set.

The injury obviously had a massive impact on my life. It meant I was unable to get to work at the RVI and my mum, bless her, was understandably worried about me. She felt the need to come and visit me every day but that involved several arduous bus journeys and I eventually persuaded her not to come so often. One of the few positives was that I made a friend for life while I was at Jesmond. Eric Arcol was older than me and we came from totally different backgrounds. But we used to spend a lot of time talking and he taught me so much about life in general during that period. He even taught me how to hold a knife and fork properly! He was a quantity surveyor by profession and was obsessed about the need never to leave yourself open to accusations about bribery and corruption. When there was a massive scandal in Newcastle during the Sixties regarding the awarding of construction contracts, Eric's strong principles served him well.

Despite all the disruption, I cannot ever remember thinking I might never play again. Of course I knew it would involve a lot of hard work to get my fitness back to the high standards required of a professional footballer but I was ready for that. And although I still had to wear the plaster for several months after leaving Jesmond, I certainly wasn't going to let it cramp my style – especially while Joe Jacques was back in Newcastle for the summer period. He was in a class of his own when it came attracting the girls and my theory was that if I stuck close to him for long enough, some of his magic would have to rub off on me. Joe was just what I needed at that particular time because he wouldn't allow me to feel sorry for myself. If it was wet or raining, we used to wrap plastic bags around my plaster and off we'd go into town. We were energetic young men on a mission.

As soon as the plaster came off, I didn't need telling what was required of me. Only through hard work, dedication and commitment could I hope to get back to full fitness and I was very aware that people were watching me closely, wondering if I had what it took to overcome the first real setback of my career. Over the next couple of months I established a very close relationship with the terracing at St James' Park. While the other lads were out enjoying their training sessions, I was pounding up and down the steps. The good thing was that I knew it was doing the trick. I could feel myself getting stronger every day.

Also, by that stage, I didn't have any distractions. When I finally turned up for work again at the RVI I was pulled to one side by the Professor in charge of the Bio-Chemistry Department. He was really pleasant about it but also firm in telling me that I had a decision to make. The part-time arrangement was not working out and I either needed to build myself a career at the RVI or choose the route that I'd been so reluctant to take... full-time professional football. In a way, I was pleased matters had come to a head. I now had a clear sense of direction.

I signed full-time forms in January 1963 for some modest weekly sum and even though I'd been on the scene at St James' for a while, I could sense that the dynamics had changed. Football was now the be-all and end-all in my life and the pressure to make the grade had been significantly ramped up. My immediate priority was to win over the dressing room and I knew there were two ways to do that. The first was through my ability, the second was to make friends and hold my own in the lively atmosphere of the dressing room. There was a group of players around the same age as me, including David Craig, Alan Suddick, Bobby Moncur and Les O'Neill who had won the FA Youth Cup the previous season. Joe Harvey recognised that between us, we represented the future for Newcastle United and as there were already some 'top' pros at the club, like Stan Anderson, Dave Hilley and John McGrath, there was genuine cause for optimism.

Eventually the day arrived when I was to make my comeback in the 'A' team. They played in the Northern Alliance and, would you believe it, the fixture that day was away to Highfield! Not only was I going back to my home village, I would also be up against my cousins, Terry and Harry Hunt, who had played to a high standard of amateur football with Tow Law Town and were still decent players. Growing up, I used to spend a lot of time with them. They were older than me and although having me around all the while must have been really annoying, they never allowed it to show. Anyway, I think being in such a familiar environment probably helped to ease my nerves and the comeback went well. That was more than could be said for our senior colleagues, because, over at St James's Park, they were being humiliated. They were knocked out of the FA Cup by non-league Bedford Town and when we arrived back at the ground, the atmosphere around the place was like I'd never experienced before. That hammered home the message that things were now different. No longer was it just a game of football. Jobs and reputations were on the line, every time you took to the pitch, and you were answerable to supporters for your actions seven days a week.

I was aware when I broke my leg that left back had been a problem spot for Newcastle for some time. Alf McMichael, a Northern Ireland international, had been a fixture there for more than 12 years but when he finished, they had real trouble replacing him. The shirt was eventually passed to George Dalton. He had been a steady, run-of-the-mill wing half, as we used to call them, but the transformation was remarkable. Within six months of switching to left back he was playing for England Under-23s but yet again I saw how cruel football can be. He was desperately unlucky to suffer a serious knee injury and never played again. By that time, I was making good progress and was certainly starting to feel the part. Joe Harvey must have had the same thoughts because he picked me for the last two games of the season. We were in the Second Division and at one stage it had seemed like a promotion challenge would be possible. But one point from four games in March put paid to that idea, and Joe probably thought he had nothing to lose by throwing me in.

It was a low profile start in front of 6,423 at Scunthorpe United's Old Show Ground but despite that – and the fact that we lost 2-0 – it was still very special. No one would ever be able to take it away from me that I'd made a League appearance for Newcastle United. All of a sudden, people started to recognise me as I walked around the city and that was something I had to learn to live with. I kept my place for our final game at home to Norwich City and a 2-0 win rounded off an incredibly eventful 12 months, on and off the field.

PLAYER - MANAGER - CHAIRMAN 47

VOICE of N.E. Industry
GATEWAY TO NORTH-EAST INDUSTRIAL ENGLAND ON TYNE, WEAR, and TEES
THE MONTHLY MAGAZINE FOR TOP INDUSTRIAL MANAGEMENT

THE JOURNAL
WEDNESDAY OCTOBER 31 1962

Crook's amateur international is tracked down—a

CLARK IS BOOKED FOR ST

United's new back can climb—fast

By KEN McKENZIE

ONE of the most persistent and harassing transfer quests ever pursued by Newcastle United for a local player ended last night, when Crook Town and England amateur international left-back Frank Clark was signed on part-time professional forms.

Clark, who was 19 last month, is 6ft. 1in., and has played three times for England youths, once for the full England amateur side, and in two international trials.

He will probably make his "Magpie" debut on Saturday in the home Central League game against Barnsley.

Mr. Alf Clark, the player's father, joked after last night's signing, which followed a long talk with United chief Mr. Joe Harvey at Gallowgate: "Well, we won't have to continue providing your chief scout, Temple Lisle, with some of his meals."

Both Temple Lisle and director Stan Seymour have

1962

Newcastle United finally get their man...
and my Dad (top left) was there to see me sign.

CRACK YOUNG FULL-BACKS

FRANK CLARK
(Left-back)
Age, 21; height, 6ft. 0½in.; born Rowlands Gill.
An England amateur international, he won an F.A. Amateur Cup winners medal when with Crook Town. An old boy of Hookergate Grammar School, he was signed by Newcastle from Crook in October 1962.
Like his partner Craig he only cost £10. Broke a leg in 1963, but recovered magnificently to establish himself in the first team. Has played every League match this season.

DAVID CRAIG
(Right-back)
Age, 20; height, 5ft. 9in.; born Belfast. This season he gained his first international honour when he played for the Ireland Under-23 side. Started his professional career at Scunthorpe, became homesick and returned to Ireland. Newcastle signed him in Ireland in 1960, and he has come through the junior and reserve sides to hold his position in the first team with extreme credit.

BOBBY MONCUR   GEOFF ALLEN

Chapter Four
DON'T GET 'SHIRTY' – TOON ARE GOING UP
1964-66

Some players have to wait for years to experience the thrill of winning a meaningful trophy – some never get to taste that feeling throughout their entire career. How lucky does that make me to have shared in a Second Division Championship triumph in my first full season as a professional?

Not only that but I also played every game during that 1964-65 season, and I'm particularly proud of that statistic because at the outset, the jury was definitely still out over whether I was good enough. Joe Harvey clearly had his doubts because, even though I'd played in the last two games of the previous campaign, he picked a number of others to play at left back during pre-season. When the time came to pin up the team-sheet for our opening League fixture, however, I was delighted to see my name up there alongside the No. 3 – in big capital letters. It wasn't until 13 months later that it failed to appear.

I got a sharp reminder when we played Charlton Athletic in the August sunshine of how passionate we Geordies are about our football. Only 12,256 had watched my home debut yet nearly three times that number turned up to see us play Charlton. No matter how bad things get at St James' Park – and there have been some desperate lows – the fans always come back the following year, full of optimism. We gave them something to cling onto that season. We lost just one of the first nine matches and were starting to look a decent side. I wasn't the only youngster being given a chance to win a regular place because David Craig figured in the other full back berth and we found a system that worked really well. Both of us were quick and strong in the tackle, and we played like full backs in the true sense – none of this getting down the line malarkey and curling the ball towards the penalty spot. We concentrated on defensive duties and left our 'non-tackling' half-back line to take the game to the opposition. That description especially applied to Stan Anderson and Jim Iley. They could really play but if ever they won the ball in the tackle... now that was a proper bonus. It might also surprise some people to know that our centre-half John McGrath wasn't the best in the tackle, either. He could also 'play' but it wasn't until he moved to Southampton that he took on his hard-man image. Consequently, David and I carried a lot of responsibility – and we were up to it.

We were top of the League by mid-September and when a spectacular 6-0 success at Swindon set us up for a club record-equalling run of seven straight wins, our confidence was sky-high. From my point of view, life was never better. I loved the training, and the lifestyle, we had a great dressing room and the captain (Stan Anderson) and coach (Jimmy Greenhalgh) were brilliant with me.

Jimmy was something of a mentor throughout my career, both as a player and manager. He was an old-fashioned, down to earth football man with no airs and graces, and it suited him that the coaching revolution was just starting to take off at that time. People were looking more deeply at how players could be taught to perform better, and how tactics could be brought more into play within a game. He was really interested in that type of thing and I owe him a lot because he always encouraged me to go on coaching courses and prepare for my future. Years later, when I was assistant-manager at Sunderland, I was pleased to get the chance to repay him. I knew Jimmy had become a bit disillusioned, working with Middlesbrough, so I persuaded Ken Knighton to take him on as our chief scout.

Like I said, life was brilliant for me. That was certainly influenced by the fact that I was developing a circle of good friends and some of us used to hang out together in the afternoons. The players didn't all eat as one after training, like they do today. Our time was our own when we'd finished work and two or three days a week some of us used to go to the Majestic, a dance hall in the city centre. Don't get the wrong impression. We weren't boozing on the quiet – I never touched alcohol in those days anyway – we were just relaxing and enjoying ourselves. And it was certainly a good thing from Alan Suddick's point of view because he met his future wife there.

Bryan 'Pop' Robson had also joined Newcastle by then. He soon became a member of our gang, as well as a very good friend of mine, and as an off-shoot of that, I finally learned how to kick a football properly. That must sound like a very weird thing for someone to say when they'd been playing regularly in the First Division but I was having a big problem with slicing the ball with my left foot, especially from free kicks. I was getting increasingly self-conscious about it and then Lenny Heppell, the father of Bryan's girl-friend, pulled me aside one day and said he thought he could help me. Lennie, a great character, was well known across the North East as a professional ballroom dancer and nightclub owner but he had no football background. I can think of plenty of players who would have said in that situation: "Who the hell is he to teach me how to kick a ball?" But I was always open to suggestions about anything that might improve me. I agreed to work with him. He was convinced that the problem was the angle of my approach to the ball and after we had worked on it for a couple of sessions in the local park, there was a massive improvement. That really boosted my confidence and I couldn't thank him enough. Lennie was a balance expert. He worked with a lot of top players and when I went to Sunderland many years later, he was working with several of their lads. He was well into his Sixties by then but could still beat everyone in the club over five yards! The one who benefitted the most though, was Bryan. Because he was dating Lennie's daughter Maureen, an international table-tennis player who later became his wife, he and Lennie inevitably spent time together. Lennie introduced him to exercises that improved his poise and reactions and the work they did together transformed him as a player. The difference it made to him was astonishing and he went on to become one of the finest goal-scorers of our generation.

One of the crunch points of the 1964-65 season came over the Christmas period when we played Middlesbrough twice in the space of three days in front of a combined crowd of more than 93,000. We were concerned about Boro because they had good players – and that led to my first real experience of tactics. Preparation for matches was chalk and cheese compared to how things are in the modern game so it was quite revolutionary when Anderson came up with a plan. Joe Harvey was happy for the skipper to have his say and Stan reckoned that if we could find a way to keep the ball away from their star midfielder, Ian Gibson, we'd be fine. His suggestion was that Trevor Hockey, our combative winger, should be detailed to man-mark Gibson. Some of us cynically thought that Stan just didn't fancy looking after Gibson himself but to be fair, his plan couldn't have worked out better. We won both games, Hockey did his job brilliantly – and it actually turned out to be the start of a new career for him in midfield.

We lost our way during February. All the good work might have gone to waste as a result but we hit back well to finish the season with a lengthy unbeaten run. It reached the point in mid-April where we knew that if we could beat Bolton Wanderers at St James' on Good Friday, promotion would be guaranteed. The crowd that day was 59,960 and even though we still had three games to go, we all knew that this was our stage. The fans had come to celebrate but that didn't quite fit with Bolton's plans. They were right up there with us, still with everything to play for, and were much better than us in the first half.

The main problem was a big Welsh lad up front called Wyn Davies. He was incredibly powerful, especially in the air where he had the ability to leap and hang there, and he was brilliant in that first period. Joe had a right go at John McGrath for not handling him better but I have to say that was easier said than done. John found a way in the second half, though, as a fierce challenge left Davies with a leg injury. Somehow we had managed to go in 1-0 up at half time, through a goal by Willie Penman, and it sparked off incredible celebrations when Jim Iley made it 2-0 with a remarkable toe-poke from 20 yards.

Skipper Stan started something as we trooped up to the Directors' Box to wave to the crowd when he ripped off his shirt and threw it to the fans. We all followed suit but when we got back into the dressing room, we were in big trouble because it left the club with only one other set of shirts! In the nicest possible way, we really didn't care... and no one was more delighted than Stan. It had caused a real stir two years earlier when he moved to Newcastle after 11 years and 400 games for Sunderland and in his eyes, leading the Magpies back to the top flight helped to justify that decision. He was a great bloke, a really good professional who always took time out to help and advise the younger players, and he certainly had an influence on me.

Our celebrations were slightly muted because we had to fly straight off to London to play Crystal Palace the following day. We'd done the main part of the job but desperately wanted to win the Championship as well. A draw at Palace and another point from the return with Bolton on Easter Monday meant we needed one more point from the final game against Manchester City to clinch the Championship. It was a rubbish game, as I remember it, but we escaped with a 0-0 draw.

The problem for me was that it was hard to imagine how things could get any better. At the age of 21, I'd been capped by England at Amateur and Youth levels, won an FA Amateur Cup Winners' medal after playing at Wembley, and been ever-present in the Championship-winning side that took Newcastle United back to the top flight after an absence of four years. Wow! It was difficult to take it all in but

I was acutely aware that all those honours would count for very little unless I could rise to my next challenge. Not everyone was convinced I could do that. No doubt many supporters had their opinions influenced by some words of 'encouragement' from Alan Sleeman, a journalist working for the Newcastle Journal. He wrote in an article previewing the new season: "Surely only Frank Clark's mother thinks he will be good enough for the First Division." Fortunately, Joe Harvey didn't share those sentiments.

Nerves can do funny things to footballers. I've known some who wilt under the pressure on a Saturday afternoon after being quite brilliant in training all week. Preparing to tackle the First Division was always going to be a test of something more than our ability to play football. I count myself as very fortunate that I never really suffered from nerves, even during the immediate pre-match period, and the fact that we were already used to playing in front of big crowds at St James' certainly helped to harden us up for the formidable challenge ahead. The bit that I particularly loved was going to grounds that I'd only ever read about – like White Hart Lane, Old Trafford, Villa Park and Highbury – and it was certainly a strange sensation when you took up your position at the far post and suddenly found yourself standing next to the likes of Denis Law or Jimmy Greaves. The secret was not to treat them with too much respect but that could be difficult. I remember one occasion when we were playing away to Tottenham and Greaves picked up the ball on the halfway line, then dribbled right through our defence to score. It was difficult to stop myself from applauding. As I soon realised, the big difference was that instead of coming up against a team with four of five good players, they all had nine or 10 in the First Division. You had to be on top of your job for every minute of every game to have a chance of surviving at that level.

There's no denying that we found it hard to adapt. By the time we'd played 23 League games in that 1965-66 season, we'd only won five of them – and Joe decided changes had to be made. Anderson was sold to Middlesbrough, Hockey to Birmingham City but the signings that everyone thought would be made never arrived. It was the home-grown youngsters who were expected to step up and do a 'man's job' and we responded well to finish the season in 15th place. None of us did better than Suddick. He was a real talent, with tremendous skill and vision, but he suddenly discovered an ability to score goals as well. We were so pleased that he did because his contribution of 15 in 31 games was massive in helping us to steer clear of relegation. He was surely destined for great things, we thought, but inconsistency held him back. And while I was disappointed when he was sold to Blackpool the following year – not least because he was a good mate – I could understand Joe's thinking. The money generated by that move gave him the chance to strengthen the squad by signing three new players. One of those was Dave Elliott from Sunderland... and talk about small world! We used to open the batting together for Lintz CC, and it was great to be able to pick up where we had left off.

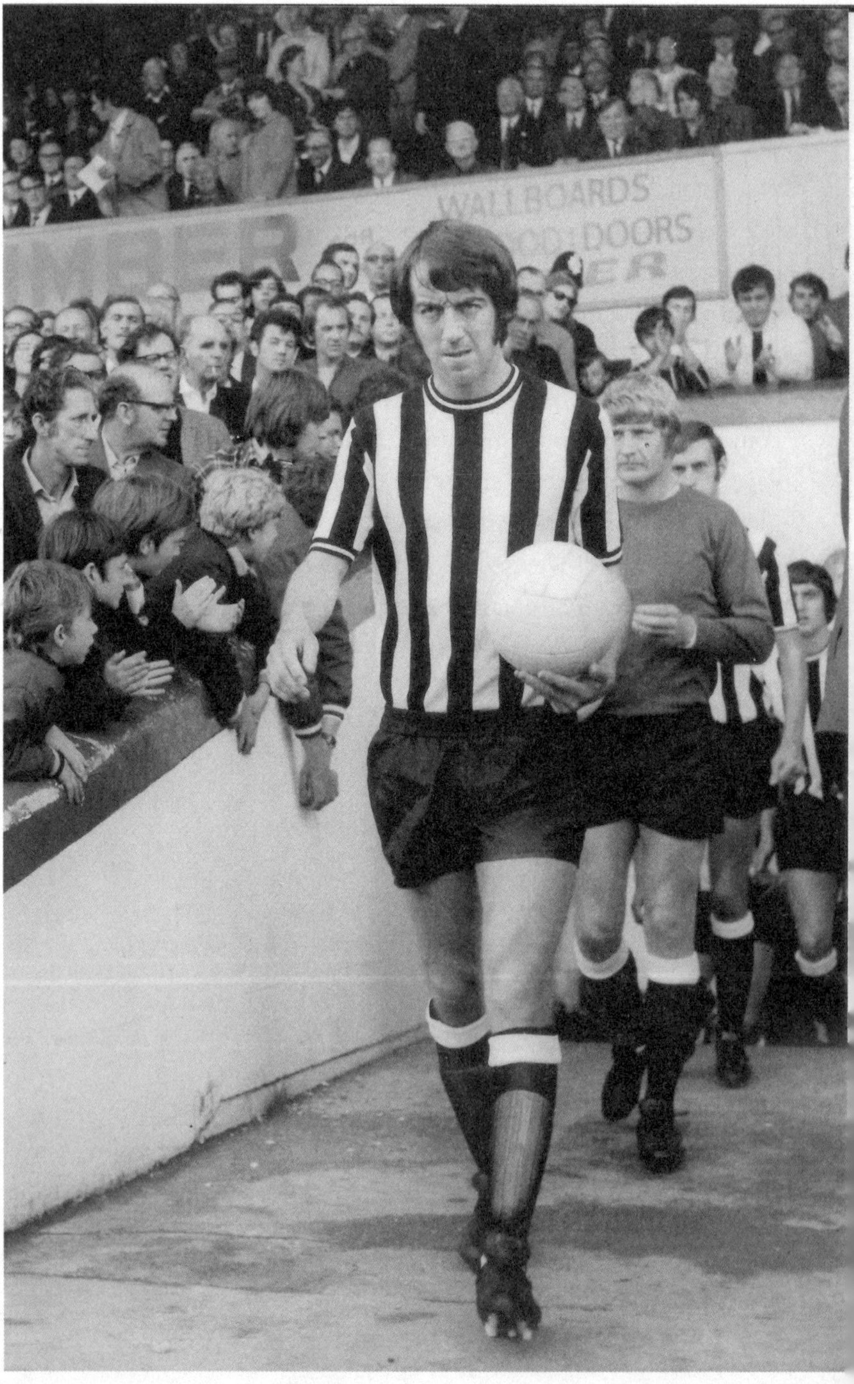
WALLBOARDS
DOORS

Chapter Five
PELE, BEST & A BACKDOOR ROUTE INTO EUROPE
1966-68

Why is it that football fans, who devote a huge chunk of their lives to supporting their team with passion and loyalty, feel the need to pick on individual players during matches? It's a subject that has always fascinated me – probably because I was on the receiving end of plenty of it for many years in my time with Newcastle. It wasn't a wholesale thing. Most supporters were brilliant with me but a certain section on the Popular Side at St James' Park deliberately set out on match-days to make my life uncomfortable. I know now that it's an issue right across football in this country, especially when the team are struggling. Every club has a player who gets dealt the hand of 'whipping boy' – and I don't recommend it. I have no idea what I did to upset that gang on the Popular Side but what I can tell you is that it's absolute b******s to say that fans will always stand by a player who gives 100 per cent effort. I was a local boy who had come up through the ranks and no player during my time with United did more in terms of taking the club out into the community. I can put my hand on my heart and say that never once did I sell the club short but although I had an excellent relationship with supporters away from the ground, that counted for nothing with some of them come 3pm on a Saturday afternoon.

I never really let it get to me. What mattered as far as I was concerned was that Joe Harvey had faith in me and the crucial thing was to let the taunting and criticism bounce off. It only made matters worse if you reacted to it. There was a spell when Tommy Gibb also 'copped' for it and when he let it be known he wasn't happy, it got even worse. Things did get easier – especially after we won the Fairs Cup – and I think I also won over a few of the cynics one Boxing Day, when we were playing at home to Sheffield United. I took a kick in the face and when I was carried off shortly before half time, it left us down to 10 men. It took 15 stitches to sew me back together and the noise was incredible when I eventually re-emerged, covered in plasters and bandages. I remember thinking at the time – "So this is what you have to do to win people over." Incidentally, I struggled to shave for about three months after that incident, which was why I grew my moustache.

The summer of '66 was so special for the people of this country, whether they were football fans or not, and I'm so pleased that I was around to witness us winning the World Cup. I really hope that at some stage, those who were born since then get the chance to go through the same experience. I didn't get to see any of the matches live because St James' Park, which was not in the best of condition, wasn't allocated any of the North East games – and I very nearly didn't get to see the final. I was supposed to have been playing cricket for Lintz at Sacriston, a mining village in Co Durham, on the day England faced West Germany. It was a nightmare situation and there seemed to be no way of getting out of it. But what a stroke of luck we had. Six drops of light rain fell at precisely the right time. Everyone instantly agreed that we couldn't possibly play in those conditions and we headed straight back to Lintz. My mate Joe Jacques lived just across the road from the cricket club and although he wasn't there, I remember sitting and watching the game with his parents.

Looking back, football in general got a massive boost as a result of England's triumph. It generated a huge wave of enthusiasm and I also think it's true to say that it elevated our profession as footballers. People who were not committed to the game suddenly viewed us in a slightly different way. Our status somehow changed and it certainly filled me with pride to think that I earned my living playing with and against the World champions.

I cannot claim that I ever got beyond 'nodding-terms' with any of the individuals involved – nor could I say that I tried any harder when I was up against the likes of Geoff Hurst, Bobby Charlton or Roger Hunt. But that's not completely true because I maybe tried even harder to kick Alan Ball than I normally did. He could be a nasty piece of work, and I think modern-day corner flags were born out of a full-on clash we had. He thought it was amusing to take the p*** and I got really angry when he took the ball into the corner and sat on it. I flew across and swung a leg that not only got the ball but him and the corner flag as well. In those days, the flag posts were made of wood and when the challenge snapped it in two, it gouged into my shin. It annoyed me even more that Ball had got the last laugh when I had to have stitches to repair the damage – and plastic corner flags were introduced not long afterwards.

After the difficult time we'd had adjusting to life in the First Division, the hope was that things would be easier in our second season in the top flight. Yet for much of the time during that 1966-67 campaign, it seemed destined to end in tears. We were entrenched in the relegation zone after winning just one of our first 11 games and as goal-scoring was our major problem, we couldn't have been more pleased to see Wyn Davies walk through the dressing room door at the back end of October. We'd seen two years earlier what a handful he could be for defenders, when he played against us for Bolton during the promotion run-in. As we soon discovered, however, it wasn't realistic to expect one man to solve all our problems. His debut was a nightmare experience as 57,000 people saw us beaten 3-0 at home by arch-rivals Sunderland, and there was no sign of an improvement as we edged towards Christmas. Desperation was setting in. That was clear for all to see when we went to play Leeds United at Elland Road on Boxing Day. Ron Lewin had been installed as coach because Jimmy Greenhalgh had gone to Darlington to try his hand at management and we couldn't believe it when he announced in the pre-match team-talk that we'd be using a new system. Basically, it involved playing with five at the back. This had never previously been discussed at any time and we had certainly never worked on it. Needless to say, our performance was a shambles. Most of us had no proper idea what our role was, and we were hammered 5-0.

Five days later we were on the move again, this time away to Tottenham, and our confidence was so bruised that we travelled south pretty much expecting more of the same treatment. There was a distinct 'smell' of relegation in the air. But suddenly, as if by magic, there was hope. Whenever we played in London we stayed overnight at the Great Northern Inn, right next door to King's Cross station, and as we were relaxing in the hotel lounge, in walked Joe Harvey with this colossus of a man. I can still hear Joe saying it now with a satisfied grin on his face…"This is big John McNamee – he's come down from Scotland to join us." The record books show that he made only 117 appearances for Newcastle after moving from Hibernian, where Jock Stein was his manager, but I think of him as playing a lot more than that. Maybe that's because he had such a massive impact during his time with us, playing a leading role in our fight for First Division survival and then helping us to European glory. We did take another hammering at White Hart Lane – Jimmy Greaves inspired Spurs to a 4-0 win – but somehow this one didn't matter quite so much. We could all see that with such a huge presence as John at the heart of our defence, we had to have a good chance of keeping clean-sheets and picking up points. He was a real gentle giant off the pitch, a lovely man, but absolutely the complete opposite on it. Fearsome is the best word I can think of to describe John. He has to qualify as the most aggressive man I ever saw on the football field and he always had a lot to say for himself – except when his wife was around. It always makes me smile when I think about that because she couldn't have been any more than 5ft tall!

That signing gave everyone a lift when we desperately needed one. It made us believe that, just maybe, we could find a way to preserve our top-flight status. But we weren't kidding ourselves... there was an enormous amount of work to be done. The biggest concern was the shortage of goals. Big Wyn had been brought in to solve that problem but was struggling to make the impact we'd all expected from him. The truth of it was that scoring goals wasn't really his strength. He was one of the bravest players I ever saw but his game was all about creating havoc in the opposition box, where he was a different class with his ability to climb. The onus was on the other players to get around him and take advantage of the confusion he was causing but it took time to get to that point. The statistics tell the story. Davies did score an FA Cup hat-trick at Coventry but he finished that season with six goals in 29 League games, while Bryan Robson was top scorer with just 10. The two of them were destined to become a formidable partnership but the problem was that we needed some of that to show through straight away.

I could never say that I got especially close to Davies. There was no problem between us, we were just different people with different interests. But we went to 'war' together for four years and won a lot more battles than we lost. I always think there's a lot of rubbish talked about team spirit. Of course it's great when you have a big group of players who get on well and that's a relatively easy situation to generate when results are good. But you don't have to be best buddies to work effectively together. What I would say about Wyn was that when we were standing in the tunnel, waiting to go out on the pitch and I looked back along the line, I was delighted to see him there. Having him with us meant we always had a chance – regardless of who we were playing against. It takes all sorts to make a football team and at the end of the day, it's about finding a way to live and work together. It's nothing unusual for players not to like each other but the secret is managing the relationship. A classic example was Stan Anderson and Jim Iley, who were key figures in our midfield for almost 100 games during the Sixties. I got on great with both of them. They were pleasant, amiable characters – very similar in many respects – and both could certainly play. Yet for some reason, they never hit it off. It was impossible to put a finger on why that should be. Sometimes it's as simple as saying that the chemistry is just not right. They were both skilful attacking midfield players and in the days of the old 2-3-5 formation, we couldn't afford the luxury of two of those. If they were going to operate in the same team, they would have to find a way around that – and they did. I felt sorry for Jim in a way because I always had the feeling that he was a fairly isolated figure. As our experienced captain, Stan carried a lot of weight around the club and that somehow overshadowed Jim's contribution.

Having said that, Jim was right in the thick of our battle to remain in the First Division and his experience was invaluable as we discovered a way to win more than we lost in the second half of the season. Confidence was gradually being restored and a run of four wins in five games during March and April meant our destiny was back in our own hands. In the end, it didn't even go down to the wire. We finished third from bottom, which in those days was good enough to avoid the drop, and we were four points clear of Aston Villa and Blackpool. But we had been severely warned. It was far too close for comfort and we never wanted to go down that road again.

Looking back, it's now possible to trace the way things gradually fell into place as we moved towards what became one of the most successful periods in Newcastle's long history. There were no relegation fears in the 1967-68 season as we finished 10th – and it should have been so much better because, incredibly, we won only one of our last 12 matches. Bob Moncur and Ollie Burton, destined to become key figures in the Fairs Cup triumph, nailed down regular places in the team that season and in an effort to bring the best out of Davies, Jim Scott – another signing from Hibernian – and Tommy Robson became automatic choices on the flanks. The changes moved us on as we won more games that season, scored a lot more goals, and real belief was beginning to develop.

Mind you, we were still prone to having very bad days, as was confirmed by two 6-0 defeats – against Liverpool at Anfield in August and Manchester United at Old Trafford in May, when George Best ripped us to pieces. I'm often asked whether he was the finest I ever played against and in all honesty, I don't believe he was. That 'honour' has to go to Pele, but George ran him a very close second. I'm actually quite proud of my record against Best. I always regarded myself as more of a thoughtful player than a hard-man. Rather than go running around like a headless chicken, I preferred to wait for my opponent to make his move and then react to it. I could certainly crunch into tackles when required but my game was about jockeying opponents, forcing them into areas of the field where they didn't want to go, and timing my challenge to nick the ball away from them. As it happened, that – most of the time – was the best tactic to use against Best. He could really look after himself, which was astonishing when you think how slender he was, and the worst thing in the world you could do was try to intimidate him. You could guarantee that if you upset him, he'd make you look an idiot and although he certainly got the better of me in that end-of-season clash, overall I think honours were about even. I couldn't say the same about my one appearance against Pele although, in fairness, I wasn't actually marking him the day we played against Santos. That came about in a close-season tour of Thailand, Hong Kong and Iran in June 1972. It was standard procedure for Santos to cash in on Pele's fame at the end of their domestic season by touring the world, playing exhibition matches, and that's how we met up with them in Hong Kong. They won 4-2, Pele scored a hat trick and he was simply magnificent. A friendly game it might have been but he showed total commitment for 65 minutes – then wandered off to a standing ovation. Quite apart from his sheer brilliance in every aspect of the game, the thing I remember most about that memorable evening was how tough he was. Challenging him was like tackling a brick wall.

We had an opportunity to influence the destiny of the title on the final day of the 1967-68 season because Manchester City came to St James', needing a win to pip United for the Championship. It was an afternoon packed with drama. I'm not sure what their thinking was but City selected Mike Summerbee to play at centre-forward that day, and moved Francis Lee out to the right against me. Lee was a real handful in his own right but at least having Summerbee out of my direct line of fire spared me from getting kicked from pillar to post all afternoon. No one ever got around to telling Mike that it was the full backs who did the 'kicking' and playing against him was a nightmare. Anyway, it turned out to be a brilliant game, a seven-goal thriller with some outstanding goals, and City just edged it in the end. I well remember the moment that they became champions because Tony Coleman, who was always a bit 'different', was in the process of trying to throttle me when the final whistle sounded. He was trying to extract revenge after I'd caught him a bit late and I eventually had to say: "Give over Tony – you've just won the Championship!"

What none of us knew at the time was that City's victory that day was part of the most complicated qualification for Europe that any club can ever have been through. Bear with me and I'll try to explain how, despite finishing 10th in the First Division, we managed to win a place in the Inter-Cities Fairs Cup. It was a competition designed to give clubs who had not qualified for the European Cup or Cup Winners' Cup a chance to still sample European competition. On paper it was a great idea but whoever dreamed up the rules had a wicked sense of humour. The first thing you needed to have a chance of qualifying was city status but the real complication was that only one club from each city was allowed to take part.

So... who would fill the three Fairs Cup places that England had been allocated? Manchester City qualified for the European Cup as champions and when United won the European Cup a couple of weeks later, they joined them in that competition the following year as holders. Liverpool, who finished third, in the First Division, claimed the first of the Fairs Cup places and although Leeds United were next in line, their place was already secured by right because they'd won the trophy the previous year. Everton couldn't qualify because Liverpool would be that city's representatives so that let in Chelsea, leaving one more place available. West Brom were already spoken for after winning the FA Cup and as Tottenham and Arsenal were ineligible because Chelsea had already claimed the capital city's spot, the incredible happened. Newcastle United had qualified for Europe in the most bizarre of circumstances – and what a magnificent adventure it turned out to be.

Meeting up with the great Pele. It was like tackling a brick wall.

The Extraordinary Pre-Match Ritual Of Frank Clark

WATCH left-back Frank Clark as he runs out of the tunnel for the game against Rangers...

He will run across the pitch to the far touchline, then down the line towards the goal United are kicking into, turn along the bye-line, and finally arrive back at his point of departure.

From there, he will head for one of the goals where he will kick a post with each foot.

A ritual unchanged from match to match. And not because of any superstition. Frank explains:

Check On Boots

"I want to get the feel of the ground. Is it hard, heavy or has it just the right amount of 'give'? I want to get the feel of the crowd. And just to make sure that my boots are tied securely, I test them against the posts. I leave nothing to chance."

Clark's not kidding! The full back actually begins his physical and mental build-up for any game three days beforehand.

He goes on: "I never wash my car, or work in the garden, or caper about during this period. Dancing, too, is definitely out. I just wait for the game.

"In fact, I could tell you exactly what I will be doing at any time on any of the two days previous to a game."

Lifting the curtain on his regular Saturday routine when United are at home, Clark continues:

Breakfast In Bed

"On the dot of 9.30 a.m., my mother will give me breakfast in bed. After that, I'll get up and read until around 11.30. Then a ten-minute walk to the lock-up for my car. Home again in time for lunch at 12.30 p.m. Then off to the ground, arriving there early so that I can rest easy, knowing everything is as it should be.

"If I played a bad game and had altered my preparation in any way, I would blame myself."

Frank feels United had their eyes opened very quickly in Europe. They'd have been out otherwise!

Clark ends: "I was unbelievably green when I joined Newcastle. I've taught myself to be a real professional. Without such an outlook in Europe, you are doomed."

Centre-half JOHN McNAMEE

Left-back FRANK CLARK

Chapter Six
WE WERE THE FAIREST OF THEM ALL
1968-69

Everyone thought it was a joke – especially the London press – and to be perfectly honest, we could hardly blame them. How could we finish 10th in the First Division and still get the opportunity to represent our country in Europe? But we were where we were, and there were only two alternatives as we saw it. We could either wilt in embarrassment and exit the Inter-Cities Fairs Cup at the first opportunity or embrace it – and make absolutely certain that one way or another, people got to hear all about Newcastle United. We'd grown as players over the period since we got promoted to the top flight three years earlier. People like David Craig, Ollie Burton, Bryan Robson and Bobby Moncur were no longer just talked about in terms of potential, and I include myself on that list. We had experience to go alongside our ability and we believed we were ready to take the club forward.

There was an extra spring in our step when we reported back for pre-season training. The whole thing was so exciting, not least for our fanatical fans, and the players got together and made a pact. Everyone agreed we would treat our involvement in the Fairs Cup as a great adventure. Of course we would be professional and do everything in our power to win the trophy. But we also wanted to enjoy every minute of the experience, on and off the field, because maybe we would never pass this way again. The thing you have to remember is that back in 1968, European competition had only been on the go for a relatively short time. In general terms, people certainly didn't hop around the continent like they do today. We'd been put in a very privileged position and were determined to make the most of it.

Maybe it was because we adopted that philosophy that things turned out so well for us. I can't say for sure but our carefree approach, spurred on by the fact that no one outside the North East wanted to take us seriously, helped us produce one of the biggest upsets in European football. We cleared every obstacle put in our way and on June 11, 1969, while most football people were enjoying their summer holidays, we finally lifted the trophy. It would be easy to belittle that achievement by saying it was "only" the Fairs Cup but that would be grossly unfair. It may have been a secondary competition by name but there were some very fine teams barring our way – and we got the better of them all. Feyenoord, Sporting Lisbon, Real Zaragoza, Vitoria Setubal, Glasgow Rangers and Ujpest Doza, who were described by Don Revie as the best team in Europe after they had knocked out his mighty Leeds United. We saw them off, one by one.

Our only new recruit of note the previous summer had been Tommy Gibb, and that signing was quite a coup because he had loads of clubs chasing him. He immediately established himself in midfield following his move from Partick Thistle and went on to create a new club record of 171 consecutive first-team appearances from August 1968. Initially, his partner was Dave Elliott but fate didn't deal kindly with him and I was very sad about that because we were good pals. Dave had suffered an epileptic fit a year earlier while out for a walk with Ollie Burton as we prepared to play at West Ham. It happened again in Scotland a year later, within hours of us facing up to Glasgow Rangers, and Dave was never a regular in the side after that. For some reason, the club chose to conceal the full facts until many years later. In today's climate, the situation would all have been dealt with in a very different way. But the bottom line was that a search was immediately launched for a new midfielder – and Dave went off the following year to join Southend. At least he did get to play his part in the Fairs Cup success, figuring in the first two rounds, but then Denmark international Benny Arentoft arrived from Greenock Morton to pair up with Gibb. Neither of them was comfortable receiving the ball off the back-four. We had to adjust a bit to cater for that but they were both great athletes, absolute workaholics, and formed a terrific partnership. Joe Harvey had done it again. Maybe he wasn't the best manager when it came to tactical nous but he really did have a good eye for a player.

Another significant change at the start of that season was that jovial Irishman Willie McFaul claimed the No. 1 spot. He'd had to be patient for a number of years after joining us from Linfield for £7,000 because Gordon Marshall was such a solid and consistent performer. But Willie grabbed his chance when it came along. He wasn't the tallest of 'keepers – certainly not by today's standards – but that seldom caused a problem and he served United well for a long time.

What quickly became apparent during pre-season was that the management hadn't been idle while we were on our summer break. Dave Smith had been promoted to the role of coach after a year in charge of the reserves and he was to have a big influence on what followed in the months ahead. The continental way of playing the game was very different to the style we adopted in this country. It was all about one and two-touch football, with lots of 1-2s that would take defenders out of the game unless you were on your guard. Very seldom did we come across that method in this country and Dave was adamant that if we wanted to make an impact in the Fairs Cup, we would have to learn how to deal with it. We were always going to play direct as our natural style, getting the ball out to Jim Scott and Jackie Sinclair on the wings as early and often as we could, so they were able to provide Wyn Davies with the best possible service. But defensively we worked for hours on stopping the 1-2s – almost to the point of it becoming an obsession with Dave – and all credit to him. There's no doubt in my mind that we wouldn't have been successful had we not done that work.

It didn't seem like such a good idea at first, though. Judging by the way we started the season, there was good reason to question whether we should have been concentrating on improving other areas of our play. By the end of September, we'd won only one of our opening 12 League games and were sitting fourth from bottom of the table. I don't remember anyone making a big deal about it at the time but we all knew that it would be crazy if the European adventure cost us our place in the top flight.

By the time the first Fairs Cup game came around in mid-September – against Feyenoord at St James' Park – our League form was so poor that no one gave us a prayer. But this is football we're talking about. You never know for sure what's going to happen. Even so, I still find it hard to believe that we won that game 4-0. They were one of the giants of Dutch football, destined that season to complete a League & Cup double. The following year, they even won the European Cup. But what they didn't know when they came to sample the Tyneside 'welcome' at its most intimidating was that we had a secret weapon. There's a saying about cometh the hour, cometh the man and in this case it was Geoff Allen. A local lad who had come up through the ranks, he'd been given an early run of matches on the left wing and on that particular night, he had the game of his life. I watched at close quarters as he absolutely destroyed their right back. I just gave him the ball and let him get on with it – and we took full advantage of the havoc he created. Scott, Robson and Gibb put us 3-0 up before half time and Davies was on target in the second period. It was a magnificent effort and that 4-0 scoreline didn't flatter us in the slightest. What made it particularly special for me was that I captained the team. I stepped up because Bobby Moncur was missing through injury and I cannot tell you how proud I was to be leading us into action for our first-ever game in Europe. Incidentally, within a few months Allen suffered a bad injury and was forced to retire from the game. It was a real tragedy for him when he had so much to look forward to, but I'll always remember that match-winning display with great affection.

The campaign was up and running and I hope you'll forgive me if I take you through the rest of it – step by step. It was packed with emotion and fun, such a brilliant experience on and off the field, and the whole journey is deeply ingrained in my memory. I just feel the need to share it all with you.

Rotterdam, Europe's largest port and the second largest city in Holland, was extensively bombed during the War and the city was still in the process of being re-built when we went there for the return leg. As with most of our trips, I was keen to explore the area as much as time would allow, and I loved the fact that my mum came to the game. She flew out with her friend on the supporters' flight and I do believe that was the very first time she had been abroad. I was delighted to think I'd helped to make that happen. It was all very strange to her, of course, and there was a lovely moment when we met up briefly before the game so that I could hand over her match tickets. She thrust a pile of Dutch gilders into my hand to pay for the coffees. She hadn't a clue what they were worth and what she was trying to give me would have bought half the café! With a 4-0 advantage, we knew that we just needed to be organised and professional to get the job done. That's more or less the way it turned out. We lost 2-0, to a goal in each half, but were never really in danger of failing to progress. We did, though, learn a valuable lesson that night, which stood us in good stead for the rest of the competition. European clubs performed to a very different standard when they were at home compared to their away leg. I limped off with a leg injury 10 minutes before the end in Rotterdam and although it caused me to miss the next four League games, I was back in time to face Sporting Lisbon.

I don't know whether you can remember the early James Bond

film, when George Lazenby put Estoril on the map with his casino scene from On Her Majesty's Secret Service? Estoril is a delightful spot, just up the coast from Lisbon, and that's where we were based before we played Sporting. We got plenty of chance to appreciate the area because, as was to become the norm with Fairs Cup trips, we flew out on the Sunday and didn't return home until the Thursday. Sporting had a tremendous pedigree so it was always going to be a massive test for us, but we were up for it. Two memories of that trip really stand out... one was that it absolutely tipped down with rain for most of the game, which was hardly ideal at a ground with very little cover for the fans. The other was that we didn't kick off until 9.30 at night. It was the longest day of my life!

We came away with a 1-1 draw and when you delve a bit more deeply into what went on, that performance in its own way was as good as any we produced in the competition. The previous Saturday we'd lost by the odd goal at Liverpool and with John McNamee injured, home-grown youngster Graham Winstanley had been drafted into the heart of our defence. By the time we flew out to Lisbon, we actually feared we might be without both of our regular central defenders because Bobby Moncur had suffered a broken nose at Anfield. Bob was our captain, a natural leader who had really developed as a player since switching from wing half to play at the back, and we needed him because everything pointed to a backs-to-the-wall struggle. Fortunately, he was passed fit for action and helped to guide the raw Winstanley through what could have been a nightmare experience. Although we were under intense pressure from the off we refused to cave in and the flavour of the game changed completely when Scott scored a fine goal. It gave us something to bite on in the incessant rain and although Sporting tried to distract us at half time by changing their shirts from hoops to a dry set of green-and-white halves, that didn't work. We edged closer and closer to victory until the very last minute when a shot rebounded from the crossbar, struck McFaul and went into the net. It was a cruel way to end a great night. But a 1-1 draw meant we had every reason to be satisfied with our efforts and we knew it had set us up for more progress. Joe was certainly pleased enough. All he said as we got changed afterwards was: "The coach leaves the hotel at 9 o'clock tomorrow morning. Make sure you don't miss it!" We'd been given license to go out and enjoy ourselves – and that became our theme wherever we went on the Fairs Cup trail.

A real feature of the Cup run was the number of youngsters who kept getting thrown in at the deep end and responding superbly. Six of us played in all 12 Fairs Cup fixtures but there will always be times when changes have to be made. Success hinges on how you react in that situation and there was something very satisfying about the fact that youngsters kept stepping up to save the day. Allen had been superb against Feyenoord, so had Winstanley against Sporting and before we were done, Alan Foggon and Keith Dyson were to add their names to the list of contributors. Foggon's 'time' was still a few weeks away but Dyson, who figured among the subs in the first leg against Sporting, was given a start in the return. As I knew from my own experience Joe was never slow to give youngsters a chance if he felt they warranted a place and Dyson, an 18-year-old local lad, had made a good impression in a handful of League games. Now he had to prove he could cope with a big European night at St James' … and he did.

Not that any 'added interest' was required but it developed into a big story when Sporting's coach, Fernando Caiado, resigned two days before the game. There was no telling how their players would react but we had to manage our own situation. Sporting kept peddling the line that they had no chance but we were not falling for that one. They had a squad packed with international players and we knew there'd be no room for complacency. What we really needed was something special to settle the nerves – and Robson provided it. We'd only been playing for 10 minutes when Davies nodded down a Gibb free kick and Bryan smashed home an exquisite volley. People still talk about it now as one of the greatest goals ever scored at St James' and certainly, in my 11 years there, I wouldn't argue with that. The partnership between Davies and Robson had taken a lot longer than we'd expected to become truly effective but this was more like it. All we had to do now was protect our slender lead to claim a place in the third round, and we did that without too much difficulty.

The idea of playing standard League fixtures on New Year's Day hadn't been dreamed up by 1969 and I guess that's why we found ourselves heading off to Spain to start the year with a game against Real Zaragoza. Yet again, we were very much the underdogs. They had a lot more European know-how than us, having won the Fairs Cup in 1964 and reached the final two years later. They were also used to playing against British teams and despite the fact that they were struggling in the League, the message was hammered home that we must not underestimate them. I remember that there was no airport in Zaragoza so we flew into a nearby military base and Joe also broke with convention by allowing us a glass of beer – just the one – to bring in the New Year.

Some of Zaragoza's play when the game got underway was amazing. I was really impressed with them – and very happy about coming away with a 3-2 defeat. We were on the back-foot right from the off. They scored after only four minutes and we had to dig really deep to come from behind twice to equalise with goals from Robson and Davies. We couldn't hold out and conceded another midway through the second half but we headed for home thinking those away goals could prove to be crucial. That's exactly how it worked out a fortnight later and the tension that night was incredible. Robson, whose 'street cred' was rising all the time, produced another early goal. It was the third time he'd done that during the campaign, and we loved him for it. But that was only the start. Their goalkeeper handed Gibb the chance to put us two-up but Zaragoza got one back before half time. That meant we were level 4-4 on aggregate and looking back, I'm still not quite sure how we survived in the second half. David Craig had to go off injured and so too did his replacement Ron Guthrie. Then young Dyson also got a painful knock and ought to have gone off but he had to battle on because we'd already used our two subs. It was really on a knife-edge but the crowd were great that night – all 56,055 of them. We needed all the help they could give us and they didn't let us down.

Next up were Vitoria Setubal, from a fishing town some 20 miles south of Lisbon. With a population of less than 60,000, it was a magnificent achievement for them to have come as far as they had in the competition. I've always loved my trips to Portugal and was pleased to get the chance to go back. But first they had to come to Tyneside and we really did have a stroke of good fortune to point us towards the semi-finals. Heavy snow was falling when they arrived and many of their players had never even seen the white-stuff before. They were keen to pose for photographs that they could keep as souvenirs, but a lot less keen to play football in it. Three of them came from Mozambique, including a flying winger that I was marking, and they just stood around shivering for 90 minutes. I actually felt sorry for them once we had got the game under control and I had to applaud the initiative of one of their lads. They didn't have any gloves to protect them from the cold but he got around that by wearing a pair of socks on his hands! Robson made his mark yet again on the tie, scoring two fine goals, and we were good value for our 5-1 win. Davies was also on target, so was Gibb and the first goal of the game came from Foggon. At 19, he apparently became the youngest player that night ever to score in a senior game for Newcastle as he headed in a cross from right back John Craggs. Young Foggon had already figured a fair bit in League games and was a talented lad who seemed destined to go all the way in the game. For some reason that didn't happen and I often wonder why? He never seemed to look like a footballer. He was prone to being overweight with long hair and his shirt always hanging out but although he was unorthodox, he certainly had talent. He did the rounds after four years at St James', including more than 100 games successfully for Jack Charlton's Middlesbrough, but he fell a long way short of what we expected when he burst onto the scene at Newcastle. We thought the tie with Setubal was as good as over when we went 4-0 up but we couldn't have been more wrong. They suddenly found two extra gears in the final 10 minutes or so, scored the best goal of the game and gave us real food for thought. They hadn't reached that stage of the competition without being able to 'play' and the very fact that they'd beaten the Italian League leaders, Fiorentina in the previous round spoke volumes for their ability. It was vital we recognised the threat and didn't base our opinion of them on that 90 minutes in the snow.

Setubal's ground was in the process of being re-built and they had no floodlights available so the game was switched to Sporting Lisbon's Jose Alvalade Stadium. We didn't mind that because it brought back happy memories. This visit, though, turned out to be a lot tougher than the first. We could tell as soon as we kicked off that they felt they had nothing to lose and were determined to give it a go. They got a goal to give them hope but it was a big moment in the tie when Davies headed us level. That restored the four-goal advantage and although Setubal scored twice more after the break, and made us work really hard, we went through 6-4 on aggregate.

All those people – especially the pundits – who had questioned our right to take part in the Fairs Cup now had to re-think their positions. I must admit we did feel a bit smug about the fact that, out of four English clubs who entered the competition, we were the one left to fly the flag as we moved into the semi-finals. The draw paired us with Glasgow Rangers and inevitably I suppose, the press labelled it the 'Battle of Britain'. Little did they know how accurate that description would turn out to be.

We had seven weeks to think about it because the game at Setubal was played on March 26 and we were not due to visit Ibrox for the first leg of the semi-final until May 14. In between, there was stacks of hard work to be done and we committed ourselves really well. Confidence was high, we were developing into a fine team, and we weren't afraid of hard work. That was just as well because we had no less than eight First Division games to play during April. We won five of them, lost only one and having climbed to ninth place in the table, we felt we were ready for Rangers.

We'd been given a good idea of what we could expect a couple of years earlier when we'd played home and away friendly matches against Celtic in the space of a month. Both clubs had gone out of their respective cup competitions at an early stage so the games were fixed to avoid having blank weekends. We won both of them – 1-0 at home and 3-2 away – and I had a couple of memorable battles with wee Jimmy Johnstone. But what really made an impression on me was the noise and passion that the 42,000 Celtic fans generated at Parkhead. It was supposed to be a friendly, with nothing more than pride at stake. I came away thinking if the fans were that committed for a match of such little significance, what on earth must the atmosphere be like when it really matters? We were about to find out. The welcome was less than warm when the coach drove into Glasgow. We didn't expect otherwise. Getting abuse from opposition supporters goes with the territory and it's like water off a duck's back for experienced professionals. Personally, I loved it. The more hostile the atmosphere was, the better I responded. You're in the wrong job if you get easily intimidated and as I always used to say... "I cannot remember any supporter ever scoring a goal". We trained at Parkhead in advance and with so much going on around the game, staying focused during the build-up was a challenge. It wasn't helped by the fact that we had five Scotsmen in our squad who were really excited about the whole thing. One of those was Bobby Moncur and he made a shrewd observation. Although he'd joined us as a kid, he pointed out that the others – especially Jim Scott, Jackie Sinclair and Benny Arentoft – would have a lot of bad memories of getting battered at Ibrox with their previous clubs.

Bob felt strongly that it was important for us to 'work' on them and make them believe that we were better than Rangers. The other Scot, big John McNamee, had to be drafted in as a late replacement for Ollie Burton, but he didn't need his confidence boosting. As an ex-Celtic player, he couldn't wait to do battle with Colin Stein – his former Hibs colleague – and was quick to let it be known that there would be only one winner of that particular duel.

We had 12,000 fans among the 75,000 crowd that packed Ibrox to the rafters. The noise that night was unbelievable. We defended superbly to come away with a goalless draw but there was no doubting our hero. The big moment of the match came midway through the first period when Rangers were awarded a penalty after Willie McFaul collided with Orjan Persson. It looked a really harsh decision to me but Willie saved the day when he flew full-length to his right to turn Andy Penman's spot kick around the post. He had more work to do as well before the night was over but we were delighted with our clean-sheet. Incidentally, I was up against Willie Henderson in both legs against Rangers and that was an interesting challenge. Although he was only 5ft 4in tall, he was a real box of tricks and made an art-form out of making full backs look stupid. We had two brilliant battles but I reckon I just about finished with the bragging rights.

The second leg was a week later and in between, we warmed up for it by playing at home to Liverpool in our final League game of the season. A 1-1 draw was enough to lift us up to eighth place, Newcastle's highest finish for nine years, and that was hugely satisfying considering how many other distractions we'd had to contend with. That wasn't the case any more. Now it was entirely about trying to bring home a European trophy.

Over the years I've been through some 'hairy' moments on the football pitch but none of them compares with what happened at St James' in the return leg with Rangers. We picked up where we had left off and for the first 77 minutes, it was a brilliant game. The atmosphere was fantastic. No quarter asked or given by either side, and even though Scott fired us in front soon after the break, no one could say for sure who was going to win. The pendulum then really swung our way when Sinclair made it 2-0 – and Rangers fans reacted by pouring onto the pitch at the Gallogate End. We headed for the dressing rooms as fast as we could but just as we approached the tunnel, McFaul skidded to a halt in front of me. He said he'd left his gloves and cap in the net and would have to go back for them. "Don't be so f***ing ridiculous." I said. "Get in that dressing room now and I'll buy you some new ones!" It took a good 20 minutes for the police to restore order and during that period, the Rangers chairman came into our dressing room and gave us an assurance that whatever happened from here, we would go through to the final. All credit to him. It cannot have been easy for him to do that.

By the time we got underway again, the atmosphere had turned really nasty and the entire pitch was ringed by police with dogs. I was determined not to put myself into a situation where I would have to go across and take a throw-in. The dogs frightened me more than the Rangers' fans! Anyway, we managed to get the job done without further alarms although it really did take the gloss off what should have been a brilliant night – not just for us but especially for our supporters.

The biggest tactical blunder I made all night was agreeing to meet up with a girl-friend to go on to a nightclub. I was still single at the time and had arranged to pick her up from a bus when it arrived at Marlborough Crescent Bus Station. The Rangers fans were running riot as I drove into the city centre. Running battles were going on with the police and there was evidence of damage all over the place. To cap it all, as I approached the bus station, I could see it was being used as a parking area for the Rangers coaches. There were thousands of their fans milling around. I slid further and further down in my car seat, desperate not to be recognised, and was so relieved to make my pick-up and get the hell out of there.

It was really strange to find ourselves in a situation where we had no League games confronting us... just a two-legged Cup Final that had to be played at a time when England's cricketers were midway through their Test Match series. But we were totally tuned in to tackling the "best team in Europe" and had absolutely no doubts about what it meant to the people of the North East. It was as if they were only allowed one topic of conversation and the buzz was incredible. But with that came pressure. We were desperate not to let them down. If we were going to win the trophy we would have to be right on top of our game in the first leg at St James'. That would be imperative but having won all five of our home games so far, we also knew Ujpest Dozsa wouldn't be too keen about the prospect of a night out on Tyneside.

Some things never changed. The bookies still had us down as hot favourites to lose and based on the fact that Ujpest had beaten Leeds at home and away, I suppose it was hardly surprising. Anyway, we liked being seen as the underdogs. It spurred us on and providing our magnificent fans played their part, we fancied our chances against anyone at home. The first half, as I remember it, was a 'real' game and we were at full stretch to contain them. They fully lived up to their reputation. They had good players all over the field and it was difficult to see how we would establish the grip on the tie that we were desperately seeking.

But one of the beauties of football is that it creates platforms for people to emerge as heroes – and so often it's the most unlikely candidates who rise up to fill that role. Geoff Allen, for example, had stepped up against Feyenoord, Willie McFaul did it against Rangers and now it was Moncur's turn as he scored twice in the space of 10 minutes early in the second period. He never scored goals. Even in his days as a wing-half, he very seldom got onto the score-sheet. It was a complete fairy-tale to see him dramatically transformed into a star striker in a match of such importance – and it couldn't have happened to a nicer bloke. The first goal was a well-struck shot as he pounced onto a loose ball after the goalkeeper had saved an effort from Davies, the second superbly taken after he'd played a neat 1-2 with Arentoft. We'd done what we had set out to achieve but there was even more to come because Scott made it 3-0 seven minutes from time. Bearing in mind the quality of the opposition, the performance that night has to be right up there as a leading contender for 'Best Ever by a Newcastle Team'.

Another ambition that we'd managed to fulfil was that right throughout Europe – and beyond – we'd forced people to recognise we were a fine team. We were attracting loads of publicity on a national level and when the media discovered Bryan Robson was getting married in between the two ties against Ujpest, and I was to be his best man, that was right up their street. His bride Maureen was the daughter of Lennie Heppell, one of the North East's big personalities, and it was actually a double-wedding because her sister got married at the same time. It was a huge occasion that brought traffic to a complete stand-still across the little market town of Hexham. For one day at least, it gave us something else to think about. We were straight back to business the following day, though, as we flew out to Hungary and I was delighted to get another new stamp on my passport. We were in good spirits as we went on a cruise down the Danube but inside we were all feeling apprehensive. I certainly was. And the extreme heat didn't help. Unusually for us, we went out for a quick stretch before the game to try and relieve the tension but couldn't have been out for more than a minute before Joe ordered us back to the dressing room. It was so hot.

Not to put too fine a point on it, Ujpest absolutely pulvarised us in the first half. They led 2-0 at the break and we certainly couldn't have complained if they had overturned our first leg lead by that stage. McFaul played out of his skin to keep us in with a chance and to a man, we were shattered when we got back into the dressing room. Joe was never at his finest when it came to tactics but he was spot on with his assessment this time. "Come on lads," he said. "You've only got to get a goal and this lot will cave in." Moncur came straight back at him. "But boss," he said. "We can't even get the ball, never mind score a goal!" Within seconds of the re-start, captain Bob did it again. Sinclair's corner was cleared back to him and when he returned the ball into the middle, Moncur smashed it into the roof of the net. Three Cup Final goals from a man whose scoring record was almost has bad as mine ... how does that work? Anyway, just as Joe had predicted, it was almost as if a balloon had been pricked. All of the enthusiasm just drained away from Ujpest. It had clearly dawned on them that now they'd have to score five to win the Cup – they were never the same again.

You may find it difficult to believe but I never really enjoyed playing football matches. I loved everything else about being a footballer but for 90 minutes every week, I hated my job. It was all about winning for me and I was so utterly wrapped up in doing what was necessary to make that happen that there was absolutely no place for enjoyment. Having said that, I do believe I enjoyed the final 25 minutes in Ujpest more than at any time during my spell with Newcastle. The pressure was off completely and the feeling of satisfaction overwhelmed me. Arentoft got us back to 2-2 on the night, which meant we led 5-2 on aggregate, and there was still time for young Foggon to go on as a substitute and grab himself a goal. The presentation of the trophy was no big deal. It took place on the pitch immediately afterwards but the lack of formalities didn't bother us. We more than made up for it during the next week or so – and could only imagine what it must have been like back home.

People turned out in force to welcome us back. There were hundreds waiting to greet us when we landed at Newcastle Airport, the streets were lined on both sides of the road as we made our way back to St James' by coach and when we finally made it to the ground, it was packed. We really had touched the hearts of the great people of the North East and I remember thinking as we slowly made our way around the pitch with the trophy that maybe even members of my 'fan club' on the Popular Side could now see some good in me! The celebrations that followed turned into one of the great nights of my life.

Fifty years on and that triumph still carries huge significance to lots of people. Some didn't feel the football club gave it as much credence as it deserved and took it upon themselves a few years back to form a Fairs Club. They used to organise an annual dinner somewhere in the North East. They invited all the Cup-winning players and their wives – all expenses paid – and a brilliant night was guaranteed. When membership expanded and the whole thing became too expensive, they went down a different track. Instead of us going to Newcastle for the dinner, they used to come to us and I was 'blown away' when a coach-load of fans and former players turned up in Nottingham to celebrate my birthday. They took over Calverton Miners' Welfare for the evening, put on a lovely spread, and we had a night of pure nostalgia. The players are always very supportive and it meant a lot to me that the likes of Stan Anderson, Jim Scott and Alan Kennedy had taken the trouble to travel down on the coach.

Stepping in to halt the danger against Rangers during another great European night at St James' Park. *Picture: Newcastle Chronicle*

TOP Fulfilling my Best Man's duties with Bryan Robson and his new wife Maureen. And joining forces to bring home the Fairs Cup together.

PLAYER - MANAGER - CHAIRMAN   85

XIII FAIRS SPECIAL, June 14, 1969

Night of triumph in Budapest

● THE goal that crushed the Hungarians. Above: Alan Foggon races through the Ujpest defence to crack in United's third goal. Right: Foggon is clasped in the embrace of Jackie Sinclair. Below: Tommy Gibb joins in the congratulations with Bryan Robson (No. 8) on the left.

Parading the Fairs Cup around a packed St James' Park.

Chapter Seven
ON RAMSEY'S RADAR – AND A BIZARRE GOAL IN EUROPE
1969-71

I don't ever recall having a conversation with Sir Alf Ramsey but presumably I did figure in his thoughts as England prepared to defend the World Cup in Mexico in 1970. On the back of our Fairs Cup triumph, I was selected three months later to play for the Football League against the Irish League at Barnsley. He was clearly using that game to run the rule over a number of players before announcing his initial squad of 40.

We won 3-0 and I thought I did myself justice – but that was as close as I came to full international recognition. I never heard another thing and although I didn't lose any sleep over it, obviously I'd have dearly liked to pull on that white shirt again. England were very well off for left backs at that time, and Terry Cooper and Keith Newton were ahead of me in the queue. They were better players than me so I had absolutely no complaints about them boarding the plane to Mexico. But I did thoroughly enjoy the experience of turning out for the Football League. It gave me an insight into what might have been. I'd only ever worked under one manager and only knew one way of doing things so, even for a brief period, it was interesting to discover different approaches. We trained together for a couple of days before the game and while I have no memory of Sir Alf being actively involved, I'm sure he would have been taking everything in. It was a shame he wasn't more 'up front' because I'd have enjoyed getting even a brief insight into the man who engineered what could well be the only World Cup triumph we ever experience.

We had a really good team at Barnsley that night. Chelsea's Peter Bonetti was in goal and I lined up at the back alongside the Leeds United trio of Paul Reaney, Paul Madeley and Norman Hunter. Colin Harvey (Everton) and Mike Bailey (Wolves) were the midfield pair and up front we had Manchester City's Mike Summerbee and Francis Lee, with Bryan Robson and Everton winger Johnny Morrissey. Three of them – Bonetti, Hunter and Lee – did make the flight to Mexico.

I was pleased that Robson got the chance to show what he could do in that company and he was on the scoresheet, along with Summerbee and Bailey. Bryan had been a brilliant player for us the previous season, scoring 30 League and Cup goals, and his contribution to the Fairs Cup success had been immense. That ought to have been more than enough to get him into the England set-up. The fact that his claims were ignored just goes to show how much talent Ramsey had at his disposal at that time. From my point of view, it was a case of knuckling back down again at Newcastle. At least I was on the international radar and only by continuing to produce consistently good performances would more opportunities come my way.

The big concern for everyone at St James' as we prepared for the 1969-70 campaign was how we would react after the unbelievable high of winning the Fairs Cup. Bearing in mind that the Fairs Final was on June 11, we only had a few weeks off before we reported back for pre-season and to be honest, we were in need of a good break. We'd played 59 matches in all competitions over an 11-months period – I'd played in all but five of them – and we were physically and mentally shattered. But it's true that winning never seems to sap the strength quite as much as losing. By the time the new season kicked off, the

Fairs Cup holders were ready to defend their trophy. We'd been paired with Dundee United in the first round but before that, we needed to get some League points on the board – and that proved to be easier said than done.

Joe invested the majority of the profits the club had apparently made from our Fairs Cup involvement in a highly-rated Scot who actually didn't command a regular place until the second half of the season. Big things were expected from midfielder Jimmy Smith when he arrived from Aberdeen to become Newcastle's first £100,000 player. Although only 22, he was already relatively experienced and a Scotland international but for one reason or another, things didn't work out as planned. 'Jinky', as he was known, could be quite brilliant on his day. He had incredible skill levels, no doubt about that, but with him, you needed to take the bad with the good and that tested our patience at times. You never quite knew what you were going to get from him when the game kicked off. I'm sure that was a big factor in us becoming a lot less consistent. We could certainly see the logic behind the signing because Joe wanted to take us to the next level. He wanted us to adopt a more expansive style of play and pass the ball more through midfield but accommodating 'Jinky' involved changing the system that had served us well. It took a while to sort it out and any hopes that we might make a Championship challenge had virtually evaporated by the end of October, by which time we were languishing in 15th place.

On the Fairs Cup front we had a series of really tight games. Two wins by the odd-goal took us past Dundee United and a goal from Jim Scott eventually saw off Porto after a goalless draw in the first leg in Portugal. Southampton were next up and after drawing both legs of the third round tie, Robson again emerged as the match-winner because his away goal took us through. Tight games or not, we were defending our title very creditably but the end of the line came when we played Anderlecht in the next round. I'd been struggling for a while with a knee injury that the medical people thought was a ligament problem and it caused me to miss the first leg in Holland, which we lost 2-0. I was fit for the return though, and it was another very special European night at St James'. Just shy of 60,000 people had come to see whether we could pull it back from the first leg. It was a really tall order against such a talented team and the atmosphere was truly fantastic as Robson scored twice in the first 20 minutes to haul us level on aggregate. The momentum was clearly with us but just five minutes later, my knee 'went' – and I was lying in a hospital bed when all the late drama unfolded. We thought we'd won it when Keith Dyson scored after 85 minutes but Anderlecht struck back to make it 3-1 and we went out on away goals. It was a massive disappointment because we believed we could go all the way again. It wasn't to be.

My problem turned out to be a cartilage and that signalled the end of the season for me. But I had a massive incentive to return to full fitness as quickly as possible because I was desperate to get myself onto the seven-game end of season tour of North America that had been lined up for May. I was in hospital for a week after the operation, then had to wear a back-splint behind the knee for three weeks or so but by the time a decision needed to be made, I thought I'd done enough to prove my fitness. Joe didn't agree. He called me into his office to say that I wouldn't be going on the trip. Career-wise, it was no big deal to miss out but the lads had a fantastic time. They won all seven games – and I would have loved to be with them to experience the American way of life.

Incidentally, despite the indifferent start as we struggled to adapt to a new system of play, there's no denying that we really did come good in the second half of the season. From mid-December onwards, we suffered just two defeats in our last 19 League games and when that edged us up to seventh place come the end of the season, it represented Newcastle's highest finish since 1951. That was something to be proud about, and I certainly was. We had moved on – even though it was only one place better than the previous season – but did we have it in us to challenge for the title? Only League champions Everton had a better defensive record than the 35 we'd conceded and if we could maintain that standard and get more goals at the other end, as we had done during the second half of the campaign, maybe we had a chance.

Joe clearly wasn't convinced because he started tinkering with the squad during the summer of 1970. For the first time in a long time, we didn't have a regular team the following season. Only three players – Willie McFaul, Bobby Moncur and Tommy Gibb – topped 40 League appearances and the chopping and changing made it hard for us to find a proper rhythm. The old goal-scoring problems re-surfaced and that no doubt influenced the decision in February to let Bryan Robson move to West Ham for their club record fee of £120,000. It left a big hole in my life when he headed south because we'd always been close and he'd given fantastic service to Newcastle. But Joe was clearly looking at the bigger picture and had five months in which to invest that money wisely and change our attacking dynamic.

What we didn't quite realise was that one half of an exciting new forward partnership had already been recruited just a couple of weeks before we waved farewell to Bryan. Although John Tudor had helped both Coventry and Sheffield United to win promotion, he was still unproven at the top level. But, and I seem to be saying this all the time, Joe's eye for a player served him well again. John and I became good friends as he eased his way into things at St James' and he went on to become the perfect foil for the marquee signing we made during the summer. He was never a prolific scorer but was good in the air and a great team player. A knee injury forced him to retire early from playing but he certainly made his mark in six years at Newcastle.

Robson will always be remembered in the North East for the massive part he played in winning the Fairs Cup. Before he departed, he got another taste of our favourite competition. We'd finished high enough in the League the previous year to qualify on merit as one of England's representatives but we landed a daunting first round tie against Inter Milan. They weren't just one of the best teams in Europe, they were a significant force in world football. Several of their players had played for Italy a few months earlier against Brazil in the World

Cup Final. The challenge was as big as we'd ever faced. It seemed inconceivable that we would be able to beat them over two legs. Right throughout the Inter team they oozed talent and it was no surprise to any of us that they went on that season to win Serie A for the 11th time. But if ever there was an example of needing more than just talent to win a football match, this was it.

We went to the San Siro first – and what an experience that was. The attendance was disappointingly small, just 14,460, and that probably reflected how the Italians felt about us. But big Wyn Davies put us in front and although Inter levelled late on, we had a 1-1 draw and an away goal to bite on. That was just the start of it because all hell was let loose at St James' a week later. Wyn had been really struggling for goals and it's incredible to think that he scored only twice in 34 League games that season. But because of his strength, courage and phenomenal leaping ability, the continentals found him a nightmare to play against. The Inter defenders tried every trick in the book to combat his threat and when they totally lost their discipline... we had them.

There was a frenzy of excitement at St James' when we ran out for the return. We wore an all-red strip that night and maybe Wyn got confused. Maybe it was the thought of pulling on the red shirt of Wales that inspired him to produce his match-winning display. That man Moncur was on target again to give us a first half lead and when Davies clashed soon afterwards with the Inter goalkeeper, it sparked off a mass brawl. All sorts was going on – including the referee being punched to the ground – and it took at least five minutes to get it sorted. In fact, it wasn't until the police piled in that order was restored. I kept well out of it. You could say that my role was to have a watching brief! When we finally got going again, Inter were down to 10 men because their goalkeeper got the blame for striking the ref and Davies was in just the mood to create more mayhem. They simply couldn't handle him. Giacinto Faccetti, an elegant attacking left-back and one of the biggest names in Italian football, had been moved inside in the hope that he could use his experience to quell the threat. But we went on to score again to make it 2-0 on aggregate and it was so fitting that Davies got the goal that killed them off. The man who'd been struggling so badly to find the target in League matches knocked in the rebound when we hit the crossbar for the third time in the game.

We were so chuffed with ourselves. Even though we'd won the Fairs Cup two years earlier we were still very much the underdogs compared to Inter Milan. Nothing that was thrown at us from then on could be as difficult. Certainly, Pecsi Doza, the Hungarian club we were drawn to meet in the next round, were not in the same class. But talk about one extreme to another!

The first leg was at home and Davies was at it again, scoring on either side of half time to give us a 2-0 win, and we were extremely confident of making further progress. But the away leg was a total disaster. Just about everything that could go wrong did so and we eventually went out of the competition on penalties, having failed miserably to do ourselves justice. It was nothing to do with lack of effort. We just couldn't get our game going. We played on a crappy pitch at a crappy ground, which didn't help the mood, and then our 2-0 advantage from the home leg was wiped out by an own goal and a late penalty. Extra time couldn't sort it out so it was down to penalties. When the first three we took were just about the worst I'd ever seen, we were out. The crowd invaded the pitch so we headed for the dressing room as quickly as we could to lick our wounds. We loved the Fairs Cup, so did the fans, and to go out in that fashion was so disappointing. Just to rub in a bit of salt, I then got tangled up in the most bizarre of incidents. The UEFA official came charging into our dressing room complaining that we had only taken three penalties and must go back out and take the other two. We thought at first that it must be some sort of sick joke but he was absolutely serious. He said he needed to keep his paperwork in order. All of our lads, except for Willie McFaul and me, were already in the bath so the two of us very reluctantly trudged back out onto the pitch. The Pecsi goalkeeper also had to come back out, of course, and he just wanted to take the p***. He leaned against a goalpost laughing as Willie and I went through the formalities. I gently rolled mine down the middle for what you could say was my first-ever goal for Newcastle. It gave me no pleasure whatsoever.

Almost certainly, that Hungarian trip was the defining point of our season. Under normal circumstances, it would have been a decent effort to finish 12th in the League but after three consecutive top-ten finishes had sown the seeds for something better, it was definitely regarded as a backward step. By the time we got to the summer of 1971, we were entering a major period of change. For me, that was true in more senses than one. It was certainly the case for Newcastle and on a personal level, Pam and I got married in the July. The ceremony took place at Whitley Bay, which was home for Pam. Joe Jacques was my best man and David Craig and Bryan Robson were ushers. Straight afterwards we headed north to Scotland for a week's honeymoon before I reported back for pre-season training. Pam's never been 'into' football. She did come to a few matches with my mum when we first started going out together but then admitted to me that she hated it. I said: "In that case, don't come... there's absolutely no reason why you should." Since then, she's hardly been to a game and I must admit that over the years, not having to take football home with me all the time helped to keep me sane.

Chapter Eight
BANDY LEGS AND BUSHY SIDEBURNS... A NEW HERO HAS LANDED
1971-73

I came across some incredibly confident characters during the course of my career as a player and manager but can say with complete certainty that none matched up to Malcolm Macdonald. He was in a class of his own. But the difference between him and so many of the others was that he always backed up the arrogance with his actions on the field. The fans immediately labelled him 'SuperMac' after his club record £180,000 move from Luton Town. By rights, that should have put him under enormous pressure but Malcolm never doubted for one second that he would be a star at Newcastle United.

It would have been easy to take an instant dislike to the young upstart. He arrived to sign in the summer of 1971 in a chauffeur-driven Rolls Royce and straight away announced to the media that he would score 30 goals that season. It was a huge gamble on his part. 'Soft' southerners weren't always readily accepted in the North East and here was a 22-year-old Londoner making rash promises within hours of arriving in Geordie-land. Virtually all of his previous experience had been at Third Division level – but that was a measure of the self-belief he had. Some of the lads didn't take too kindly to his brash style, on and off the field, and I could well understand why. I have to say though, that it never bothered me. As soon as we got down to work, I could see that he was capable of making a real difference to us and we always got on well together.

Malcolm came in to replace Wyn Davies, who had gone to Manchester City as part of a major overhaul of the squad. Joe had hinted at what was to happen the previous season when he signed Stewart Barrowclough, John Tudor and Tommy Cassidy but that was only the start. Irving Nattrass stepped up from the youth ranks to show real potential and apart from Macdonald, three other significant signings were made before the end of October. It proved to be a great piece of business when Terry Hibbett was tempted north from Leeds United for just £30,000 during the summer and a month into the season, central defender Pat Howard arrived from Barnsley. What promised to be the final piece of the jigsaw was fitted into place in October when Scottish midfielder Tony Green, rated at £150,000 in a part-exchange deal, was signed from Blackpool. The problem was that when we lost 1-0 at Everton on the day Green made his debut, we sunk to the bottom of the First Division. All the upheaval, with so many new players and a change of style, had taken its toll but Joe knew what he was doing. By the time we got to the end of the season we'd climbed to 11th place and people really didn't fancy playing us.

Defenders certainly hated having to contend with Macdonald and Tudor, who were developing into a terrific partnership. The three of us often used to go to a local café for lunch after training and invariably at some stage, the conversation would get around to Malcolm's work-rate. We kept on telling him that if only he would work a bit harder when he didn't have the ball, he could become one of the all-time greats. His stock answer was always the same: "Put your goals on the table". What he never actually said, but was clearly inferring, was that John was in the team to do his leg-work. He would be standing still while John was buzzing around all over the place and when the ball eventually came to Malcolm, he'd smash it into the net. Only years later, after I'd become a manager, did I fully grasp that he was right all along. When you have a player who is outstanding in a certain area of the game, they should be left to concentrate on that – not waste time trying to improve the bits and pieces that others could do equally as well.

Malcolm was an out-and-out match-winner, brilliant in the air with a fantastic left-foot, and he was an absolute powerhouse. Boy, was he quick! When he got up a head of steam, it was virtually impossible to stop him and he was once timed at 10.9 secs for the 100m when he took part in the TV series, Superstars. Mind you, ask him to run much further than 100m and he was rubbish. We had a crazy situation during his first pre-season when he was so far behind the rest of us in a cross-country run that he got lost. We had to send out a search party to find him. I guess that summed him up in a way. All about concentrating on your strengths.

The fans absolutely adored him, with his bandy legs and bushy sideburns, and there's no doubt that he was the biggest Newcastle United star since Jackie Milburn. True to form, he was quick to cash-in on his huge popularity. He opened a fashion shop in Newgate Shopping Centre not long after he arrived and to be fair to him, they did sell some very good stuff. I was probably his best customer.

The best thing you can do when you join a new club, especially if you've been making outrageous predications, is to hit the ground running and Macdonald instantly won over the fans by scoring a hat-trick in his home debut against Liverpool. I might actually have spoiled that particular party when I brought down Kevin Keegan to concede a penalty. But Willie McFaul came to my rescue by making a brilliant save and the stage was set for Malcolm to convert a spot kick at the other end, then fire two more goals with his favourite left-peg. We won 3-2 and there was a painful end to the game for the new hero when he was carried off with concussion after a nasty collision with Ray Clemence. Those goals were to be the first of many – 95 in 187 appearances – as he topped the scoring charts in four of the five seasons he spent at St James' Park. But although all the plaudits he received were richly deserved, it should never be forgotten that his working relationship with Tudor – and Hibbett – was vital to his success during that period.

Hibbett was a great character in his own right, capable of causing a riot in an empty house as well as being a very fine player. He infuriated me when he first arrived to play down the left-side of midfield because he insisted on coming back and taking the ball off my toes. I kept saying: "If you just stay 10 yards in front of me I'll give it to you." For some reason it took ages for that message to get through. Anyway, he had the ability to ping balls all over the place with his superb left-foot and his perfectly weighted diagonal passes over the top of defenders to set Macdonald free were a great source of goals. Those two worked well together but it wasn't always sweetness and light between them – as a really funny incident illustrated after training one day. Terry had a bit too much to say for himself, as he often did, and Malcolm, strong as the proverbial ox, simply picked him up and hung him on a clothes peg!

Despite all the changes there was a familiar look about us defensively. McFaul missed only one League game, David Craig and I were still automatic choices as full backs and so was our skipper Bobby Moncur in between us. But although we were becoming a very efficient and attractive team, we couldn't be totally trusted. That was underlined early in the New Year when we were nationally humiliated as non-league Hereford United knocked us out of the FA Cup. We brought it on ourselves to a large extent by not getting the job done when they came to St James' for a third round tie. Tudor and Macdonald both scored but it finished 2-2 – and the consequences were horrendous. Maybe we should have guessed what was coming because three times we travelled all the way down to Hereford only for the game to be rained off. That area of the country had been hit by terrible flooding and in the end, it was decided we would stay down in a Worcester hotel until such time as the pitch was declared fit. It meant that our preparation, not that anyone was really to blame, was awful. We didn't even have any other clothes to change into and boredom really set in as we lounged around the hotel for hours on end. Of course that was no excuse for us becoming the first top flight club to lose to non-league opposition for 23 years but the whole thing was horrible. It was the coming together of a series of difficult circumstances. When we finally got the game played, on the day fourth round ties were due to take place, Edgar Street was packed. The tight little stadium only held just over 14,000 and people were swinging from the surrounding trees and hanging onto the floodlight pylons. In all honesty, the pitch would never normally have been passed fit for action. But it was the same for both sides – no argument about that.

It took us 82 minutes of the replay to edge in front when Malcolm produced a far-post leap that Wyn Davies would have been proud of but Ronnie Radford equalised three minutes later with his famous wonder-goal, playing a neat 1-2 and firing the sweetest shot you will ever see. Why did he have to do it to us? It was a sensational strike that has haunted us Newcastle lads ever since. Football people always talk about third round FA Cup day as one of the great events of the season but I dread it because I know damned well that they'll be dragging up that Radford goal all over again. It's now become part of FA Cup folklore and for many years was included in the opening shots for Match of Day. Ricky George went on to score the winner in extra time and the whole thing was so embarrassing. Everyone outside of Newcastle took delight in seeing us humbled by the little non-leaguers and our fans understandably hated the fact that we were a national laughing stock. I'd never seen Joe Harvey so upset and we had to stop the coach on the way home so that he could get off and be physically sick. Then, when we stopped for a meal in Cheshire, we had to take some fearful abuse from a group of fans and I finished up pinning one of them against the wall. It all blew over within seconds but if we didn't already know it, that highlighted the degree of pain and anguish we had caused them.

Hereford had tried to do the right thing and I remember their chairman bringing a bottle of Champagne to our dressing room straight after the game. He seemed genuinely surprised when we bombarded him with muddy football boots. It still upsets me to think about that defeat and Colin Addison, who was their player-manager, cannot seem to understand why I turn him down every year when he invites me to their re-union, which involves watching a recording of the game and then having dinner. He's a lovely bloke, Colin, and any other time, I'd be delighted to have dinner with him. But I've been trying for more than 40 years to wipe that disastrous day from my memory. The last thing I need is a kick-by-kick reminder of how our downfall came about.

Winning back the respect of our supporters would be no easy thing and we were pretty relieved that our next League fixture was well away from St James' Park. There was no hiding away from what had happened though. All we could do was start repairing the damage at the first opportunity. That presented itself the following Saturday, against Manchester United at Old Trafford, and few results have been more pleasing than the 2-0 win we produced that day.

Come the end of that season, despite the Cup catastrophe, I had a good feeling about things. Macdonald and Tudor looked full of goals and the way the new lads had settled in gave me a feeling that maybe we really could hoist ourselves up to the next level the following season and finally mount a serious challenge for the title. Although Barrowclough was a typical winger, who struggled to find a consistent level of performance, he was a good crosser of the ball and provided some great service to the front pair. Howard was strong, quick and reliable alongside Moncur at the back, and the really interesting one for me was Green. I would actually go as far as to say that he was right up there among the finest players I ever played with – the type that you could genuinely build a team around. He could well have qualified as the worst trainer I'd ever seen and getting him to do any sort of running in a session was virtually impossible. But Joe soon realised that he could live with that because come the Saturday afternoon, it was like slipping a coin into a slot machine. The transformation was quite remarkable. As soon as that whistle went he was off ... 90 minutes of perpetual motion that often ran the opposition ragged and his dribbling ability was second to none. He drifted past players as if they weren't there. Tony's only weakness was that he didn't score enough goals for an attacking midfielder but I was looking forward to seeing him improve that department of his game.

I was eager for the 1972-73 season to get underway to see if we could move forward as a team but just seven games in, disaster struck for Tony when he suffered an injury that ended his career. I remember the moment so vividly. We were away to Crystal Palace and he was dribbling his way through in typical fashion when he trod on the ball. It looked innocuous enough but his twisted knee was so badly damaged that he never played again. It was that nightmare situation that had made me so reluctant years earlier to become a professional footballer. Three months later he announced his retirement. He was just 27, only 35 games into his career with Newcastle, with so much more to offer. As far as I was concerned he was irreplaceable and I didn't envy Joe as he set about trying to fill the gap. Even so, for much of the second half of that campaign we were sitting in fifth place in the First Division and would have finished in that spot had we not allowed a two-goal lead slip from our grasp in the final game at Tottenham.

We'd grown into a force to be reckoned with and although we suffered another embarrassing FA Cup defeat – 2-0 at home to Second Division Luton Town in the fourth round – we did enjoy a bit more cup success. For the second successive season we reached the semi-finals of the Texaco Cup, a sponsored competition for English and Scottish clubs who had just missed out on a place in Europe, and we won the Anglo-Italian Cup. Strangely, bearing in mind how they relished our Fairs Cup involvement, the fans never took to the Anglo-Italian and attendances were disappointing. But we saw it as a fantastic experience – on and off the field – as we visited some great places and got an insight into a very different football culture.

David Craig was my regular room-mate and never had we known such luxury as when we got drawn to play away to Como. We enjoyed magnificent views from our room overlooking the lake and breakfast was served on the balcony. Who needs football? We did click into gear when we needed to and won that game, just as we had against Roma and Bologna before that, and the Roma clash in the Olympic Stadium was particularly memorable. Their fans were getting increasingly restless as we coasted to a 2-0 win and they staged a mass protest afterwards. Our team coach had driven right into the stadium and down a ramp to the dressing room area. We were warned that on the way out, we would be best advised to get down onto the floor as we went back up the ramp. As it happened, the Roma fans all began to applaud as we emerged into the sunlight … it was their own players that they intended to hurl rocks at.

A 5-1 win over Torino took us into a two-legged semi-final against Crystal Palace and after a goalless draw at Selhurst Park, Macdonald scored a hat-trick as we notched up another 5-1 win in the return. When we went back to Italy for the final at the start of June, we walked into another interesting situation as we prepared to take on Fiorentina in front of a passionate 45,000 crowd. Keith Burkinshaw had become our chief coach by then and the day before the final, he had a huge row with Joe. What caused it was that two or three of our players had broken the curfew the previous evening. Keith was furious that the manager declined to discipline them. As the man in charge of tactics, Keith always took responsibility for giving our final 'pep' talk but he was so annoyed that he went on strike. We were all sitting in the dressing room 10 minutes before kick off, waiting to see what would happen. Keith had made his position clear so it was over to Joe, who was never at his best in these situations. In the end, he got to his feet and said: "I've been connected to this club for a long time and never lost a f****** cup final. I don't expect you lot to allow that to change." And then he walked out.

Malcolm was missing because he was away with England so

we needed to find another hero. Up stepped Craig to fill that role by scoring a rare goal. When a Fiorentina player then planted the ball into his own net, we won the game 2-1. Maybe the competition hadn't captured the public's imagination but I had another medal to add to my collection and was delighted about that. I'd like to be able to say that we celebrated in style but that wouldn't be true. Gigi Peronance, the agent who had negotiated the moves of John Charles, Jimmy Greaves and Denis Law to Italy, had helped to organise the Anglo-Italian Cup. He told us that if we won it, he'd treat us to a slap-up meal. Steak and chips in the Fiorentina canteen wasn't quite what we'd expected – but hey-ho.

Yet again it had been a busy season but my body, I'm pleased to say, was holding up well. I'd played in all but one of our League games, and all the various cup ties. I'd managed to stay largely injury-free and clear of suspensions, not that disciplinary issues were ever a problem with me. People have often told me that no self-respecting full back should be able to claim they were never suspended or even sent off, and only got booked twice throughout their entire career. I can live with that. You have to remember that we are talking about an age when you virtually had to commit GBH to get booked and not far short of murder to get sent off. Although I had my 'moments', it's a fact that I was only booked twice. One of those was scrubbed off my record and the other took place in the dressing room! I cannot remember who we were playing but I was upset about a decision the ref had made right on full time and when I called him a "Bald old bastard" as we left the field, he followed me to the dressing room and booked me.

With the other incident, I was guilty of a bad tackle and could have no complaints when the ref asked for my name. But when his report arrived at the club a couple of days later, it said that I'd been booked for an horrendous tackle from behind. No way was it a tackle from behind and knowing that the Tyne Tees cameras had covered the game, I decided to appeal and use the TV film as evidence. When I went to the hearing, I was surprised to find that Alan Hardaker, the Football League Secretary and a very powerful figure within the game, was sitting there as an observer. There was a Subbuteo pitch laid out on the table in the middle of the room, with 22 players and two stands, and unbelievably, the first 20 minutes were taken up with people trying to decide exactly where the stands should be situated. When the referee and his linesmen were eventually asked whether they were sure my tackle was from behind, they all confirmed that it was. It was game, set and match when the film revealed that clearly wasn't the case and that there must have been been some collusion between the officials. The case was instantly thrown out and I remember Hardaker being absolutely furious about the fact that we'd shown the workings of the FA to be less than perfect.

RIGHT Winning an aerial duel with Kevin Keegan, in one of our epic battles with Liverpool.

TOP RIGHT Receiving a silver salver from John Gibson, the legendary sports editor of the Newcastle Chronicle, to mark my 350th appearance for United.
Picture: Newcastle Chronicle

PLAYER - MANAGER - CHAIRMAN

Happy days with Joe Harvey – the Newcastle manager throughout my time with them. *Picture: Newcastle Chronicle*

Chapter Nine
ALL DOWNHILL AFTER CUP FINAL SHAMBLES
1973-75

I was no different to any other boy obsessed with football. The one thing I really wanted was to play in an FA Cup Final. I'd already been to Wembley to represent Crook Town in the FA Amateur Cup Final but I was desperate to discover how it felt to be in that queue of proud players, striding into the early May sunshine with the eyes of the nation upon you. The FA Cup was incredibly close to the hearts of success-starved Newcastle United fans. We all harboured great memories of Jackie Milburn & Co taking the trophy back to the North East three times in five years during the Fifties. That remarkable achievement was – and still is – central to the club's folklore. The fans longed to experience it again. But when we did finally create an opportunity to make that dream come true, in the last throws of the 1973-74 season, we absolutely blew it. Liverpool romped to a 3-0 win in a totally one-sided final and our performance, not to put too fine a point on it, was a disgrace. Even more of a disgrace was the circumstances leading up the final. To this day, more than 40 years later, it still makes me very angry to think about it.

As soon as we got within sight of a place in the final, nothing else seemed to matter. The FA Cup consumed everyone, inside and out of the football club, and the result was that we turned off from everything else. That should never have been allowed to happen. It's easy to see now that we had no chance of doing ourselves justice at Wembley because our preparation, from a very long way out, was awful. The only good decision the powers that be made during the build-up was to get the players away from Newcastle at an early stage because the anticipation and the demand for tickets was suffocating us. We couldn't turn around for people wanting a piece of us, even though most had probably never been to St James'. It came as a relief when Joe announced we would be heading south on the Monday before the game. We would be staying in a hotel near Croydon. That was fine because it was the same place Sunderland had used when they won the Cup the previous year. Surely that would be a good omen.

The problem was, difficult though you may find this to believe, absolutely no arrangements had been put in place for us to do our work each day, nor to occupy the players during their leisure time. What on earth were they thinking of? It was always going to be a recipe for disaster. How did they believe we could get ourselves into the right frame of mind to take on Liverpool and work up a plan for winning the game when we had no-where to train? I'm not talking about a fully-fledged stadium – I mean a pitch of any description. In the end, we managed to get the use of a small stretch of grass that was on a slope. It was totally unsuitable but at least we could do some work. That was only half the problem because the decision not to put some sort of programme in place to cover our leisure time led to a major rift between the players. Unless you make a plan to occupy professional footballers they'll be off in search of a good time and a small group of them disappeared into London every night. It was a crazy situation and for some reason, Joe did nothing to stop it. Much as I liked and respected him, he got it desperately wrong in that instance. One of his great strengths as a manager had always been the way he instilled strong discipline but he'd mellowed to an incredible degree. It just seemed as if he trusted the players to behave responsibly and do what had to be done to put on a performance in the final. That was never going to happen. I'd always been a bit of a dab-hand with a guitar and our coach Keith Burkinshaw suggested before we set off for London that I should take it with me. I was happy to do that and on the Tuesday evening, I put on a show at a local pub. It was a great evening but the aim of turning it into a bonding session failed miserably. There were only six of our players there. We were comfortably outnumbered by the North East media lads, who always travelled with us. By the time we got to Thursday, Keith knew we had big problems. Although it never came to blows, we made it very clear to the 'good time Charlies' that they were bang out of order and their behavior was jeopardising our chances of beating Liverpool. We'd become split into two pretty distinct groups, basically the older lads and the younger ones, and Keith was desperate to do something that would bring us back together. He asked me if I'd put on another show down at the local and I said: "No chance". In my prime, I could perform for two hours without ever repeating a single song but it really took it out of me. Bearing in mind that it was a golden rule with me that I never went out after Wednesday if we had a Saturday game coming up, there was no way I was getting involved in that. The whole thing was a nightmare. We even had a fiasco with the tracksuits that had been specially made for us to wear as we emerged from the tunnel. They were truly awful in every respect and we all refused to wear them.

Then, on the morning of the game, Joe dropped a bombshell when he announced the team. We'd been operating for most of the season with a loose 4-3-3 formation with Terry Hibbett tucked in on the left of midfield alongside Tommy Cassidy and Terry McDermott, and Stewart Barrowclough up front with Malcolm and John Tudor. My feeling was that if Liverpool had a weakness, it was at left-back. Alec Lindsay was a fine player but I reckoned that Barrowclough's pace would cause him a problem. Given the right service, he could be our match-winner. When Joe read out the names, Barrowclough was missing. He'd picked 'Jinky' Smith instead. That decision directly affected me because I had to switch to right back for the final. Unlucky David Craig missed out because of injury and I moved across with Alan Kennedy coming in at left back. It wasn't ideal but nor was it a big problem to me. Although I spent the vast majority of my career at left back I was predominantly right footed. I actually liked to think of myself as two footed but if players wanted to have a go at me on my right side, I was comfortable with that. The switch meant I would be marking Steve Heighway in the final and he was renowned for being quick and tricky. That in itself didn't cause me to have a sleepless night but as soon as Joe confirmed the team, I was very aware that I'd need to be right on top of my game. Jack Charlton was part of the TV commentary team and I've been told that he had a 'go' at me at half time for not getting forward more often. That was fine in theory but how could I trust 'Jinky' to fill in behind me when necessary? I had enough on my plate trying to contain Heighway.

I've never been able to understand why Joe left out Barrowclough but his decision played right into Liverpool's hands. I can only assume that he pinned everything on 'Jinky' taking the big stage by storm. That didn't happen. To be fair to him, not one of us did ourselves justice on the day. Somehow we managed to get to half time without conceding and I remember saying that we couldn't possibly play as badly again in the second period. The plain fact is that we did – and I don't think we had a single shot on target in the entire game. Our performance that day was far and away the biggest disappointment of my career and as I've often said in the intervening period, we prepared for six weeks to play as badly as that. We had totally turned off in the League – we actually won only two of our last 19 games – and the build-up to the final was an embarrassing shambles. I could live with losing to a very fine Liverpool team but the circumstances surrounding what should have been a dream-day left me with a feeling of bitterness that still lingers. We will never know what might – and should – have been but the most painful aspect for me was that we had failed the great people of the North East so badly. When we got back to the hotel after the game, our wives had already booked into the rooms and I remember hurling my loser's medal into the corner. It meant nothing to me and I really didn't want it. Pam retrieved it and slipped it into her case. Incidentally, many years later I loaned that medal to a museum in Newcastle City Centre and I was surprised to discover when I went back there that it had closed down. No one ever bothered to contact me and tell me it was closing so somewhere out there is my Cup Final loser's medal. I would quite like to know where it is and who has it.

We stayed down in London and went to an open air Elton John concert at Watford on the Sunday. Music has always been a massive part of my life so that was a fantastic experience. But it was impossible to enjoy it as much as I would have liked. I was still hurting from the previous day – and would do for months afterwards. We travelled back by train on the Monday and the reception people gave us at Newcastle Central Station – and all the way back to the ground on an open-top bus – was unbelievable. We really didn't deserve it after the way we'd performed and some of the players were moved to tears by the warmth of the reception. How hypocritical was that? Seeing that reaction from some of them just made me even angrier. They should have thought about that when they were selling the people short during the build-up to Wembley. The fans deserved so much more.

We had started that season really well. For a month from the closing stages of October, we occupied second place in the League. That was definitely a step up but inconsistency plagued us. At our best, we were as good as any team in the country but we didn't play to that standard often enough to make people take us seriously. In the end, as I mentioned earlier, we fell away badly and with that run of only two wins in the final 19 games, had we not started well we'd have been in big trouble. We ended up in 15th place and cup ties dominated our season.

Yet again we had problems at home against lower division opposition in the early stages of the FA Cup. Hereford and Luton had embarrassed us the previous two years and this time it was the turn of non-league Hendon. They left St James' with a 1-1 draw and although we won comfortably when the replay was staged at Watford, why did we never learn? It was exactly the same in the 4th round when lowly Scunthorpe also went away from Newcastle with a 1-1 draw. Again we were convincing winners in the replay and I can only think that spoke volumes for the make-up of the team at that time. We 'changed hats' completely for the 5th round against West Brom because we won 3-0 at The Hawthorns and the performance that day was absolutely top notch – right up there with the best I was ever associated with.

After the events of the next round, against Second Division Nottingham Forest, it was impossible not to start thinking that our name must surely be on the trophy. They deservedly led 3-1 at St James' and when Pat Howard got himself sent off in the second half, we certainly couldn't see a way back. Our fans then invaded the pitch, one or two at first and then hundreds and thousands, and we headed for the dressing rooms as quickly as our legs would carry us. We were told after a lengthy break that we would have to go out and finish the game. It was totally wrong. We had nothing to lose so we threw people forward while the Forest lads, understandably rattled, started to panic. We finished up winning the game 4-3 but I left the field thinking it would all be academic anyway. We were sure to get kicked out of the competition. Given the same situation at Glasgow Rangers in the Fairs Cup, when their fans invaded the pitch five years earlier, their chairman said that no matter what happened, we would go through. Our hierarchy opted not to do that and it did them no credit. It was a massive injustice to Forest when an inquiry ruled that the first match was "null and void" and the FA missed a big trick in reaching that decision. Football hooliganism was just starting to kick off at the time. It wouldn't be long before fences were introduced to try and put a stop to pitch invasions. If the FA had instantly expelled us from the FA Cup – and thrown the book at us – it would have sent out a strong message that no good could come from invading the pitch. As it was, their message was exactly the opposite. They then compounded the situation by announcing that the re-match would take place at Everton. Where was the logic and fairness in that as far as Forest were concerned? Then, when we drew that game and they announced that the replay would also be at Everton, that was beyond a joke. We were paid to play football, not to have opinions on politics, and when a Macdonald goal finally settled things in our favour, it set up one of the great days of my career.

I'd always been told that there was nothing worse for a footballer than to lose in the semi-final of a major cup competition. To be honest, having gone through what we did against Liverpool at Wembley, I'm not sure if I agree with that. Anyway, that theory added to the pressures as the build-up gathered pace for our meeting with Burnley on neutral ground at Hillsborough. They were a top side in those days. We knew it would be tough and they were the better team for the first hour. The atmosphere was fantastic, a mixture of tension and excitement, and with so much at stake we knew we had to hang in there, and hope for a flash of magic. 'Supermac' provided it – not once but twice – and we were elated with our 2-0 win. It meant we were through to the final and that was becoming a lovely habit because we'd already booked our place in the Texaco Cup Final in late April.

Before we move onto that, I have to share my memories of our League Cup campaign that season because I finally scored my first goal! It was goal No. 5 in a 6-0 win over Doncaster Rovers in a second round tie at St James' and what a reaction it prompted. Forget about the way things are done today. Basically, I never crossed the halfway line and if you'd ever seen me when we were doing shooting practice in training, you wouldn't argue with that. There were very few attacking full backs around at that time. My strength was defending and supporting the ball from behind – and I knew my place. Even from set-piece situations, I was always the one left standing on the halfway line. For some unknown reason against Doncaster, I found myself a few yards outside the area as the ball came my way and I just let fly. The place erupted as it flew into the top corner. The players mobbed me, the fans poured onto the pitch and after the game, they were all hanging around outside, chanting my name. James Rush, one of our directors, even came into the dressing room with a bottle of champagne. As for the Doncaster lads, they were totally baffled by it all. In the context of the game, it was hardly surprising. Terry Curran, who played on the right wing for Rovers that night, later became a colleague of mine at Forest, and he told me they couldn't see what all the fuss was about when the game was already well and truly won. It was a lovely moment and well worth the wait. I have to tell you that although the official attendance was given as 15,948, at least 25,000 people have told me over the years that they were there on the night I scored my first-ever goal.

We went out of the League Cup at the next stage when we lost in a replay to Birmingham City and incredibly, they were two of seven fixtures we had against them that season. They were a nasty team to play against at the time, very competitive and physical, with the likes of Roger Hynd, Garry Pendrey and Kenny Burns in their ranks. If you're looking for reasons why we collapsed in the second half of the campaign, maybe that was one of them. Apart from those two League Cup games and two League meetings, we also played them three times in the Texaco Cup. It should have been two meetings but the second leg went to extra time and the game had to be abandoned after 100 minutes because of bad light! That must be a 'first'. The Miners' Strike was on at the time and people were working three-day weeks to save on electricity. Football clubs were banned from using their floodlights and those who fixed the kick-off time for that midweek tie must have forgotten to factor in the possibility of extra time. Anyway, I'm very pleased that we did have to go to an extra game because it allowed me to double my career goals tally. We finally saw Birmingham off with a 3-1 win at St James' and this time my goal was nothing like as spectacular. I think it was the fifth bobble that fooled City's goalkeeper Dave Latchford.

Scottish clubs were also involved in the Texaco Cup and we came out on top in two-legged clashes with Morton and Dundee United to earn the right to play Burnley in the final. We won the toss to have home advantage and there were 36,076 people there to see me boost my growing medal collection as we lifted the trophy after a 2-1 win. Not only did we win it, we also retained it the following year and it was my job to step up and receive the Cup on that occasion because by then, I'd been appointed club captain. We came out on top in group matches against Sunderland, Carlisle and Middlesbrough, then fought our way past Aberdeen and Birmingham (again) before defeating Southampton in the final. We were 1-0 down after our trip to The Dell but sparked another great night of St James' Park celebrations with a 3-1 win in the return.

It was a sensational story in the North East when Bobby Moncur announced live on national television that he was leaving Newcastle to join Sunderland. Bob was working with the ITV panel providing coverage of the 1974 World Cup when he told the nation it was time for a change. He'd worn the black & white stripes at one level or another for 14 years and the fact that he was joining our closest rivals took our breath away. I've never really dug too deeply into how Bob arrived at his decision but I suspect, like me, that he was becoming increasingly frustrated about the way the club was being run. Joe had lost his sparkle and there was a real lack of ambition being shown at Board level.

I suppose I was the obvious choice to take over the captaincy. I'd filled in for Bob on numerous occasions over the years when he'd been forced to miss matches and by then, I was the senior figure in the dressing room. On the back of the bad atmosphere that the Cup Final build-up had caused, I was conscious that I could be setting myself up for a difficult time by taking the job. But I'd never have forgiven myself had I turned down the chance to become the captain of Newcastle United and me being me, I was determined to make a success of it. The problem was that in taking my responsibilities seriously, I got myself well and truly branded as a trouble-maker. Because of the way the club was being run, many of the players – not just the youngsters but experienced lads as well – had all sorts of issues that were not getting resolved. I suppose when they turned to me for help I could have shrugged my shoulders but that was never my way. I did what I could to help them fight their corner and inevitably, I got myself a reputation with the hierarchy for being a shop steward. On reflection, that did me no favours.

That season was comfortably the worst of my Newcastle career. I'd always prided myself on the fact that I seldom missed matches. But I only played 19 League games that season because of a series of niggling injuries, and several of those were as a centre back. I mentioned at the start of this story that I had an opportunity midway through the season to go to America and make a fresh start. As Joe had advised, I went to see the chairman, Lord Westwood, to discuss it with him. He assured me that I had a future at Newcastle and he did not want me to go. Based on that meeting, I turned down the American offer but come the end of the season, I was given a free transfer at the same time as Joe was moved 'upstairs' and Keith Burkinshaw was sacked. My last game was in David Craig's testimonial against Sunderland, which was tagged onto the end of the season. By then, word had leaked out that I'd been released and although most of the fans gave me a warm send-off, my 'friends' on the Popular Side didn't pass up the chance to have one last go at me.

So that was it... time to move on. The vast majority of the previous 13 years had been a privilege and a pleasure and I was leaving with a sackful of medals and so many great memories. I'd managed to chalk up 486 League & Cup appearances – only two players had ever played more times by that stage – and apart from the 42 when we won promotion in my very first season, every game in the League had been in the top flight. I trust that proved a point to that journalist at the

Newcastle Journal who wrote: "Surely only Frank Clark's mum thinks he will be good enough for the First Division."

I just had one last opportunity to run out at St James' Park wearing the black & white stripes. That came exactly a year later. I'd been promised a testimonial and the club stuck to their word. As usual for such occasions, Sunderland provided the opposition and a crowd of 19, 974 turned up to see us record a 6-3 win in a thoroughly entertaining game. It was an incredibly special day for me and I cannot thank the players and supporters enough for the reception they gave me. I was totally overwhelmed by it.

Bearing in mind that I was long-gone from Newcastle by that stage, I didn't organise any other testimonial activities, except for a night with Jasper Carrott that Malcolm Macdonald kindly offered to front up for me. Jasper at that time was a folk singer with ambitions to become a comedian and when I met him at a function in Birmingham, he offered to put on a night for me. It attracted a big turnout at City Hall and I was disappointed I wasn't able to be there because Nottingham Forest had a game that night. When I rang Malcolm late on to ask how it had gone he was his usual bull-shitting self. He said there was good news and bad. The good news was that they'd had a brilliant night. Unfortunately, they hadn't made any money.

Some you win, some you lose – and I'll forever count my lucky stars that I won a lot more than I lost during my time at Newcastle.

Making music as we build up to the FA Cup Final.
Picture: Daily Mirror

PLAYER - MANAGER - CHAIRMAN

TOP Farewell Newcastle – it's been great. *Picture: Newcastle Chronicle*

Chapter 10
INJURY-PRONE? IT HELPS WHEN YOU WORK FOR A GENIUS
1975-76

Brian Clough often referred to the fact that he left school at 14 and was poorly educated. In fact, it cropped up so often that I suspect he might well have had some deep lying hang-up about it. But a lack of 'O' levels didn't change the fact that he was one of the most intelligent men I've ever come across and the sharpness of his brain put him right up there with the finest legal judges in the land. I was always in awe of the speed of thought he showed in reacting to any situation. It didn't seem to matter how much pressure he was under. He was an incredibly decisive man and I gave up wondering if he ever got things wrong. Of course he must have done somewhere along the line during his time as the Nottingham Forest overlord, but he covered his tracks so quickly that we never got to see it. He certainly never lost an argument. Larry Lloyd tried to take him on, so did Martin O'Neill but no one to my knowledge ever got the better of 'Cloughie'. The more I got to know him, the more I came to realise there was an ulterior motive to virtually everything he did. We'd often wonder why he'd said or done a certain thing and days later – sometimes weeks later – all was revealed. It was quite remarkable. Stories are legendary about how

Brian hammered players at times for falling below the high standards he required of them yet they always seemed to leave his office feeling 10ft tall because of a little compliment he'd cleverly handed out at the end of their 'chat'. He certainly had a temper and could be vicious at times. At the other extreme, it was amazing to see him turn on the charm – and he was totally sincere about it.

Even now, years after he died, people still want to speak to me all the time about Brian. They love to hear the stories about how he and Peter Taylor lifted the club from rags to riches and everyone wants to know what made him so special.

Brian was very much a man of his time. By that I mean that I don't think it would have been possible to adopt his style of management in today's world. The methods he used to motivate players would either have been seen as non 'pc' – or simply wouldn't have got the same reaction from people whose vast wealth means they're not the slightest bit influenced by the carrot and stick way of doing things. But back in the Seventies, Brian had 'gifts' that set him apart from his peers. He had an incredible ability to squeeze the absolute maximum out of those who worked for him. Not only that but we also got a huge amount of satisfaction from knowing we had given him our last drop. For me, football management is primarily about two things. The first is acquiring the talent, the second is bringing the best out of the players you have at your disposal. Peter Taylor was the main man when it came to acquisitions and there was no one better at man management than Brian. If you are looking to sum up their amazing success in one sentence … there you have it.

Brian was no great tactical genius. What he did have though, was a thorough understanding of the basics of the game and an unwavering belief that in order to be successful, you need to have 11 players on the field all doing their jobs properly. We all knew exactly what was expected of us and as long as we tried to do that to the best of our ability, we were OK with him. He never asked us to do things we couldn't do. In fact, we could be in big trouble if we tried to step outside of our brief. I remember an occasion when John McGovern went charging forward to get involved in an attack and most managers wouldn't have given it a second thought. But Brian made it abundantly clear that his job was to sit in the centre of midfield, not get all gung-ho, and he warned that if it happened again, he would immediately pull him off. That was another of the incredible things that set Brian apart ... he never missed a trick. He saw – and remembered – every single thing that happened in a game. When you think that he always sat on the bench at the City Ground, which meant he was looking at the pitch at eye-level, it was all the more staggering. We never got away with anything and knowing that we would have to take the consequences for any act of stupidity kept us fully on our toes. Kenny Burns fell foul of that in a game against Manchester City when Brian seized on an opportunity to make a point. We were well in charge of the game when Kenny got the ball on the edge of our area and instead of just clearing it, he tried to be clever and chip a pass to me. Dennis Tueart intercepted it. Fortunately, he couldn't control the ball and it went out of play. When we got to the dressing room at half time, the boss handed 'Burnsy' a white envelope with a red Forest 'tree' on the front. As soon as the incident happened, he'd told the club secretary, Ken Smales, to go and type out an official letter, notifying 'Burnsy' that he'd been fined. That act of stupidity cost him £50 and he was told in no uncertain terms that any repeat performance would cost him £200. It was expensive for 'Burnsy' but every single one of us got the message that day.

Having said that, I don't want to give the wrong impression. People have often suggested to me that Brian ruled by fear. That's nonsense in my view. There's no way we could have performed as well as we did over such a lengthy period if we'd had a fear culture within our dressing room. On the contrary, the atmosphere throughout the whole club was terrific. We had a healthy respect for Brian and although you certainly didn't want to get on the wrong side of him, the relationship wasn't based on fear. We knew what the rules were and providing we played by them, we were fine.

Looking back, there was nothing complicated about things during that era – on or off the field. He'd developed a style of play that worked brilliantly for him when Derby County won the League Championship. Very little changed when he came to Forest. He expected his defenders to win the ball and in his words, "give it to someone who can play". He was obsessed about certain elements, like breaking your neck to stop opponents from crossing the ball. Knowing what a huge percentage of goals stem from crosses, no one could argue with that. Equally, few things angered him more than if the front players failed to get hold of the ball when it was played up to them. That's why Garry Birtles was such a success with Forest, because he had phenomenal work-rate and would hold the ball up and turn away from defenders.

Like I said, we all knew our jobs inside out. In fact, we all knew each other's jobs. That's why players could switch positions so effectively, as John O'Hare did when the Scottish international centre-forward had a terrific spell playing in midfield. We kept the same shape, no matter what. We never even had a Plan B. His philosophy was that if it's right in the first 10 minutes of a game it must be right in the last 10 minutes as well. Brian would say that if things are not happening for us, we must work even harder to make sure they do. We just stuck to the basics, passed the ball to a red shirt and made sure there was always at least one player supporting the man in possession. Of course, an element of the way we did things was to do with it being a different era. For example, we operated with a squad of 16 players in those days and as you were only allowed one substitute, you tended to hold back on using him in case someone got injured. Another thing that people today find difficult to accept is that we never ever worked on set-pieces. When David Needham joined us he came from Queen's Park Rangers, who were renowned as a progressive club in coaching terms through the influence of Dave Sexton. In one of Dave's early games, he just went and stood at the near post when we forced a corner because it was what he always did at Rangers. But that wasn't something that our central defenders ever did. John Robertson, being 'Robbo', responded to that by plonking the ball onto Dave's head and he flicked it into the net. Peter Taylor was quick to tell the media afterwards that it was a move we'd worked on for a while in training. Yeah, Yeah!

You'd be astonished to see the lengths that most managers go to in the modern game to try and establish the strengths and weaknesses of the opposition. Scouts, analysts and Uncle Tom Cobley feed in every scrap of information they can unearth. In the four years I spent working for Brian, only once can I remember him even mentioning the opposition as we prepared for a game. He decided before we went to Liverpool for the second leg of the European Cup to switch Archie Gemmill to play wide on the right, presumably hoping that his stamina and gritty determination would curb the attacking flair of Ray Kennedy. Other than that, the opposition didn't matter. It was all about what we did and whether he believed it or not, Brian always gave us the strong impression that he fully expected us to win if we did our work properly.

Standards were a huge thing with him and in many ways, he was quite old fashioned in his approach to life. Discipline and respect were right up there on his list of priorities, as he illustrated in the way in which he dealt with referees. It was an absolute no-no for us to show dissent to officials in any way. Maybe that was a tactic and Brian believed that if you treat referees with respect, you might get the odd favour in return. I think he simply felt it was the right way to behave. He was never slow to 'have a word' if he thought we needed a haircut, or caught us standing with hands in our pockets. He set himself high standards and demanded the same from others. I'm sure that disciplined approach had a big influence on our performances and results. Even when we played in testimonial matches – and there were lots of those – he was obsessed with doing things properly. He always fielded a full-strength team and our orders were to treat it just like a cup tie. On one occasion we flew to the Middle East to play

Maccabi Tel Aviv and the eyes of the world were on Israel at the time because Anwar Sadat, the president of Egypt, had just arrived. He was the first Arab leader to visit Israel and address the Knesset and I've never known such tight security. There were gun-toting soldiers everywhere we turned. Anyway, we won the game 6-1 and as we left the field, it seemed like every single person in the stadium stood up and applauded us. When I asked one of their officials what we had done to deserve that sort of reception he said that we were the first overseas team who had ever gone there and taken the game seriously. That was a great tribute to Brian. He taught us that we had a duty to represent Nottingham Forest to the very best of our ability at all times and equally important, be true to ourselves.

I'd only ever had one boss before I moved to Nottingham. Joe Harvey had been in charge throughout all my time with Newcastle United and I suppose it's pretty amazing in itself that I only played for two managers throughout my entire 17-year professional career. That probably means I'm not best qualified to talk about the merits or otherwise of managers. But I do know that I was incredibly fortunate to work with two of the best in the business in the eras in which they operated. I'm also very proud of the fact that in both cases, I was a part of relatively long-term projects to build something special.

Initially, it was a bit like footballing chalk and cheese when I signed for Forest. I'd been used to regularly putting my work up for scrutiny in front of 50,000-plus crowds for as long as I could remember. Now I was joining a Second Division outfit who had hit on hard times. That was underlined when the attendance for my debut at home to Plymouth in August 1975 was just 13,083. It was a very different environment but I certainly wasn't complaining. 'Cloughie' had shown faith in me when no one else would. I was determined to repay him. I'd also seen enough of him already to make me think we were in for a lively ride. What I didn't know, of course, was that by the time I retired four years later, I would have figured in a promotion from the Second Division, won the League Championship and also added an Anglo-Scottish Cup, two League Cup and one European Cup winner's medals to my collection.

The minute we arrived in Nottingham, Pam and I had a good feeling. Alan Hill, one of the coaches, took her and our young daughter Lisa for a walk alongside the River Trent while I completed my negotiations – if you can call them that – with the manager. We both already knew it was a done deal, not least because apart from a couple of luke-warm inquiries from Hartlepool and Doncaster, no one had shown the slightest interest since Newcastle announced that I was being given a free transfer. The word on the grapevine was that I'd become injury-prone. That was enough to make everyone steer clear of me. I couldn't dispute that I'd missed a lot of games the previous season because of various muscle injuries. That was a fact. And although I was very confident about my ability, the doubts about my fitness were really starting to play on my mind.

I remembered reading a magazine article with Mohammad Ali in which he'd been asked whether he trained less as he was approaching the end of his career. He said he'd actually trained more and it made me think if that was good enough for him, it had to be good enough for me. That was my plan.

Brian was known within the game for not working his players too hard but that, I can assure you, was a fallacy. My first pre-season at Forest was as physically demanding as any I ever experienced. Much of the work revolved around running and although Wollaton Park is a delightful area of Nottingham, we were seldom in any fit state to appreciate it. Alan Hill was a really strong runner and always led from the front. We were constantly screaming at him to "slow down" but it fell on deaf ears. The manager's theory, and it obviously worked, was that if you put in the hard graft during pre-season, you would only need to top up your fitness as you went along – especially if you were playing two games a week. Consequently, he gave us lots of days off because he believed rest periods were essential.

I could understand that but I also wanted to be as sure as I could that I wasn't going to be hampered by another season of injury troubles. Consequently, I regularly went out for a 'recovery run' around the streets near my home but that came back to bite me when a supporter sent a letter to the local newspaper, praising me for being such a good 'pro'. When Brian got to know about it, I was hauled into his office to be bluntly told: "When I give you a day off you take a day off... or I'll fine you." In my first two seasons at Forest I never missed a game. Including Cup ties, that added up to more than 100 consecutive appearances. His memory, as I've already mentioned, was incredible and straight after we won promotion in my second season he pulled me aside and said: "Well? Now who was right?"

We settled immediately in Nottingham. We bought a new house in a village called Lowdham and quickly established a circle of brilliant neighbours and friends. I loved the 10-mile drive through the countryside to work and back every day and the heartache and fears we had about swopping our native North East for the East Midlands were quickly dispelled. I must admit, though, that my first impressions of the playing side of things at Forest were not very favourable. They seemed a decent enough set of lads but were not much of a team. Sammy Chapman and John Cottam, a couple of bully-boy central defenders, ran the dressing room. I let it be known straight away that they wouldn't be running me and we had an 'understanding'. McGovern and O'Hare, who had been part of the Derby County success story, had been bought for a cut-price fee from Leeds in order to, as the manager put it: "Show the rest how to do it". But looking around our dressing room, I didn't see much to fill me with confidence that we could mount a promotion challenge. Martin O'Neill was already there, so was Ian Bowyer... and then there was John Robertson. My first impression of 'Robbo' was that he and his mate Jimmy McCann were a couple of scallywags who were not serious enough about their football. To be honest, I saw no inkling in those early days of the fantastic talent he possessed. We went to Germany in pre-season for a five-game tour that I thoroughly enjoyed, then skipped over to Ireland to play Ballymena and Coleraine. It was an ideal way for me to get to know my new colleagues. I remember being really conscious of the fact that the majority were so much younger than me. I was sure that was part of Brian's thinking when he signed me on. He was very clear about the fact that he wanted me to use my experience to have an influence in the dressing room and on the pitch.

I had to smile less than two weeks into the season when Brian announced the team for a League Cup tie against Rotherham and I was down to play as a central defender. Liam O'Kane had suffered an injury at Portsmouth so I moved into the middle and 17-year-old Bryn Gunn took over my No. 3 shirt. It took me back to the original meeting I'd had with Brian at Scotch Corner Hotel. I mentioned in our talks that I'd played a number of games as a central defender for Newcastle because I thought it might impress him that I had another string to my bow. He didn't want to know. He cut me off in mid-sentence with a curt comment about signing me to play at left back. Now here I was, striking up a new partnership with Sammy Chapman. I didn't mind. Sammy was something of a legend at the City Ground and was in his testimonial season. He loved his hard-man image, which was certainly justified because I hate to think how many players he left his mark on over the years. He could be downright vicious but was also very skilful and read situations well. The problem with Sammy was that he didn't always pick the best moment to demonstrate his skill. That was a flaw that was always going to cause him to have problems with Brian. As for young 'Gunny', he had a decent run in the team and certainly looked the part. I actually got to know him well because, right out of the blue, Brian asked me one day if I would take him in as a lodger. I cannot remember the circumstances – maybe it was back to this business of me being a good influence. Anyway, I took the idea home to Pam, fully expecting her to dismiss it out of hand, but she agreed to it. Bryn stayed with us for a few months and was never a minute's problem. Actually, that's not strictly true because we had terrible trouble getting him to drink. I don't mean alcohol. I'm talking about fluid of any description.

We just couldn't understand how he managed to keep himself hydrated.

Bearing in mind the love-hate relationship I had with a small section of fans at St James' Park, I was delighted that the City Ground supporters seemed to take to me straight away – and that rapport never wavered. I think it was influenced by a little incident in one of my early games. One of the opposition players got clear down the middle and although our goalkeeper John Middleton came out to block the shot, the ball came off him and was looping towards our goal. I managed to get back and, for the first and only time in my life, I cleared it with a spectacular overhead scissors kick. The place erupted and I collected enough 'brownie points' in that precise moment to keep me going for ages. Even to this day I still get people coming up to me and saying they remember that clearance.

It was evident at a very early stage that we didn't have enough about us to mount a promotion challenge and that was a testing period for 'Cloughie'. Forest were not a wealthy club by any means and although he was desperate to re-shape the squad, the only way that would happen would be if he could beg, steal and borrow. He was good at doing that. A player-exchange deal led to Terry Curran joining us from Doncaster Rovers and Brian was clearly excited about pulling it off. Curran certainly offered us something different with his speed and skill down the right and I think we all felt that he was going to become our main man. Sadly, injuries and illness got in the way of that happening but although he only stayed for two years, he did give us a spark in those early days.

Our other significant signing was Colin Barrett, a play-anywhere type who initially joined us on loan from Manchester City just before the March transfer deadline. We became really good mates and we must have been because even when we found ourselves competing for the same left back spot, we were still close. Colin was a good footballer, very competitive and an excellent team man. I thought Brian produced a master-stroke by signing him. Colin didn't want to join us at first but Brian's persuasive powers sorted that and I thought he made a big contribution in the four years before a knee injury tragically wrecked his career at the age of 28. He certainly gave fantastic value in return for the £29,000 it cost to make his move from City permanent.

That was peanuts compared to the sort of fees Brian would be shelling out on a fairly regular basis three years down the line and I always think that somehow gets lost when people talk about his incredible achievements. Forest were unique at that time because they were run by a nine-man committee who, as I understand it, had no obligation to fund the club out of their own personal accounts. There was certainly no sugar-daddy on the scene, pumping in millions like they do today, so the long and short of it was that any money Brian spent had to be generated through gate receipts, commercial activities and transfer dealings. With attendances dropping to less than 10,000 on occasions in my first season, that was a measure of what he was up against. I know the lack of buying-power was a source of huge frustration to him and was much to do with the fact that he regularly threatened to resign when the committee wouldn't back him. But he stuck at it and somehow transformed the club's finances every bit as much as he did our playing performances. I have nothing but admiration for the way that he did that and kept Forest in the forefront of English football for the best part of 18 years. Of course he was a brilliant football manager but he also had a brilliant business brain.

We eventually finished eighth in the Second Division in my first season but truthfully, I don't think we were that good. There were, though, some promising signs that Brian was moving things in the right direction. We kept clean-sheets in six of our last seven games of the season. We only lost once in that period – and we also won our last eight home games on the trot. On top of that, some key round pegs were being fitted into round holes... especially John Robertson.

Lining up with my new team mates at Nottingham Forest
Picture: Nottingham Post/Nottingham Local Studies Collection

Chapter 11
'ROBBO' SEES THE LIGHT AS WE FLY TO PROMOTION
1976-77

I've often wondered what would come out on top if you carried out an in-depth survey about Peter Taylor's greatest contributions during his time with Nottingham Forest. Would it be his ability to identify unlikely heroes like Kenny Burns, Larry Lloyd and Peter Withe? Would it be his central role in getting John Robertson to finally see the light? Perhaps it would be his insistence on signing Peter Shilton at a key stage in our development... or maybe it would simply be the fact that he always managed to make Brian Clough laugh. The pair had gone their separate ways after the messy end to their incredible spell with Derby County but there was an unbelievable buzz around the City Ground when they were re-united in the summer of 1976. Peter had resigned a few weeks earlier as manager of Brighton and he wanted everyone to know he was delighted to be back in his home city, renewing his partnership with Brian. The biggest problem I could see as we built up towards the new campaign would be managing expectations because we were starting out with basically the same set of players. It didn't stay that way for long.

I 'got' it straight away that Peter was a big man and a big character – and there was something in his make-up that prevented him from ever taking things at face value. Whatever the situation, he always seemed to think there must be something more to it, and he believed his role in life was to dig until he found it. For example, he was convinced every player must have a vice. Whether it be drink, women, gambling or something more obscure, there had to be at least one vice and he was determined to find it. He had a way of getting under people's skin and his theory was that unless you got to fully understand what made a player tick, you wouldn't be able to bring out the best in them in every given situation. That was how he got his kicks in a football sense – from helping to turn players into 'big' winners when people had virtually given up on them.

Larry Lloyd was a classic case. Everyone in football knew he had all the attributes to become a top defender – that's why Bill Shankly had paid out a hefty fee to take him from Bristol Rovers as a successor to Ron Yeats. But Larry was never the easiest to manage and had this thing about challenging authority. He played for England while he was at Anfield, and helped win the UEFA Cup, so on the surface it seemed a really strange decision when Liverpool allowed him to move to Coventry for £240,000. It seemed even more peculiar when he dropped a division to land at the City Ground for a quarter of that fee. As a business deal it was brilliant but that was only the half of it because Peter was convinced that with him and 'Cloughie' as controlling influences, they would get big Larry to push on to fulfil his potential.

It was a similar tale with Peter Withe. He'd been knocking around the lower leagues for some time and also had spells in South Africa and America. But there was nothing in his track record to suggest he was a potential League Championship winner – or that he would eventually go on to score the winning goal for Aston Villa in the European Cup Final. He was already 25-years-old when he signed for Forest and frankly, his record of 12 goals in 52 appearances for

Wolves and Birmingham was very ordinary. But Taylor had done his homework in his own inimitable way and in my book, the signing of 'Withey' was one of the best he made. I really rated him. He was an excellent team player, a great athlete and top-notch target man. I particularly liked the fact that he had the ability to turn average passes into good ones when the ball was fired in his direction! 'Withey' was a brilliant pro and I think it summed him up when we went on a 'bender' to Cala Millor – Cloughie's favourite haunt in Majorca – and he went for a run every morning while the rest of us were still in bed.

So many of the signings Taylor lined up at that time concerned players that others doubted for one reason or another. That would have been partly to do with the fact that Forest were still strapped for cash so they had to take gambles. There's no doubt that he loved nothing more than to pull the proverbial rabbit out of the hat. That didn't just involve bringing new players to the club. He was equally influential in re-shaping the careers of numerous players already on the books.

Seldom, if ever, during the course of my lengthy playing career can I remember a manager or coach getting stuck into a player quite like he did to John Robertson soon after he'd arrived at the club. We were in the middle of a training session on a pre-season trip to Germany when he stepped in and emptied both barrels. 'Robbo' got the full force – and Peter then sent him packing, back to the hotel. Once we'd finished our work, the two of them sat down and carried on their 'discussion'. This time it was conducted in a far more constructive way and the key words Peter said were: "I'm only bothering with you because we think you can play." According to 'Robbo' that was his Saul on the Road to Damascus moment. That was the comment that changed his life and put him on the path to becoming one of the finest players this country has ever seen.

He'd already made the switch from midfield player to out-and-out left-winger but all of a sudden, he began to demonstrate the full extent of his unbelievable talent. For the best part of three years, it was my privilege to watch a master craftsman at work from very close quarters. I'd actually like to take some credit for helping 'Robbo' to achieve some of the great things he did – but I know my place. The left-sided role was still quite new to him and he had some rough edges to work on. But he steadily matured and the better he became, the more our understanding developed. One of the things I most admired about him was how courageous he was on the pitch – not in terms of going into tackles but the fact that he always wanted the ball. Invariably there would be two players marking him but no matter how bad things were in a game, never once did he go into hiding. He was always available, always demanding the ball, and I was always happy to give it to him. It was standard procedure for teams to double-mark him and in an age when 'nailing' a troublesome opponent was regarded as part and parcel of the game, I'm sure they will have often planned to take 'Robbo' out by illegal means. Yet in all my time playing behind him, I don't ever recall anyone managing to do so. That was more than coincidence. 'Robbo' was so good that he could dodge tackles before they landed. It was a tribute to his amazing ability.

I'd had a similar relationship at Newcastle with Terry Hibbitt. Like 'Robbo', he liked to get on the ball early and if I could give it to him while he had half a yard of space to work in, that boosted his chances of getting the upper-hand on his marker. The fact that I was naturally right-footed was really helpful in that regard. It meant that if the ball was coming to me, I could just help it on to Terry or 'Robbo', rather than waiting for it to come across my body and maybe take a touch before moving it on. As always with these situations when you work together for long enough, 'Robbo' knew what to expect from me and I from him. Very rarely did I make a run in front of him because that meant I was invading the space he wanted to hit, so he could deliver one of his teasing crosses. But he always knew I'd be backing him up and help was at hand if he needed it. He gradually developed into the most influential player in a team packed with quality internationals. No matter what plans opponents came up with, they just couldn't deal with him. He'd simply drop his shoulder, weave his way around them, and when he got to the by-line the cross was delivered. There was always an end product with him. Nothing too elaborate – he never overdid things. He had an uncanny ability to get his angles and timing just right so he was guaranteed to cause maximum damage. Right foot or left foot, it was all the same for him.

'Robbo' was such a good player in the period when we won the League Championship and then two European Cups. We were all in awe of him. The only one who wasn't was the man himself. He genuinely used to look at the team-sheet when it was pinned up on a Friday morning and thank his lucky stars that he'd been picked. Incredible! I always thought that the scruffy tramp image he had to live with was unfair. Clough and Taylor used to refer to him affectionately as "the little fat bloke" and he did have problems keeping his weight under control. But he was also a very intelligent lad who took that into his game. I've played with so many wingers over the years whose legs worked faster than their brains and virtually everything they did was instinctive. You couldn't pin that one on 'Robbo'. He knew exactly what he was doing at all times and it's totally beyond me why he doubted himself.

The atmosphere around the City Ground was very different as we prepared for the 1976-77 season. That had to be down to Taylor's arrival. The playing staff was virtually unchanged by the time we kicked off the League programme but there was much more energy around the place. No one was going through the motions any more and it was easy to see that the boss was delighted to have his mate back to aid and abet him. Taylor could be a very funny man and Brian thrived on the humour he brought to the scene. When I talked to John McGovern and John O'Hare about it, they felt that Brian had been coasting the previous season, by his standards. There was something missing compared to their time working under him at Derby but Peter re-lit his flame. Together, they were an irresistible force. I'm so grateful that at a stage of my career when most players were being put out to grass, I had a front row seat as football's finest double-act put on a show. It's common knowledge that they were very different people in all sorts of ways but the chemistry between them created a dream partnership. I was fascinated by the way they worked their 'good cop, bad cop' routine. I'm sure they sat down in advance and planned it out. Whether we liked them as individuals was irrelevant – the players were all desperate to please them and it made our day if one of them paid us a compliment. You could guarantee though, that just as you began to feel pleased with yourself, the other one would say or do something to drag you back down again. They instilled confidence in us but never allowed us to get carried away. It was a brilliant exercise in how to keep people on their toes.

Training sessions most of the time were left in the capable hands of Jimmy Gordon. He was an old-fashioned fitness trainer, big on discipline. He was also very organised and kept things simple. Having been part of Derby's success, he understood how the management wanted things done. I'd always enjoyed training but I particularly loved going to work in my time at Forest. Sessions tended to be fairly short but they were very intensive, with lots of five-a-sides and virtually no functional coaching whatsoever. That just didn't fit into Brian's scheme of things although he argued that every time he opened his mouth, he was coaching. He didn't need half-hour sessions to get his point across. Colin Barrett, for example, tells a story about the day he got an earful for playing a square pass. "If you can play the ball forward, do it," screamed the boss. "If you can run forward with the ball, do it." Message received and understood. That's coaching.

Very rarely did we see Clough and Taylor at the training ground. They were too busy scheming, back at the City Ground. They were constantly plotting and planning, striving to find ways of making us better and setting up deals that would have an impact both on and off the field. If it was a nice day, though, there was always a chance they would take a stroll alongside the Trent and we had to be on our guard. If they suddenly appeared at training without us realising and one of us was taking a breather, woe betide the player concerned.

There was an encouraging start to the season as we fought our way impressively through our qualifying group in the Anglo-Scottish Cup, drawing at Notts County and beating two top-flight outfits in West Brom and Bristol City. I was already the holder of two winners' medals in this competition, from my time at Newcastle when it was known as the Texaco Cup. For some reason, that didn't impress my Forest colleagues too much! Anyway, that form didn't spill over into the League because four games in, we'd drawn three of them and had our weaknesses brutally exposed by Wolves in a 3-1 home defeat. But things did get better as Terry Curran kept giving us a spark with his exciting wing-play down the right and a couple of key re-enforcements were drafted in. Withe's impact was immediate as he marked his debut with a goal in a 5-1 win over Carlisle and was on target again when we beat Sheffield United 6-1 in our next home game. Big 'Lloydy' was the other new-boy and he brought something very different to our dressing room. It was impossible not to get the impression that he felt he was doing us a favour by coming to Forest but we all knew that with him in our team, our chances of being successful were so much brighter.

It was a perfect platform for the moaners when we were drawn to play Kilmarnock and then Ayr United in two-legged affairs in the Anglo-Scottish Cup because the coach trips to Scotland seemed to take forever. Crossing the border had become a fairly regular thing during the latter years of my time with Newcastle but there was a big difference between heading up from the North East and the long haul from Nottingham. Tedious journeys are an occupational hazard for footballers and it was made worse if, like me, you didn't get involved in the card schools. I used to in my early playing days but quickly learned the folly of arriving home with no cash in my pocket. I either used to read or sleep, or – if I was really lucky – find some stimulating conversation, but long trips were definitely a down-side to playing for Newcastle. Anyway, we got the job done against Kilmarnock and Ayr and that took us through to meet Leyton Orient. Hardly the most glamorous of fixtures, I admit, but it was a Cup Final. Forest had not appeared in one of those for a very long time. We drew 1-1 at Brisbane Road in mid-December and just two days later, won the second leg 4-0. The prospect of seeing us lift the Anglo-Scottish Cup didn't exactly excite the Nottingham football public. Only 12,717 turned up to watch – but the significance was certainly not lost on Clough and Taylor. It had given us a taste of success and helped to develop a winning mentality. Now the challenge was to push on and try to win promotion.

Our chances of doing that had been severely hit by a serious injury Curran sustained during a win over Burnley in October but, for not the only time in the Clough-Taylor reign, as one door closed another one opened.

I couldn't understand what Brian had against a lad called Tony Woodcock. He impressed me every time I saw him play for the reserves or working in training but for some reason, the boss was reluctant to give him a chance at first-team level. He clearly didn't rate Tony, who came very close to signing for Doncaster and Lincoln after doing well during loan spells with them. Taylor was much more on my wave-length on this one and kept telling Brian he should give him a go. Part of the problem might have been that Brian was undecided about what was his best position and one day he asked Tony where he wanted to play. "In the hole boss," said Tony, after giving it due consideration. There was no due consideration required from the manager as he instantly fired back: "You won't find any f***ing holes on my pitch!" Tony was really quick. His close control was good, he could turn defenders, ride tackles and was a decent finisher. What was there not to like?

Eventually he did get his chance to contribute to the Anglo-Scottish success, scored in his first game in the 2-0 win at Ayr ... and his partnership with 'Withey' was up and running. Come the end of the season, Tony was voted Player of the Year by supporters and the front pairing had produced 36 valuable goals between them. Everything pointed to the fact that losing Curran at that time would be a massive blow that could even wreck our promotion hopes but the problem had been solved, without spending a penny. Was that purely down to luck? It probably was but then again, it was by no means the only time that happened during the golden era.

'Lloydy' was still playing hard to get. He went back to Coventry when his loan spell expired and got back into their team. He eventually signed for us permanently in December. By that stage, we were storming up the Second Division table. We arrived in second place after a 2-0 win at Millwall but couldn't maintain it. We'd slipped down to seventh by mid-March and had completely lost our momentum.

There are always loads of twist and turns during the course of a 42-game season. You learn to take the rough with the smooth but some incidents really do have a massive influence, like the night when we played Southampton at the City Ground in February. They'd won the FA Cup the previous year and had some terrific players at that time – Mick Channon, Peter Osgood, Alan Ball and so on – and if you happened to get them on a day when they all fancied 'playing', you had problems. Collectively, they were far too good for the Second Division and on that particular night, they were ahead and totally controlling the game when all of a sudden, a blanket of fog covered the pitch. When the referee complained he couldn't see both goals from the halfway line, we couldn't get back to the dressing room quickly enough. Visibility was no better some 20 minutes later, so he abandoned the game and although the fog lifted very soon afterwards, the decision had already been made. We really got out of jail with that one and it was the start of people claiming 'Cloughie' was so brilliant he was even capable of divine intervention. We won 2-1 when the re-arranged fixture took place in late March and by then, a concerted push to get ourselves involved in the promotion shake-up was underway.

There was no such thing as Play-offs in those days, of course. The top three got automatically promoted. By the time we reached Easter we occupied the third spot and were neck-and-neck with Notts

County. As it turned out, we were due to meet them on the Saturday, just across the river at Meadow Lane. They were only one point behind us with seven games remaining and whoever won that clash would be right in the driving seat. Compared to what I was used to when Newcastle played Sunderland, I thought the Nottingham derby games were pretty low-key affairs. I'm sure that view was influenced by the fact that I wasn't a native of Nottingham but those games never seemed to generate the same degree of passion. Having said that, the significance of that Easter clash did get people going. There were 32,000 crammed in that day and the atmosphere was tremendous. County needed to win more than we did so the 1-1 draw meant we still had a slight edge. That didn't last for long, though, because we lost our next two matches against Chelsea and Cardiff and that left us feeling we'd surely blown it.

Although I'm not suggesting it was a factor in our results, there were regular distractions as Brian and Peter were linked with just about every managerial job that became available. That was inevitable, I suppose, and we did learn to get used to it over the next couple of seasons. It became a frequent topic of conversation in the dressing room but there was nothing at all the players could do to influence decisions about their future. Our task was to focus on trying to take Nottingham Forest back to the top flight.

I mentioned before about Brian and Peter always scheming, trying to get one over the opposition. They certainly did that when it came to the final run-in. We were due to complete our programme with away games against Bristol Rovers and Plymouth, plus a City Ground clash with Millwall, and incredibly, the management persuaded the League to let them bring forward the Plymouth game by 12 days. It was an amazing decision that certainly wouldn't be allowed today. They argued that by playing Plymouth on the Monday, two days after we'd faced Rovers, we could save money and not have to contend with two long trips to the West Country. Plymouth agreed to it but must have wished they hadn't as we drew 1-1 with Rovers and then won at

Home Park before finishing with a victory over Millwall. Plymouth were relegated that season, and a win over us would have saved them!

What that little bit of skulduggery meant was that our season had finished while our rivals still had work to do. It set up the now famous situation where promotion was clinched while we were flying to Majorca for an end-of-season jaunt. Only Bolton could ruin our day and I must admit that I didn't fancy our chances. They were playing Wolves, who had no great motivation because they'd already won the League. I thought that would swing it Bolton's way. It didn't turn out like that, though, and a 1-0 defeat meant we were promoted with the incredibly modest total of 52 points. The memory can play tricks after all this time. Some players claim they discovered in mid-air that we were promoted but I don't remember it that way. I reckon it was confirmed after we'd landed through a phone call to the wife of our chairman, Stuart Dryden. Needless to say, it set off the party of all parties.

As always when a team win promotion, nagging doubts set in for the players. In this instance, that was especially true. We'd had a good season but definitely not a brilliant one. It was a certainty that Clough & Taylor would be looking for better next time around. They oozed ambition and if we wanted to stay on board, we'd have to significantly 'up' our game. That's easy enough to say but in my case, did I still have it in my 34-year-old frame to meet the requirements of the top flight? I'd played in 57 games that season – including every League match – and that was more than any of the others. But would that be enough to persuade them to keep faith in me?

Chapter 12
CHICKEN 'N CHIPS – OUR RECIPE FOR THE DOUBLE
1977-78

People tend to look at me in astonishment when I tell them I always look back on the 1977-78 season with slightly mixed feelings. That was the year Nottingham Forest stunned English football by winning the League Championship in the season straight after we'd won promotion. Not only that, we also completed a brilliant double by winning the League Cup. It really was a phenomenal achievement and the manner in which we did it was especially satisfying. The quality of the football we served up was a different class and having topped the table pretty much from start to finish, we had the whole thing wrapped up with three games to spare.

The problem was that from a personal point of view, for the first time in my career I wasn't at the sharp end. I only started 12 League games – comfortably the lowest number I'd ever played throughout a season – and as Brian Clough discovered, I didn't like being stuck on the fringe. I used to bang on his door on a fairly regular basis to let him know my feelings. Eventually, it tested his patience a bit too far.

"Will you f*** off," he told me. "I'm signing all these brilliant players, we're the best team in the country by a mile and you are a part of it. Why can't you just be satisfied with that and enjoy the ride?"

"I know boss," I kept saying. "But I want to play!"

It was a whole new ball game for me and I didn't like it. Part of it was that I thought I only had one, maybe two more seasons left in me – especially at the top level – but more importantly, I knew I was missing out on something incredibly special. While I did walk away at the end of that season with two more sparkling medals to stick in my trophy cabinet, mentally I struggled to find the right balance.

Although the thought had never actually entered my head, I was aware there were rumours doing the rounds before the season got underway that I was ready to retire and move into coaching. On the back of that, I'd had an approach from Colin Murphy, who'd been appointed manager of Derby County a year earlier when Dave Mackay was sacked. His appointment was a huge surprise because 'Murph' had never played the game to a high level, had no real management experience and all of a sudden he found himself in charge of the League champions. It was hardly surprising that he was having some problems keeping Derby's big stars in check – especially the discontented ones who were not in the team – and he thought I could help with that. I'd met his assistant Dario Gradi on a coaching course a few months earlier and presumably he'd put in a word for me. 'Murph' wanted me to become his reserve-team coach and because the call came at a time when I was on a bit of a downer, I was really interested. As it happened, I didn't follow it through. That turned out to be a great decision because 'Murph' was sacked a few weeks later. It does, though, indicate just how I was feeling at the time.

'Cloughie' was absolutely right in what he said about me being a part of all the good things that were happening at the City Ground. We had a squad of 16 or 17 players and even if we weren't on the team-sheet, he kept us fully involved. Bearing in mind that tickets to watch us play – home or away – were like gold dust I had every reason to think of myself as incredibly fortunate... and I did.

We were such a good team in every department. The quality of the football we produced, often on pitches that were nothing more than mud-heaps, was sensational. We had strength, skill, pace, an incredible work ethic, and stacks of confidence in our own ability. Package that lot together and you have the complete team – which we were. What we also had at the time, which maybe gets overlooked, was a team full of potential match-winners. If, for whatever reason, one of the players didn't 'do' it on the day, you could guarantee that someone else would step forward to turn the game our way. So often you find that teams have two or three players they rely heavily on to swing it for them. We had match-winners all over the field.

The big talking point as we prepared to take on the First Division was the arrival of Kenny Burns from Birmingham City and I wasn't the only one who struggled to see the logic. Knowing how effective Peter Withe and Tony Woodcock had been in getting us promoted, why would the management make a striker our priority signing? 'Burnsy' had scored 19 top-flight goals for Birmingham the previous season. There was absolutely no doubting his quality, but other areas of the team surely needed strengthening ahead of that. I don't know to this day whether it was always Clough and Taylor's intention to use him at the heart of our defence, but regardless of how they arrived at that decision, it was an absolute masterstroke. We were all a bit wary of Kenny at first because of his wild-man reputation but he didn't take long to win me over. He was a great lad and I thought his image was way overcooked. Admittedly, we were never quite certain what he would do next during the course of a game and it's true that he had the odd aberration. But he was never a problem off the field.

Actually, that's not strictly true because there was a little incident that I inadvertently got involved in after he'd only been with us a couple of weeks. We prepared for the new campaign with a trip to Germany that also involved games across the borders in Austria and Switzerland. One of the games in Germany took place at an enclosed ground within a park. I cannot remember why but Kenny and Larry Lloyd didn't play that day. It was a recipe for disaster because there was a beer festival taking place in an adjoining field. Needless to say, they found a visit to the festival much more appealing than watching us perform and by the time they linked up with us at the end of the game, 'Burnsy' was looking the worse for wear. Despite his reputation, he wasn't a big drinker and those giant-sized tankards they use in Germany had got the better of him. I was sitting next to him at a long trestle table when we went for a meal and 'Cloughie', who had some of his family with him, was on the table behind. At the split second in which a plate of chicken and chips was put in front of 'Burnsy', he collapsed head first into it! Two of us tried to get him out as quickly as possible, one on either side, and find somewhere for him to sleep it off. We were desperately hoping the manager wouldn't notice. We thought we'd got away with it because he didn't appear to show the slightest interest. How naïve was that? He'd taken in every single detail and it wasn't the chicken and chips that was causing him to lick his lips. It was exactly what he was looking for. 'Burnsy' had given him the perfect opportunity to get stuck into him at an early stage in his Forest career. He certainly didn't pass that up. You would never have believed that man with his face in the food was destined nine months later to win the Football Writers' 'Player of the Year' award – the highest individual accolade available in our professional game.

A lot of our lads had never actually played at First Division level and although we were still on a high to some extent after winning promotion, there was definitely a feeling of apprehension about what was in store. Maybe the management felt the same way because they had a late change of heart on the make-up of our team. All-out attack had appeared to be the plan with Terry Curran and John Robertson as out-and-out wingers but when the line-up was announced for our opening game at Everton, Martin O'Neill got the nod over Curran. Clough and Taylor clearly felt that would make us a more solid unit and Martin performed his role brilliantly over the next couple of years. He was never slow to say how frustrated it made him to spend 90 minutes belting up and down the right-side while the ball was constantly being fed out to 'Robbo' and to a large extent, he did have to sacrifice himself for the good of the team. But we were all very aware of how important he was within our pattern of play. I can remember having a chat with Martin during a break in play at Everton and we were gasping for breath. We couldn't believe how quick the game was … but it didn't stop us from winning 3-1. That was a fantastic statement. It was also a massive boost to confidence and we followed it up with home wins against Bristol City and Derby and a 5-0 thrashing of West Ham in the League Cup.

We'd managed to hit the ground running, which I thought would be crucial, but the next game at Highbury was a setback for the team and even more so for me. Malcolm Macdonald had joined Arsenal by that time, amid the inevitable blaze of publicity, so there was plenty of good-natured banter between us. Sadly, it didn't last too long. We lost that game 3-0 and I limped off with a pulled hamstring. That signalled the end of my unbroken run of 88 League matches and the long-term consequences could have been serious for me.

Colin Barrett slotted in to replace me at left back for the next game against Wolves and took to the job superbly. He'd been 'Mr Versatile' for the majority of his career, filling in wherever he was needed, and although players who are good at that role are priceless, they undoubtedly make personal sacrifices. Given the choice, Colin certainly wouldn't have chosen left back as his favourite position. I'm not even sure he'd ever played there before but he looked a natural when he took over from me and played so well that I was genuinely concerned that I might never get back into the team. I didn't play in the first-team again until we went to Bury for a League Cup tie in January and didn't play again in the League until the start of March. By then, we were well on the way to Double success. All those 'experts' who predicted in the early weeks of the season that it was only a matter of time before our bubble would burst were being forced to think again. Particularly with the London-based media, it was almost as if they resented these upstarts from the Midlands showing the others how to do it. They kept coming up with examples of clubs like Carlisle United, who went top of the League immediately after winning promotion but were relegated at the end of the season. It took a long while to win them over – and for much of that time I was little more than a spectator. Initially, of course, I had to recover from the troublesome hamstring injury and it was my longest spell out of action since I'd broken my leg as a teenager.

It was during that period that Clough & Taylor made one of those headline hogging moves they enjoyed so much by buying Peter Shilton from Stoke. We already had the England Under-21 goalkeeper in John Middleton. He'd done well in helping to win promotion and settle into the top flight – but that wasn't enough for them. They wanted the best in the business and although it took some doing to get the deal over the line, they eventually managed it in the September when their offer was upped to £325,000. That move typified their courageous approach to management. Shilton was there for everyone to see. He wasn't just the best goalkeeper in England but probably the world yet people in those days didn't pay out big money for goalkeepers. Clough and Taylor did... and their courage was amply rewarded. I'm sure Taylor will have led the way on that deal. As a former goalkeeper himself, he understood how many extra points could be gained during the course of a season by having a top-notch performer between the sticks and his judgement was spot-on.

The day after 'Shilts' joined us, I was the only senior player at the ground when he arrived for training. I was there for treatment and the rest of the lads were off – as they so often were. He asked me if there was any chance that I could organise a session for him because he felt he needed to work so I rounded up a group of youngsters. The whole thing was an eye-opener for me but even more so for the kids. He absolutely worked his socks off in that session. He was an obsessive when it came to preparing himself properly and doing everything he possibly could to make himself better. After the session I called those young lads together and hammered home the message that if you want to be the best, that's what you have to do – not just today but every day. 'Shilts' tended to keep himself to himself and was a bit aloof from the other lads. But although I could never claim we were close, we did get into the habit of going out together after midweek games. Neither of us could sleep after midweek matches so we used to go to the Victoria Club in the centre of Nottingham. I wasn't a gambler but I used to watch 'Shilts' lose his hard-earned cash. He did win occasionally – but not too often. When he arrived at the City Ground he was already a terrific goalkeeper but I believe he improved during his time with Forest. The amazing statistic of only 24 goals conceded in 42 League games on our way to the League Championship is a tribute to him and the bottom line for 'Shilts' is that he won things with us… that's what he'd come to do.

Next on the shopping list was Archie Gemmill, who arrived soon afterwards. He was already a proven winner with Derby County and I found it fascinating to watch from the sidelines as the dynamic of our dressing room took on a different complexion. All of a sudden we had loads of experience – not just at League level but internationals – and plenty of players who knew how to win things. Archie was a fiery little bugger, capable of causing a riot in an empty house, but that was a big part of making him the player he was. He needed a strong will to win to help him overcome his lack of height and he had that in abundance. He continued to live in Derby and was never what you could call 'one of the lads'. But he was the latest in a growing number of strong characters in our dressing room and we blended well. If anyone got above themselves, there were always plenty of others ready to shoot them down.

It was a regular thing in my Newcastle days that a small group of us would head for a local café for lunch after training and I have fond memories of those times. We developed the same situation at Forest. Several days a week we would go to Mackay's Café at the bottom of Musters Road, alongside Trent Bridge cricket ground. 'Robbo' and Martin O'Neill were part of the regular gang, so were Colin Barrett and Ian Bowyer, and numbers had to be quite select because it was only a small café! A pot of tea and chip butties all round was our normal fare and we would chew the cud for an hour or so, with football always the main topic. Almost without realising it, we'd created a situation that was great for team bonding. I reckon we probably kept Bill Mackay in business for a few years. Bill was a lovely man and I often gave him my two complimentary tickets that the players got for every game. Pam didn't want them and he was always very appreciative. Incidentally, a few years later Bill's dingy little café – complete with a temporary new frontage in German lettering – featured in an episode of Smiley's People, the BBC spy drama series. Alec Guinness sat in the cramped corner that we used to occupy, negotiating an exchange of spies that later took place at nearby Lady Bay Bridge.

All I could do as the lads were storming towards the title was to make sure I kept myself in the best possible condition, ready to step up if needed. The team was picking itself and the way Colin was performing, he must have been one of the first names on the sheet every week. As for the team performances, they just got better and better and reached a new peak in December when we won 4-0 against Manchester United at Old Trafford. I wasn't there that day because my father-in-law had died suddenly but I recall 'Robbo' telling me it was the best overall display he was ever involved in. And what about David Needham, who made his debut for us that day? No stranger to our scene because he'd played more than 400 games for Notts County, he'd been signed from Queen's Park Rangers to cover for the injured Larry Lloyd and he simply couldn't believe what he'd come to as United were torn apart. I think that was the performance that finally won over any remaining doubters.

It's a fact that success can sometimes cause problems every bit as great as failure and performances of that kind were the best possible advert for Brian Clough to take with him when he headed off to London to be interviewed for the England manager's job. We'd grown accustomed to him being linked with all sorts of jobs but this time, I thought we'd lose him. He loved to play games with people and would use job opportunities as a way of manipulating situations to suit to himself – and the club. This was different. I'm sure that he really did want the England job and especially during that period, what 'Cloughie' wanted, 'Cloughie' got. We all feared the worst. I still cannot believe that he failed to land the big one. But the FA chose Ron Greenwood instead – and we got on with the job of becoming the best team in Europe.

I finally got a first-team recall in January, four months after I'd last played at that level, and helped to beat Bury in the League Cup. At that time, people were even talking about us completing a unique treble. The trouble was that wintry weather caused a number of games to be postponed and we were left with a ridiculously heavy workload. Bearing in mind that we operated with such a small squad, it was bound to catch up with us. I got a recall to figure twice in three days in FA Cup replays against QPR because Barrett was injured. We eventually got through to qualify for the 6th round but our treble dreams ended at West Brom, as we lost 2-0. We couldn't have any complaints. We didn't perform to anything like our normal standard and although we were missing a number of injured players, there were obvious doubts about how the defeat would affect us. The following Saturday we were off to Wembley to play Liverpool in the League Cup Final but the fixture list had become so congested, we even had to fit in a midweek League game against Leicester before we could concentrate on that.

Quite apart from the injury problems and general fatigue, Shilton, Gemmill and Needham couldn't play against Liverpool because they were all cup tied. If ever we needed someone to step up and be a hero, now was the time. What we didn't expect was that Chris Woods, our novice 18-year-old goalkeeper, would take on that role. It was an incredible story because he had never even made a single League appearance. Yet here he was, deputising for the best goalkeeper in the land at the home of football and putting on something close to a one-man show. Liverpool murdered us on the day. They threatened to totally overwhelm us but we did our best to stay solid at the back and young Chris proved to be unbeatable as we held out for a 0-0 draw.

It was a disappointing occasion for the Forest fans, who hadn't had a big day-out at Wembley for 19 years, and I came away regretting that I still hadn't experienced the thrill of a victory beneath the Twin Towers. I'd missed out all those years ago when Crook Town could only manage a draw in the FA Amateur Cup Final and again when Newcastle failed to get out of the starting gate in the FA Cup Final against Liverpool. At least there was still a chance of getting my hands on a League Cup winners' medal. I desperately hoped I'd be picked again for the replay at Old Trafford, just four days later. Another game, another chance for someone to be a hero, and this time it was another unlikely one … John O'Hare. In contrast to Woods, he was a vastly experienced Scottish international, a fine player who I knew wouldn't let us down when he was drafted in as the only change to replace the injured John McGovern. And he was to be right at the heart of a controversial incident that led to 'Robbo' winning the game with a second half penalty. It looked a clear-cut decision from where I was when Phil Thompson hacked down O'Hare as he got clear through the middle. I would say that, wouldn't I? But television showed it was a really tight one. Did the offence take place inside the area or not? The debate still rages on to this day. It wasn't a great game but we'd won the Cup and with McGovern missing it was stand-in captain Kenny Burns – he of the chicken and chips fame – who went up to collect it. It was also a big moment for me when I went forward to collect my medal from Newcastle chairman Lord Westwood, the Football League president. We didn't get around to discussing why he'd handed me a free transfer a few weeks after assuring me I had a future at Newcastle. My thoughts were best left unsaid and I settled for a knowing look.

Victory guaranteed us a place in the UEFA Cup the following season but as always, Brian and Peter wanted more. They were only interested in us using the Cup triumph as a platform to push on and win the Championship. The good news for me was that my patience had been rewarded – I was back on the scene again. I kept my place for the League game three days later and ironically, it was at home to Newcastle. I was delighted with our 2-0 win but took no pleasure from giving Newcastle a further shove towards relegation.

The schedule of matches was unrelenting – eight during March and the same again in April – and although it wasn't so bad for me, some of the lads had hardly missed a game all season, and 'Robbo' had played in every one. Knowing that everyone wanted to beat the champions-elect merely added to the challenge and it was just as well the management were masters at dealing with a glut of games. We hardly did any training at all. We just turned up for games, added a few more points to our tally and moved onto the next one. We'd only lost three games all season – four if you include the FA Cup game at West Brom – and it was an amazing feeling to be involved with a squad of players who had total belief in each other. Liverpool still had a chance of catching us as we moved into the home strait but realistically, the only threat to us claiming the title was that some of our lads were running on empty. That became increasingly obvious but we all pulled together to help each other over the line.

It came to a head on April 22, 1978 when we went to Highfield Road knowing that a draw against Coventry City would clinch the title. I missed out that day and watched on anxiously as we produced one of our poorest performances of the season. But for not the first time, those who had questioned the wisdom of paying out a record fee for a goalkeeper were shown exactly why it was done. Shilton picked the perfect stage to demonstrate his incredible talent and it was mainly down to him that we claimed a goalless draw. The sense of satisfaction was enormous and inevitably, as we sped our way back to Nottingham, all the talk was about what could possibly be next.

In my case, you would have got incredibly steep odds on what was about to happen because three days later, against Ipswich at Portman

Road, I scored my one and only League goal. It had only taken me 14 years! I was our substitute that day, remembering that only one was allowed at that time, and our first half performance reflected the fact that the lads had been celebrating since Saturday. 'Cloughie' went ballistic when we got back into the dressing room and all but one of the players took it on the chin because they knew full well they had been shocking. Only Peter Withe was daft enough to go back at the boss, who was in no mood to be tangled with. "You! F*** off to the showers," he said to 'Withey' and then told me to get warmed up. I was trying to work out where I would play and there were various things that could have been done to accommodate me. By the time the buzzer went to tell us to take the field again, there had still been no mention of what they wanted me to do. I was halfway out the door when I raised the subject. "You'd better play up front," said the boss as he cocked his famous thumb in the direction of 'Withey'. "You can't do any worse than him."

So there I was, lining up to kick off the second half, and not even in my schoolboy days could I ever remember seriously playing up front. As luck would have it, playing centre half for Ipswich that night was Allan Hunter, a strong and very capable Northern Ireland international, and I just happened to know him. He was Willie McFaul's cousin and we enjoyed a number of good nights out together when Allan came to visit him in Newcastle. First opportunity I got, I sidled up to him and said: "You know that I haven't got a clue what I'm doing up front and I know you're due to play in the FA Cup Final in a couple of weeks. I'd hate to be accidentally responsible for you missing the final so let's stay well away from each other shall we?" We had a pact. He agreed that would be sensible and we got on with the game.

Anyway, we forced a corner soon afterwards and I had no idea where to stand. None of our lads ever had pre-defined positions from corners and it was especially strange for me because I never even went up for set-pieces. I got myself into the penalty area and when the cross from 'Robbo' dropped in front of me on the edge of the six-yard box, I knocked it into the net. I didn't know what I was supposed to do next. Clough and Taylor were both up celebrating and the lads all came running after me. It didn't take them long to catch me! That opened the scoring and when Paul Mariner put through his own goal, we'd conjured a 2-0 away win out of no where. There was a nice moment afterwards when Taylor went to try and get me the match-ball and Ipswich boss Bobby Robson was reluctant to give it to him. He refused to believe that after all those games I'd played for Newcastle, I'd never previously scored a League goal. Eventually he did relent and that ball is still one of my favourite trophies.

That little cameo was a welcome diversion but much more pertinent was the reaction of our management to our below par first-half display at Ipswich. Surely they would allow us some slack after we'd grafted incredibly hard to bring the title home with three games to spare? Not a bit of it. Standards were standards and there was no way we would be allowed to let them slip. In a nutshell, that summed up what Brian and Peter were all about. I don't know whether they celebrated after we'd done the business at Coventry. Maybe they did in private but they certainly didn't get involved with us. It could have been, of course, that unlike most of us, they'd already won the Championship at Derby so our triumph didn't affect them in quite the same way. What they hadn't done, though, was win the European Cup and the day after we went to Coventry, they were already trying to find ways to put that right.

I should have known better than to think that maybe my goal-scoring feat might earn me the No. 9 shirt for our final home game, when we collected the Championship trophy before taking on Birmingham. There was absolutely no chance of that happening. In fact, I didn't even make the team-sheet but I did play in the last game of our spectacular season.

That just happened to be away to Liverpool, who were convinced there had been a massive injustice in both games when we beat them in the League Cup Final and would have liked nothing better than to put us in our place. They'd been the powerhouse of English football for some time. They'd won the League Championship the previous two seasons, were the reigning European Cup holders and were destined to win it again a couple of weeks later. In theory, there was nothing riding on that game at Anfield but it meant a huge amount to the players – especially the Liverpool lads. Our unbeaten League run stretched back over 25 games to October but they had stormed up behind us to claim runners-up spot by winning nine and drawing two of their previous 11 games. It was little wonder there were 50,021 people there to see a veritable battle of the giants. From what I can remember, the game didn't match expectations. But true to form, we were rock solid at the back, held out for a goalless draw, and I was incredibly proud about playing my part.

I just couldn't believe what had happened to me since I'd left Newcastle, wondering where my next pay packet was going to come from. Although I'd missed out on a big part of the season, I'd come back strongly to prove a point to myself and to others. I still had two more years to run on my contract – and I fully intended to see it through.

PLAYER - MANAGER - CHAIRMAN   **159**

TOP Down on 'all fours' at Wembley as a Liverpool effort flies into our net. Fortunately, it was ruled out for offside.
The irrepressible John Robertson coolly slots in our replay winner against Liverpool to land us the League Cup.
Pictures: Nottingham Post/Nottingham Local Studies Collection

Parade of the trophies.
Picture: Nottingham Post/Nottingham Local Studies Collection

Chapter 13
THE BIGGEST PRIZE IN EUROPE – WHAT A WAY TO SIGN OFF!
1978-79

Nice people, according to popular theory, don't make good football managers. That's a massive generalisation, of course, but I do understand the thinking. History shows that without a ruthless streak that allows you to make tough decisions without getting sidetracked by sentiment get, you can't do the job successfully. Quite often those decisions have a huge impact on the lives of others, not just immediately but for years to come, and the fact that everything within football is played out in such a public way makes it worse. Managers who cannot rise above that are in the wrong trade.

Brian Clough and Peter Taylor never had a problem making decisions and although I was one of three players agonising over what their line-up would be for the European Cup Final of 1979, I can't imagine they will have lost a second's sleep over it. Basically, the situation was that three into one wouldn't go. Archie Gemmill, Martin O'Neill and I were all competing for the last available spot against Malmo. Trevor Francis hadn't been eligible to play the previous rounds following his £1million move from Birmingham City but he could play in the final. He was sure to be selected... but who would get the other place?

We'd all been suffering from injuries. Martin and Archie had been out for some time and in my case, I'd made a quicker than expected recovery from a groin strain for which I'll be forever grateful to the Leeds United club doctor. He came down from the directors' box to see me in the physio's room at Elland Road after I'd limped off in our penultimate League game of the season, immediately 'iced' the groin area and told me what I needed to do going forward. I was convinced the injury would cost me any chance of playing in the final but I followed his advice to the letter, went into the ground for treatment every day and made an excellent recovery. By the time we set off for Munich to play against Malmö, I reckon I was about 95 per cent fit.

Stating the obvious, all three of us were desperate to play and when Brian asked if we were fit, there was no way we were going to say "no". There were all sorts of possible permutations that would allow any one of us to slot into the line-up so there was no obvious way for the management to go. The 'will we, won't we' scenario was far more tense than the general build-up to the game. Martin, Archie and me spent several days eying each other up and down, wondering which of us would get the chance to play in what was the absolute peak for a player – Europe's biggest football occasion of the year. It all came to a head on the morning of the match. Brian called all the players together and said: "Frank's playing and Trevor will operate down the right".

I felt desperately sorry for Martin and Archie. I could only imagine how I would have felt had it been one of them selected and not me. Archie took it particularly badly. He claimed he'd been told that if he got himself fit he would play. I don't know if that was true but I do know that Clough and Taylor were always capable of having a late change of mind. I'd had previous experience of that the year before because my name was on the team-sheet to play in the League Cup semi-final at Leeds and by the time we arrived at the ground, I was out and John O'Hare was playing.

Anyway, the management hadn't allowed sentiment to get in the way as we completed our preparations for the final and neither could

I. Many years later, I did pluck up the courage to ask Brian how he'd arrived at the decision to pick me. "Because you were the one most likely to tell me the truth when I asked if you were fit," he matter-of-factly said.

The magnificent journey with Nottingham Forest just rolled on and on. Promotion, the League Championship and now we were on our way to conquering Europe. I honestly couldn't believe what was happening to me. I wasn't an automatic choice any longer – far from it – but I did play significantly more games than I had the previous season and tended to get picked for the big ones. Life was good. No, life was brilliant and by that time, I was able to see the bigger picture. I'd come to terms with the fact that at my stage of life, I had to enjoy every second of the very special atmosphere and step up and perform whenever the opportunity arose.

There was a crowd of 41,000 at the City Ground on the opening day of the season – and they weren't just there to see the reigning champions get a new campaign underway. Tottenham provided the opposition and Keith Burkinshaw, my former coach at Newcastle, had started a new trend. Foreign footballers were a rarity in this country so it was a huge story when he signed a couple of Argentinians. Everyone wanted to be a part of it. While Ossie Ardiles and Ricky Villa were strutting their stuff in Nottingham, I couldn't have been much further away from the glare of the cameras. I was playing for the reserves against Sheffield Wednesday in front of a few hundred people at Hillsborough but it turned out to be a very significant day. I've no idea what the result was but I have vivid recollections of being on the team coach afterwards and seeing Garry Birtles looking thoroughly depressed. I went and sat next to him and told him to share his troubles. He was incredibly 'down' and said he was ready to pack in football and go back to laying floor tiles. Signed from Long Eaton United for £2,000, he'd made his League debut two years earlier as a left-sided midfielder but had struggled to make the step up. He couldn't see any way that he had a future in the game and it was making him so unhappy that he thought the best thing was to walk away from it. I asked Garry what his contract situation was and he said he still had a year to run. I stressed that he would always regret the decision if he gave it away now and said he should just keep working hard and see where it led. He really didn't have anything to lose. I'm sure I wasn't the only one who had an influence but that time I spent with Garry turned out to be one of the most valuable contributions I made during my period with Forest. Within five weeks, he was writing a little fairytale all of his own.

Peter Withe had let it be known during the summer that he wanted to leave and we were staggered that the management said they wouldn't stand in his way. I knew that he'd asked for a pay-rise and Clough and Taylor could be quite unforgiving in those situations if it didn't fit with their thinking. But even so, I always felt 'Withey' was an important cog in our success and he underlined that by playing his part in a 5-0 Wembley win over Ipswich in the Charity Shield. Within a fortnight, he'd gone to Newcastle for £250,000 and we were scratching ours heads about who was going to replace him. They gave the No. 9 shirt to Stephen Elliott, a promising young player with virtually no previous experience, and although he hit the post a couple of times in his five appearances, he failed to score and we only won one of them. By that time, we'd been drawn against Liverpool in the opening round of the European Cup and were in no fit state to take them on. Our management had finally made a mistake. They'd surely got it wrong to allow Withe to leave without signing up a suitable replacement.

I've said it before but I'll say it again... I know that Clough and Taylor were incredibly astute but they were also unbelievably lucky. I just refuse to believe that when they allowed Withe to leave, they thought for one second that Birtles was the answer to their problems. But just as with Tony Woodcock when he was plucked off the scrapheap two years earlier, Garry's impact was massive in a totally unfamiliar role up front. Instead of going back to laying floor tiles, he helped to beat Arsenal in his top-flight debut and four days later, he dramatically scored his first senior goal in a 2-0 win in the European Cup.

Ever since we'd clinched the Championship, it seemed that the only topic worth talking about for the good people of Nottingham was our venture into Europe. I'd passed that way before with Newcastle but this time, it was different. We had a pact at St James' that we would be totally professional and do our utmost to win the Inter-Cities Fairs Cup but above all, as a group, we were determined we would enjoy the whole experience. In all honesty, we didn't think we could actually win the competition and we were not weighed down by expectancy. It was different with Forest. Despite the fact that we would be facing up to the very best teams from each of the countries of Europe, our management expected us to win it ... and so did we. After all, we hadn't lost a League game for 10 months and winning was what we did.

What we certainly hadn't bargained for, however, was that we would come out of the hat at the first round stage with Liverpool. They had won the Cup for the previous two years, were vastly experienced at handling two-legged ties, and they were desperate to do us some damage. My instant reaction was that we wouldn't even need our passports and the fans were bitterly disappointed. But Clough and Taylor were at their best in situations like that and the way they transferred the pressure onto Liverpool was brilliant. They kept stressing the point that they'd failed to beat us in four meetings the previous season and said that if we were disappointed about the draw, how must Liverpool be feeling? By the time the tie came around, they had us all believing we would win.

The great irony was that on the night when Birtles stepped forward to announce himself on the European stage, I was the one completely out in the cold. I was yet to figure in the League team that season but I did at least expect to be involved against Liverpool because five substitutes were permitted in the European Cup. When the team-sheet was pinned up, I wasn't even in the 16. I was absolutely gutted. I watched from the stand as the lads produced a memorable performance to win 2-0 and I couldn't have been more pleased that it was Birtles and Colin Barrett who scored the goals. Colin broke all the rules when he charged forward at a time when we were defending a 1-0 lead, kept on running until he arrived in the area and when Tony Woodcock nodded a cross down to him, he scored with the sweetest of volleys. I couldn't stop laughing and I was so pleased for him. He'd battled away all his career to establish himself in a regular position and he had grabbed the chance to take over my left back spot superbly. That goal quite rightly propelled him to celebrity status but never was there a better example of how cruel football can be. Just 10 days later, he suffered a serious knee injury against Middlesbrough. Although he did briefly make a comeback, he was never the same again and had to retire at the age of 28.

What that injury inevitably meant was that a replacement left back would be required when we went to Anfield for the return leg at the end of September. Could there possibly have been a more daunting time and place to make my first appearance of the season? The last time, in fact, that I'd played in the first team was when we drew at Anfield on the final day of the previous campaign. We got a goalless draw that day and presumably that influenced the decision to play me. They really didn't like us at Liverpool and although you always got a hostile reception when you went there, it was ratcheted up a good few notches for this game. Personally, I loved it. Backs-to-the-wall struggles like that really brought out the best in me and when I looked around that night, and could see how well our lads were coping with the ultimate challenge, it made me realise how far we'd come as a group. Viv Anderson, for example, was a young local boy striving to make a living from the game when I arrived at the City Ground. You wouldn't believe it if you met him now but he was quiet and introvert. He'd developed into an excellent player, a beautiful mover who made it all look so easy. I ought to balance that by saying he was never happy getting the ball off the goalkeeper. It always made me smile when he used to turn his back and run away when 'Shilts' got possession – but you can't have everything.

The occasion was being billed as the biggest club match in the history of English football and I suppose it was hard to argue with that. I'd lived to tell the tale of figuring in two Fairs Cup clashes between Newcastle and Rangers and for sheer passion and noise, they really did take some beating. But the whole of Europe wanted to know if we could finish off the job and topple the mighty Liverpool. Brian and Peter did their best to give the impression that it was just another game but no amount of kidology was going to convince us of that. Our build-up on the day was just the same as normal... with one exception. While we were en-route Brian asked our coach driver Albert if we had any beer on board. "We have – but it's on the boot," said Albert. Before we knew it, we'd pulled onto the hard shoulder of the M62 to bring on the boxes of beer. Goodness knows what that was all about. Whether it was really for Brian's benefit I'm not sure but the players were given the option to grab a can. Some did but I wasn't one of them.

People often referred to the special atmosphere of a European night at Anfield and for want of a better word, there was a distinct tingle in the air when we arrived. It's hard to describe but that set it apart from a typical Saturday afternoon. I'm not sure whose idea it was but we decided the only way to deal with it was to meet it head on. With best part of an hour to go before kick off, the ground was already more than half full as we strolled out onto the pitch and headed towards The Kop. The reaction from Liverpool fans was utterly predictable and wasn't helped by the fact that we stood there laughing and joking. We were supposed to be quaking in our boots, not out there enjoying ourselves, but even the Liverpool fans were laughing along with us when 'Robbo' produced his first bit of magic for the night. Someone on The Kop threw a tennis ball in our direction and 'Robbo' instinctively flicked it up and volleyed it into the back of the net. It brought the house down and by the time we arrived back in the dressing room, we believed we'd given ourselves a psychological edge.

It was certainly a night for finding out what people were made of – and we didn't have a bad player. Everyone did their job superbly but the way Viv and Archie Gemmill defended the far post was key to us getting a goalless draw. It was a favourite tactic of Liverpool if they were struggling to find a goal that they would feed the ball to the far post where Ray Kennedy was very clever at making late runs. We knew we had to guard against this and time and again the threat was snuffed out. I fully expected them to target me, knowing I was short of top-level match practice after not playing at that level for four months, and they didn't let me down. Jimmy Case left his 'signature' on my shin and seven stiches were needed to repair the gash at half time. But we stayed really solid and disciplined and they just couldn't break us down. It was a phenomenal result. No one had fancied us. European Cup opposition didn't get any more difficult than Liverpool.

The shin injury caused me to miss our next game and I was in and out of the team for the rest of the season. But most of the time when it came to European ties, I was in. I figured in successive League wins against Wolves, Bristol City and Ipswich and both legs in the next European round against AEK Athens. We won the first leg in Athens 2-1 and that was especially memorable because it featured the one and only occasion when I overlapped 'Robbo'. They employed a really tight offside trap which we were having trouble dealing with. Our strikers had to keep coming back as their defenders pushed up so someone had to break in behind. I set off on a run after feeding the ball to 'Robbo' on the halfway line and predictably, he delivered it back to me in inch-perfect fashion. All of a sudden I was approaching the left edge of the penalty area and was starting to panic when I spotted Birtles making ground in the centre. It wasn't the best of crosses, slightly behind him, but he made it look good and his goal gave us a handy lead. That was stretched to 7-2 on aggregate as we cantered through at the City Ground but I failed to go the distance in that game. I had to limp off with a strained hamstring, which meant another spell on the sidelines.

I was back, though, in time for yet another trip to Anfield and at long last, Liverpool managed to beat us. A 2-0 scoreline signalled the end of our remarkable unbeaten run that stretched back for 42 League games – the equivalent to a complete season. What a staggering achievement that was, especially when you feed all the other bits and pieces into the equation. We'd done it with a squad of 16-17 players on mud-heap pitches while competing for various cups at the same time. It really makes me laugh when people go on and on about rotating tired players these days. Ending the run wasn't the end of the world in my book because I felt it had become a bit of a burden to the lads. They didn't appear to me to be playing with quite the same freedom and I thought it was a good thing to be able to clear our heads and start all over again. That's the way it turned out. We lost just one of the next 19 League games and by the middle of March, we were up to third in the table and defending the title with style. We'd also retained the League Cup and impressively cleared another hurdle in the European Cup. Oh, and we'd also doubled the British record transfer fee in signing Trevor Francis.

Knowing how Clough and Taylor were never satisfied, it had been a surprise to all of us that they'd done nothing to strengthen the squad the previous summer. If fact, they had weakened it if anything by allowing Withe to head off to the North East. But just as the signing of Shilton had done, it rocked the football world when they prised Francis away from St Andrew's to inject fresh energy into us. The first I knew about it was when I heard on the radio that Trevor was signing and I didn't envy him. He was coming into a very tight-knit dressing room, full of 'big' players, and was clearly going to cost one of us our place in the team. That can be a difficult situation to deal with but the management instantly threw down the gauntlet. They made it absolutely clear that a £1million price tag wouldn't be enough to get him an automatic place in our team. Just to underline the point, he was told he would be playing the following morning in an 'A' team fixture against Notts County on The Embankment. That's a wide open public space alongside the River Trent, containing at least half a dozen pitches, and because it was a popular area with dog-walkers, there were always plenty of calling cards around. Whatever Trevor had in mind as his debut for Nottingham Forest, I could guarantee this wasn't it. The majority of players in both teams were apprentices and young pros but I played, and so did Ian Bowyer, who was then substitute for the first-team in the afternoon. How did the management get away with that? Just imagine telling one of today's established Premier League players that he would be playing in the 3rd team in the morning, and then sub for the first-team four hours later!

The Notts County lads couldn't believe their eyes when Trevor suddenly appeared from the ramshackle changing rooms and although he tried hard to make an impression, it was asking too much. I'm not quite sure why Clough and Taylor went to such extremes because although Trevor was clearly a superstar, you could never accuse him of being a 'Big-time Charlie'. Rather than make it easy for him to settle in, it probably made it harder. He was a terrific player who gave us options up front and extra penetration. The only issue with him was that his speed could cause problems as much to us as it did to the opposition. He was so quick that he would take possession and spin, get to the by-line and deliver a cross before anyone could get up to receive it. He needed to improve his understanding of the game when he first arrived and in time, he did that.

Four days after Trevor was finally given his first start – a 1-1 draw at Ipswich – we faced up to the Swiss champions. We managed to take the sting out of the tie against Grasshopper Zurich by winning 4-1 at home – then claimed a 1-1 draw in the return. I only played in the first leg and picked up yet another injury. But it was nothing serious and I was delighted to learn that I'd be off to Wembley again to play in the League Cup Final against Southampton. This time, I desperately wanted us to do ourselves full justice and from a personal standpoint, to finally experience the thrill of a Wembley victory. I didn't need to be told that there was a job to be done and the management were trusting me to do it. The biggest threat to our chances of winning was the Saints' right-winger Terry Curran, who clearly had a point to prove to Clough and Taylor. Where better to do it? Although Terry had been one of the stars of our promotion from the Second Division a few years earlier, he'd been cast aside at the gates of the top flight. He was struggling to get his career back on track after a brief spell at Derby but had real talent. We all knew he was capable of causing us serious damage but I backed myself to out-think him. That's how it turned out.

Our regular routine for away matches was to meet up late afternoon on the Friday and eat together at Antonio's, the Italian restaurant on Trent Bridge. We'd then travel to the overnight hotel and more or less go straight to bed when we arrived. Normal procedure was being followed but when we got to West Park Lodge to the north of London, the boss told Jimmy Gordon to round up the players in the lounge. Archie Gemmill was already in bed and was less than pleased to be told he must get dressed and join the rest of us. Anyway, 'Cloughie' suddenly produced a crate of Champagne and he and Peter put on a double-act for the next hour of so, telling one humorous football tale after another. People would have paid a fortune for tickets to watch it. As always, there was a method in their madness. Brian, as he later told me, thought we were not comfortable with being red-hot favourites. They believed the tension was showing and simply wanted to do something to relax us.

They certainly did that. In fact, they very nearly overdid it because we were awful in the first half. No one was cracking jokes when we got back to the dressing room at half time. We were subjected to a barrage of choice words instead, and they had the desired affect. The quality wasn't up to much but it turned out to be an entertaining final for the fans as Birtles inspired us to come from behind and win 3-2. That little chat I'd had with Garry in August seemed such a long way away.

Somebody really had it in for me that season because although I managed to get through the 90 minutes, I was injured yet again. In fact, it led to me becoming the first footballer ever to have a wound stitched live on television. I don't know if that's strictly true but I like to tell people it is! It was normally a complete no-no to have cameras anywhere near our dressing room but they were in there that day. I think it stemmed from Brian's friendship with the ITV commentator Brian Moore, and they got close up shots of me wincing as my shin was sewn back together. It became slightly less painful when I heard Brian being interviewed and tell the world that I was the best player on the pitch.

Incidentally, I was really pleased that John McGovern, our club captain, was there to pick up the Cup after missing out through injury when we beat Liverpool the previous year. He wasn't short of critics during his time at Forest. Some fans gave him a really hard time but you would never have found any critics in our dressing room. We were fully aware that he was a vital cog in the machine. No one understood what 'Cloughie' wanted better than John because he'd been with him throughout his managerial career. As the anchor-man in our midfield, he had great discipline, a great engine and a great eye for the simple pass. It's not always about being the best player. It's more important to be the best at doing your particular job and he was the epitome of that. Throughout my career in management, I always wanted to find a player like John McGovern and I never managed it. That's an indication of how good he was. He was the undemonstrative type, never a fist-shaking captain, but earned our respect for the way he conducted himself – on and off the field. When I was playing in our under-11 school team I overheard the teacher tell my dad that although I wasn't very graceful, I was incredibly effective. I always think the same about John.

There was no time to really celebrate the Wembley triumph because we had bigger fish to fry. The lads flew out the following day to Zurich to complete victory over Grasshopper – but I wasn't with then. The gashed shin caused me to have another spell on the sidelines and I didn't figure again until the semi-final of the European Cup.

What a night that was when Cologne came to the City Ground. Peter Taylor had apparently seen them play and told us we had nothing to worry about. We weren't thinking that when we found ourselves 2-0 down and were being run ragged as they kept hitting us on the break. I was on the bench but went on when Archie got injured. Considering how much there was riding on the game, it was incredibly open and fantastic entertainment for the crowd. Birtles and Ian Bowyer scored to haul us level and a collector's item put us in front – a brilliant diving header from 'Robbo'. It was a great effort to turn it around the way we had but just as we thought we'd got something to hang onto for the second leg, they made it 3-3 with a goal out of nothing. Even to this day I cannot believe that 'Shilts' dived over a fairly tame shot from Cologne's Japanese substitute Yasuhiko Okudera. He never did things like that... it was clearly a night for collector's items.

That was a huge blow. There was no denying it but as soon as we dragged ourselves back to the dressing room, Taylor started. "We will win over there – no doubt about it," he said, and he and the boss never wavered from that at any time. I've no idea whether they actually believed it with such confidence but by the time we landed in Germany, we believed them. It's often said that the worst thing in football is to lose a semi-final and having come so far, we really didn't want to miss out now. All it needed was one of our trademark defensive displays, mean and disciplined, and one moment of magic at the other end. We were always capable of that.

There was more work to be done before we jetted off to Germany – four League games in the space of 10 days – and when we emerged undefeated from that demanding stretch, it wasn't out of the question that we could retain the League Championship. Inevitably though, the European Cup was the prize we all wanted and we knew it was going to take a monumental effort to rescue the situation in Cologne. Not that we needed anything extra to motivate us but you couldn't fail to notice an air of inevitability when we arrived there. People were even handing out leaflets, urging supporters to join the official parties when they travelled to Munich for the final. A little bit premature, we thought, and when we arrived at half time with the game still goalless, I could sense a change in the attitude of the Cologne players. Suddenly, doubts were creeping in. They'd had a decent chance early on that they failed to take and although they had plenty of possession, 'Shilts' was hardly troubled all night. It was all down to whether or not we could get a goal and when it came, some 20 minutes into the second half, it was scored by yet another unlikely hero. One of the lovely features of Newcastle's Fairs Cup success had been the number of 'lesser lights' who had stepped up to make a crucial contribution and the trend was continuing. Garry Birtles and Colin Barrett had thrust themselves into the limelight with their goals against Liverpool and now it was the turn of 'Bomber' Bowyer, who headed in after Birtles had flicked on a 'Robbo' corner. I couldn't have been more pleased for 'Bomber' – a great lad and a really good player. Like Colin, he'd missed out slightly over the years through being a 'Jack of all trades' and had filled the left-back spot for much of that season. He was a brilliant competitor with bags of energy and his versatility was priceless to us when we were operating with a squad of just 16 players. We hung on quite comfortably to book our place in the final and could only imagine what a reaction it must have caused back home. It seems that everyone I've met since in Nottingham has a story to tell about where they were and what they were doing on the night we won in Cologne. It's a great feeling knowing that we made so many people happy.

    Mentally and physically, that game took a lot out of us and I believe the way we finished the season from there on in spoke volumes for what Clough and Taylor had built. We'd played nine games in March and 10 in April. The lads were genuinely running on empty. It wasn't so bad for me because I'd been in and put of the team but with such a small squad, most of us had been playing two games a week for the whole of the season. In all, we played 62 League and Cup games in the course of that campaign – not to mention a fair sprinkling of testimonials – and 'Robbo' had appeared in every single one of them. Physically it was a massive 'ask' but we also had to contend with the fact that everyone wanted to beat Brian Clough and Nottingham Forest. Games were played with enormous intensity. Just three days after the game against Cologne, for example, we were at home to Liverpool. It was a huge game. We occupied the top two places in the table and the winners would be virtually certain to win the Championship. In finished 0-0, which was a fantastic effort from our lads, and although Liverpool took the title, we won four and drew the other of our last five games to finish as runners-up.

There was a 12-day gap between the last League game and the European final and some said it was too long. I certainly wasn't one of them. I needed every hour I could possibly get to give myself a chance of recovering from the groin strain I'd picked up at Leeds and as each day went by, I was getting closer to fitness. In general, our build-up to Munich was typically relaxed but the tension from my point of view – as it was for Martin and Archie – stemmed from not knowing who would be the final piece in the jigsaw.

Malmo had been a real surprise package in working their way through to the final and it was a great achievement by the Swedish champions. The problem was that everyone seemed to be taking it for granted that we would win and I remember 'Cloughie' getting very irritated when a television reporter put his question in that way. Brian jumped straight back at him, saying that was incredibly disrespectful to Malmo who had beaten some very fine sides in qualifying for the final. He was absolutely right, of course and we'd be stupid to think it was going to be easy.

Malmo were coached by Bobby Houghton, an Englishman who had come from no where to put them on the European stage and because he had them so well drilled, the contest at the Olympic Stadium was always likely to be a dour affair. To be honest, it wasn't that good. We played our normal way but they really did a job on us. I don't think any team we'd played all season made a better fist of keeping 'Robbo' quiet and although there was never much chance of Malmö scoring against us, we were way short of doing ourselves justice. In the end, a moment of classic 'Robbo' won us the game. He shimmied his way past two defenders and delivered a delicious cross to the far post that was begging to be headed into the net. Our £1million-man famously arrived to do that – and yet another fairytale had been written.

Despite the victory, we were all feeling deflated when we got back to the dressing room. We'd been desperately keen to put on a show in the biggest game of our lives but just didn't have the energy to take apart a team intent on stifling us. The celebrations were distinctly muted and for once, it was Brian who was dishing out the sympathy. He knew we had given him every ounce of energy we had left and kept stressing that 12 months from then, people would only remember the result.

In every respect apart from the result, it was a massive anti-climax and arguably the biggest drama of the night came when suddenly Peter Taylor announced they would be gathering up the medals and would give them back to us later. "You're not having mine, Pete," I said sharply, and others started to follow suit. There was no way I was letting it out of my sight and I think I even took it into the bath with me.

From my point of view, the anti-climax actually continued for the rest of the day. As always with us, no official celebrations had been organised so all the lads met up after the game with their wives and partners and went off to mark the achievement in style. Pam hadn't been able to come out to Germany because our youngest daughter Nicky was only six months old at the time, so and I was left at the hotel with Archie, Chris Woods and Tony Waddington, the former Stoke City manager who was there as a guest of Brian. Archie was still steaming at the decision to leave him out and no words I could think of would console him, while young Woods was a very shy and retiring lad. I just had a modest meal with them... and took myself off to bed. Surely that wasn't how it was supposed to be?

At the end of the day, though, no one could take away from me the fact that I was the proud holder of a European Cup winner's medal, which beautifully rounded off my career. Although I didn't know it in the time, that game against Malmö was my last as a professional footballer.

A Wembley winner at last as we celebrate retaining the League Cup.
Picture: Nottingham Post

Ian Bowyer stoops to head our winner in the European Cup semi-final in Cologne. What a moment that was!
Picture: Nottingham Post/Nottingham Local Studies Collection

PLAYER - MANAGER - CHAIRMAN 179

TOP Celebrating our triumph in Munich with Larry Lloyd. *Picture: JMS Photography*
And we're The Kings of Europe.
Picture: Nottingham Post/Nottingham Local Studies Collection

Garry Birtles in his pomp. Hard to believe he so nearly
walked away from the game.
Picture: Nottingham Post/Nottingham Local Studies Collection

PLAYER - MANAGER - CHAIRMAN

The Manager

Sunderland (Assistant: July 1979-April 1981)
Leyton Orient (Assistant: October 1981-May 1983)
Leyton Orient (May 1983-May 1991)
Nottingham Forest (May 1993-December 1996)
Manchester City (December 1996-February 1998)

Honours
1979-80 – Second Division promotion
1988-89 – Fourth Division promotion
1993-94 – Championship promotion
1994-95 – LMA 'Manager of the Year'
1995-96 – UEFA Cup quarter-finals

Chapter 14
ROKER ROAR WAS SPECIAL – PITY IT DIDN'T LAST
1979-81

The call came out of no-where in the summer of 1979. Ken Knighton had been promoted from first-team coach to manager of Sunderland when Jimmy Adamson left and he wanted to me be his assistant. I still had a year to run on my Nottingham Forest contract and as we basked in the glory of winning the European Cup, it never occurred to me that the Final against Malmö would be my farewell appearance as a player. The more I thought about it though, the more I felt the time was right to enter the next phase of my career.

I hardly knew Ken. We'd met a time or two at management and coaching courses and got on very well but I couldn't make such a big decision based on that alone. Ken was really excited about what the future might hold when we met to discuss it further. It didn't take long for me to get caught up in the enthusiasm. It really was a fantastic opportunity and an ideal way to ease myself into management. Sunderland are a terrific football club. They're one of those perennial sleeping giants and sooner or later, someone would have to get a grip of them and make them fulfil their vast potential. Why shouldn't it be us? Even though people in the North East automatically associated me with Newcastle, joining their big rivals wasn't an issue. There'd been plenty of movement between the two clubs in my time as a player – Stan Anderson, Bobby Moncur and Dave Elliott to name but three – and the intensity of feeling between the two groups of fans was nothing like as confrontational as you get today. I chatted it through with Pam and we decided to give it a go. We'd been very happy living in a village on the outskirts of Nottingham but I was 36-years-old. My career had arrived at a crossroads.

It wasn't quite as straight-forward as it appeared, however, because I wasn't free to make that decision. I still 'belonged' to Forest. I had another 12 months to run on my contract and when I went to discuss it with Brian Clough, he made it very clear that he didn't want me to leave. In fact, he even offered me a year's extension to my deal. He admitted they were looking for a new left-back so I'd no longer be a regular in the team. But he wanted me to use my influence in the dressing room and help bring the youngsters through. Our conversation was going no-where. Eventually he said he was committed to do a weekend's coaching in the North East in a few days time, with an after-dinner speech thrown in, and I would be going with him. I had no option but to agree to this and he spent the whole weekend telling me why it was right for me to stay at Forest. He wasn't used to people saying 'no' to him but I stood my ground. My mind was made up. In the end, he cancelled my contract and I left with his blessing.

Sunderland were in the second tier of English football but had the makings of a good team. And although it didn't influence my decision in any way, I was delighted at the prospect of working again with my old mate Bryan Robson. He'd just returned to Roker Park for a second spell after three years at West Ham. I knew we'd be able to bank on him to get us some goals.

I wasn't the only new arrival behind the scenes. Peter Eustace was brought in to run the reserves, George Herd took charge the youth team and when Mick Docherty announced his retirement as a player, he also worked in the youth scheme. We needed a new chief scout as well and I pushed for Jimmy Greenhalgh to be given the job. He was my mentor for a big part of my time at Newcastle and I was delighted to do something for him in return. It was a really strong backroom team and the more work we did with the players, the more we fancied our chances of achieving something.

Although Ken liked to be hands on with the coaching, the majority of my time was spent on the training ground, which was how I wanted it to be. Looking back, I made a lot more noise than I should have done at the start but I was learning every day. It very quickly dawned on me that no amount of management and coaching courses, nor 600 appearances at the top level of the game, could thoroughly prepare me for the job I'd taken on. I had to back my judgement and be sure to learn from the mistakes I inevitably made. I'd crossed the great divide between player and management and although I was always 'up' for a laugh and joke with the lads, it was essential to know where to draw the line because no longer was I one of them. We certainly had a laugh on the occasion that I was called upon to show my sprinting prowess. Barry Siddall, a good goalkeeper but always full of himself, kept going on about the fact that he was the fastest man in the club over 100 yards. As part of the banter, the lads threw out a challenge to the staff to take him on. I was nominated to represent us, bearing in mind that I'd not long finished playing, and my 'street cred' went through the roof when I beat him!

We got away to a decent start to the season, established ourselves among the front-runners, and strengthened the squad as we went along. Everything was falling to place. We broke the club's transfer record in November to sign Stan Cummins, a 20-year-old attacking midfielder from Middlesbrough. His manager, Jack Charlton, had predicted he would eventually become the first £1million player. We got him for £300,000 and he proved to be an excellent signing. Joe Hinnigan also joined us three months later from Wigan and I rated him very highly. He was great lad, a real powerhouse who could operate anywhere along the back. I was convinced he would go on to play for England. Injuries got in the way of that happening but he certainly played his part as we surged on towards the top flight, as did Robson. He was well past his 30th birthday by that stage but hadn't lost his incredible knack for scoring goals. I rated him as one of the finest strikers of his generation when we were together at Newcastle and although he – like me – never got any further than the night we lined up together for the Football League, I really thought he should have got a full England cap. Bryan made a huge contribution towards our promotion success, popping in 20 goals that season. As an aside, though, I got a sharp reminder the following year that I'd crossed to the 'other' side. Ken and I left Bryan out of the team when he was struggling for form and his wife and mother stopped speaking to me. Football really does strain relationships at times.

In between the arrival of Cummins and Hinnigan we also broke our transfer record again by paying £380,000 for Argentina international Claudio Marangoni. A South American agent had tipped off Ken that Marangoni was available and urged him to make inquiries about buying him. It was a big decision that didn't need to be rushed but he immediately made arrangements to fly out and watch him play. I felt that put him under pressure to try and get the deal done and Marangoni duly arrived in early December. It turned out to be a bad piece of business.

The common denominator about my time at Sunderland is that my inexperience at handling certain situations – and people – had a big influence. For example, I should have done a lot more than I did to help Marangoni settle at Sunderland. He found it very difficult to cope with the English culture, and the game, and we should have reached out more than we did. On Fridays, for example, we would always do a few gentle laps of the pitch, followed by some short sprints and then knock a ball around. Claudio would say: "On Fridays, I do not sprint." On one occasion we 'lost' it with him over that. We were wrong and had that happened 10 years later, I would have handled it entirely differently. The one thing that mattered was that Marangoni performed on the Saturday afternoon and it was all about putting him in the right frame of mind to do that. He never did fit in at Roker and stayed for just 11 months.

Another mistake we made that still haunts me to this day is that we rejected the chance to sign Chris Waddle. One of our local scouts tipped us off that there was a promising lad playing for Tow Law Town so we extended an invitation for him to come and train with us for a couple of weeks. Sunderland's training ground at that time was situated in a valley. It was a horrible place to be in mid-winter when the wind was blowing in from the North Sea. Chris spent the entire two weeks shuffling around the training ground with his hands down his shorts, trying to keep himself warm, and absolutely no attempt was made to make him feel welcome. At the end of his trial period, the staff got together and unanimously agreed he wasn't good enough for us. To make matters worse, we didn't even send someone to watch him in action for Tow Law. It was classic bad management. We couldn't possibly have handled it worse and I vowed I would never allow that to happen again. It's not unheard of for players to be a bit 'cold' towards trialists because they can see them as a threat but we should have had a better policy in place to give Waddle the best possible chance to impress. Presumably Arthur Cox and his staff dealt with the situation far better when he went to Newcastle.

Anyway, we were closing in on promotion and it all came down eventually to the very last game of the season. We could have tied it up a few days earlier by winning at Cardiff but a 1-1 draw meant that we would need a point from the home game against West Ham to finish runners-up behind Leicester. The game was played on the Monday after the FA Cup Final, in which West Ham had beaten Fulham. The big question was how would they react to their special day out at Wembley? They could have been celebrating for two days and not give a damn about how things worked out at Roker. Alternatively, they could arrive determined to put on a show before a sell-out crowd of 47,000. I was obsessed with us playing with a quick tempo. I thought that was the best way to make sure they didn't enjoy the occasion. It was a real game, no half-measures from either side, but eventually we won 2-0 and I experienced the famous Roker Roar like never before. This was a proper football club, capable of becoming one of the giants of the game in this country. I wanted to be a part of making that happen.

The next day, we flew to America for an end-of-season tour... and Ken made his first big mistake. We'd agreed in advance that there would be no wives or partners on the tour and then, at the last minute, he decided to take his wife and family. They stayed in separate hotels to us but even so, he spent much of the trip with his family. Instead of being the brilliant bonding exercise that these trips so often are, an atmosphere developed of almost 'him and us' and I just felt that people viewed him slightly differently from then on. Incidentally, it was during that trip that the Miami Race Riots broke out and we were stuck in the middle of it at one stage. I remember looking out of my hotel bedroom window and the whole city seemed to be on fire. It was a scary business and we couldn't wait to move on.

We signed Sam Allardyce from Bolton during the summer and immediately made him club captain. He was a commanding central defender who we knew was well capable of being an influence at the top level. He helped to bring out the best from the likes of Cummins, Joe Bolton, Shaun Elliott and Kevin Arnott. They stepped up impressively following our promotion and we made a decent start to the season. Behind the scenes, though, things were not all they might be. Long-serving Keith Collings had decided to take a back seat and the working methods of new chairman Tom Cowie were different. He was a self-made millionaire who liked to have things his own way, and the chemistry between him and Ken was not good. We were regularly summoned to his business premises for meetings and they invariably developed into a shouting match between the two of them. You hope your results will protect you in situations like that and for a while, they did. But little things become big things. When that happens, they get stored away until such time as results are not good – then they are brought out and used in evidence against you.

Come December, we were due to play at home on the Boxing Day and Ken wanted to take the players to a hotel on Christmas Night. Cowie wouldn't sanction it so Ken took it upon himself to arrange it. He knew the hotel manager and restaurant manager well and they agreed to give us the rooms for the cost of the linen charge. Ken leaked the story to the newspapers and said that he and I were going to pick up the bill. It was the first I knew about it! When Cowie found out, he simply asked whether we would be prepared to do the same thing every time a hotel stay was required. If Ken thought he'd put one over on him, he was very wrong. It was just a bit more ammunition to store away.

When I took the Sunderland job Pam wanted to live back in Northumberland so we bought a house in a lovely development at Darras Hall, just north of Newcastle. It was 20 miles from Sunderland but the journey was comfortable and knowing my background, it was no surprise to anyone that we moved there. But Ken, whose family had initially stayed in Sheffield, then decided he also wanted to buy a house in Darras Hall and as a journalist pointedly said to us: "That could cost you two your jobs."

All of a sudden, things were not going our way. I thought it was a great piece of business when we managed to sign Ian Bowyer from Forest because he was just what we needed. We were starting to wobble but he would be able to use his ability and experience to settle things down. I was confident we would pull through the sticky patch. But then 'Bomber' needed an operation after getting injured and that was a massive blow.

It was incredibly tight towards the bottom of the table and with four games to go, the directors – or one in particular – lost their nerve. There had been rumblings for a few weeks and I even got a call from someone in the know who said that if I was to distance myself from Ken, I could get the manager's job. I wasn't prepared to do so and made that plain to Ken. It seemed only a matter of time before something would have to give and I guessed what was coming when we organised a full-scale practice match at Roker Park and all the directors were there. Before the day was out we were sacked – Mick Docherty took temporary charge – and it was a horrible experience. Those situations never can be pleasant but I felt especially sorry for Ron Linney, the club secretary and a nice man. He was ordered to stand over us as we cleared our desks and then collect our car keys as we departed. The humiliation was complete the following week when Ken and I had to 'sign on' at the dole office in Wallsend. We had to walk past a building site to get there and when the workers recognised us, the stick we took was incredible.

I was at Sunderland for less than two years and I packed so much into that period. I had personal tragedies as my mum died suddenly of a heart attack and my best mate Joe Jacques died at a ridiculously young age, but Pam and I loved being back in the North East where we re-connected with a lot of close friends. On the football front, I experienced the highs and lows of winning promotion and getting the sack and went through a massive learning curve. I had come out the other end far better equipped to manage a football club. Now the challenge was to persuade someone to give me a job.

I didn't have to wait too long for my first opportunity but when I went for a job interview for the one and only time in my life, I blew it. I saw that Halifax Town were looking for a manager, sent in my application and they invited me to go and meet them at the chairman's house. The first question they asked at the interview was: "How much money do you want". Being a clever bugger, I said I thought we were wasting each other's time and asked whether they wanted the cheapest or the best. Even though they were clearly not convinced about how I'd cope with players at their level, I left the meeting feeling optimistic. I'd got that wrong, though, because the vice-chairman called me later to say that I hadn't got the job. They appointed the youth coach instead.

A couple of weeks on I bumped into Ron Fenton and Liam O'Kane on a course for managers and coaches. Jimmy Gordon had just retired so Ron had been promoted to first-team coach at Forest and Liam was still running the youth team. It meant there was a vacancy with the reserves and I told them I fancied that. They were taken aback but as I said: "I'm out of work!" They fixed up for me to see Brian Clough and Peter Taylor and we met up at Peter's house in Tollerton. I was gob-smacked when they told me what they were prepared to pay me. I knew the coaching staff at Forest were not well paid but it was less than one-third of what I was on at Sunderland. I told them I wasn't sure if I could live on what they were offering … but they knew I needed a job.

I reported for duty back at the City Ground in time for pre-season and Brian's greeting was: "Two things. The first is that Liam is taking the youth team to play in a tournament in Rimini and you are going with them. The second is that as soon as yet get back, you're running in the inaugural Robin Hood Half Marathon around the streets of Nottingham." The first was no problem, of course. I'd be delighted to spend a few days on Italy's delightful Adriatic Coast but as for the second … oh dear. I'd always hated long-distance running and it would be absolute torture. I certainly wasn't wrong in that respect. It nearly killed me. The only thing that kept me going on the final three miles was the knowledge that Jimmy Sirrel, Notts County's legendary manager who was more than 20 years my senior, wasn't far behind me. I knew that I would never live it down if he finished ahead of me – and 'Cloughie' would have been furious. Liam and Ron were also under orders to take part in the half-marathon and when we'd finished, we hauled ourselves tentatively back to the City Ground. We went straight to the Referee's Room, submerged ourselves in the three individual baths and in my case, I really struggled to get out again an hour later. Thanks Brian! The only good thing about it was that at least I picked up another medal to add to my collection as I crossed the finishing line.

The job at the City Ground was a dream – not least because Brian's attitude to training meant that most of the time, I was only working three days a week. Given the chance, I would have preferred to work five days because I felt sure I could have helped to improve the technique of the youngsters with more time on the training ground. But if Brian was around, he'd immediately put a stop to that and tell me to send the players home to rest. I did find that frustrating and so was the fact that I could never prepare the players properly for matches because I invariably didn't get to know the team until late in the day. Having said that, I thoroughly enjoyed working with the likes of Chris Fairclough, Steve Hodge and Steve Sutton and I knew that with players of that calibre coming through the ranks, the future of Forest was in safe hands.

Mind you, I'm not so sure the players themselves were in safe hands on match-days because the biggest shock I got when I went back to Forest was being told I would be responsible for treating the injuries. That basically involved running on with a sponge and bucket of water whenever a player went down. To this day I struggle to get my head around that. I had no medical knowledge and certainly hadn't been trained in any way yet the careers of highly-valued players, many of them internationals and European Cup winners, were being left in my hands. I thank my lucky stars that I was never put in a situation where my lack of knowledge was exposed.

Yet again, I could put that down to experience and although I was only back with Forest for three months or so, the whole episode was another massive learning curve. Working in that environment, you couldn't fail to gather information and I loved that aspect of it. For example, if the first-team were playing and the reserves weren't, I was expected to sit with the other coaches on a bench just along from the dug-out and I was fascinated by how Clough and Taylor handled certain situations. One little story about that which sticks in my mind concerned a pre-season game against foreign opposition. Stuart Gray, who was really a midfield player but was filling in at left back for some reason, was having a tough time and all of a sudden, Cloughie's head appeared and he glanced down the line. "Frank!" he screamed. "If you don't teach him how to play left back, I'll sack you!"

I never quite got to grips with where the demarcation lines started and finished between the coaches and management at Forest, when and when not to speak up. The newspapers were full of the fact that Forest were set to pay £1million to sign Justin Fashanu from Norwich and although I had views on that subject, I wasn't sure how welcome they would be. I was staying at that time in Alan Hill's hotel and used to arrive at the ground early. One morning I got there at the same time as Peter Taylor. I thought that was my ideal opportunity so I mentioned the fact that when we'd played against Fashanu at Sunderland, Rob Hindmarch had battered him and I felt Fashanu had thrown in the towel. Had our roles been reversed I would have appreciated that input. Peter didn't see it that way. He came at me aggressively, prodding me in the chest, and said: "Listen. You have to make your mind up. Do you want to be a coach or a scout?" The deal was done a few days later and turned out to be a disaster for Forest. The Fashanu saga caused a lot of disruption at the City Ground over the next 12 months and might well have been the start of Clough and Taylor going their separate ways the following year.

Ken Knighton and I had plenty to laugh about
in our first season at Sunderland. *Picture: Newcastle Chronicle*

PLAYER - MANAGER - CHAIRMAN

Celebrating Sunderland's promotion with local lad Barry Dunn.
Picture: DM Brannigan

Chapter 15
NEW LIFE AS HONORARY EASTENDER
1981-93

I spent 12 years with Leyton Orient, from October 1981 until the summer of 1993. In some ways it didn't seem that long – in others it seemed like an eternity. But I certainly packed a lot of life into that that period, plus experience of all aspects of football. By the time I left Brisbane Road I was a much more rounded person. Apart from anything else, moving to London and working in the East End introduced me to a very different existence.

I'd thoroughly enjoyed my brief 'time out' period at Forest but I knew there was no future in that. I needed to return to management as quickly as possible to keep my career moving and when Ken Knighton landed the Orient job we were back in business. He offered me a pay-deal worth four times what I was getting at Forest so that was instantly attractive. What I didn't quite realise was that I'd need every penny of that to pay my way in London. Initially Ken and I shared a flat in South Woodford, 15 minutes from the ground, and it was really difficult on the family front with Pam and my two daughters living 300 miles away in Newcastle. But I needed to earn a living and somehow, we had to find a way around it.

Things were not good at Orient. They'd been in the old Second Division for 12 years and competed strongly but the tide had turned. Jimmy Bloomfield, who was ill, had recently finished as manager and although Paul Went replaced him, he lasted for just three weeks. They only won one of their first 12 League games of the season. They were bottom of the table when we arrived, really struggling, but my first impression was that they had two big things going for them. The first was that they had a mixture of promising youngsters and decent experienced players like Tommy Taylor, Mervyn Day and Barry Silkman. The second was that Brian Winston was the chairman. He impressed me immediately as a 'sound' man, who understood football and had the interests of Leyton Orient very much at heart. We became good friends.

The challenge for Ken and me was to change results quickly, before the rot really set in. That was far easier said than done because it was a difficult dressing room. From my experience, the dressing rooms at London clubs tend to be different from what you find elsewhere in the country. There's an 'edginess' about the atmosphere that's difficult to put into words. It seems to be a way of life that people are striving all the time to put one over the others. We could sense from Day 1 that the senior lads were questioning what entitled these two country bumpkins to come in and tell them what to do. They were constantly testing us – and that seemed far more important to them than winning matches and getting us out of trouble.

Results did improve, though, and we steadily closed the gap on the clubs above us. There was good cause to feel that we could work our way into a position of safety. Alongside that, we made a few bob by reaching the fifth round of the FA Cup. We knocked out Charlton, then beat Huddersfield after a replay, and took Crystal Palace to two games before being unluckily beaten. Crowds were increasing and there was a much better feel around the place. But the turning point was one of the most difficult situations I faced in my managerial career.

During the replay with Palace, Tommy Taylor had a confrontation with a linesman. At half time we made the point to him that he shouldn't get involved with officials – he should leave that to us. He reacted by going into a rant which included comments that were bang out of order. That put us in a really difficult position. We had a lot of youngsters in our squad at that time and we were concerned that if we did nothing, it would not only undermine our authority, it could be seen as condoning Taylor's actions. We took it to the chairman and recommended he should be sacked. The directors didn't support that view and felt the right course of action would be to drop him from the team and strip him of the captaincy.

Even to this day I struggle to decide whether Ken and I were right or wrong. On the one hand, we were definitely right to take action and I'm sure Tommy regrets the episode. But we showed our naivety in massively over-estimating what the effects of his rant would be. Any disharmony that followed in the dressing room was caused more by what we did than what he said. Tommy had played more than 300 times for West Ham before going back to Orient for a second spell. He was a very good player and was key to the sweeper system we'd adopted as the platform to dig us out of trouble. The fizz went out of the team when he was dropped. We hardly won another game all season and were relegated. That was the first time in my career that I'd tasted relegation. It was a blot on my record that hurt intensely. It could well have been avoided had we decided not to take a stance.

Inevitably, losing our Second Division status had consequences. The playing budget had to be slashed which led to major changes and we struggled again the following season. A lot of clubs would have sacked us after we took a 6-0 hammering at Huddersfield and then lost successive home games 5-1 against Newport County and Bristol Rovers. That was a horrendous experience and by the end of October, we were bottom of the League. But the Board stuck with us and we managed to avoid a second successive relegation on the final day of that 1982-83 season with a 4-1 win over Sheffield United.

We didn't realise quite how bad the financial situation had become. By then, Winston and his vice-chairman Adrian Harding had taken a step back and Neville Ovenden, a local paper merchant, had taken over the controlling interest of the club. The position was close to crisis point and Ken and I were told at the end of the season that one of us would have to go. Our contracts were written differently and if Ken went, he would get his full entitlement. If I went, I'd leave with nothing. That possibly influenced the decision but the directors, I later discovered, wanted me to get the manager's job because they thought I'd be more receptive to working with the severe cuts that had to be made. Ken accepted the decision and I'm pleased to say that we parted amicably.

We were right down to the bare bones when we reported back for pre-season. I had 15 players and no coaches. Shortly after Ken and I had taken over we sacked a chap called Jimmy Hallybone. He'd had a very modest playing career, had no proper coaching qualifications and we couldn't see what his function was. After a month, I said to Ken: "We need to bring him back." Fortunately, Jimmy agreed to return. By then I'd realised that his function was a willing pair of hands. He was Leyton Orient through and through, happy to do anything that would help the cause, and he was brilliant throughout the rest of my time at Brisbane Road. Billy Songhurst came in as physio and we managed to develop an 'all in it together' mentality. We didn't have demarcation lines – we just got on and did whatever job had to be done. We'd had to dispense with the services of our youth coach, Dario Gradi, the previous year to save money. But someone had to look after the kids and I later gave that job to Patsy Holland, the former West Ham player, on condition he agreed to combine playing with being youth coach. The problem was that his knee was shot to pieces and he prayed that I wouldn't have to pick him. I remember his face being an absolute picture when he was on the bench for a game at Wimbledon and I told him to get warmed up!

Amazingly, we finished 11th in the old Third Division that

season. We had massively over-achieved and I told the Board they had to find me some additional budget. They said that wasn't possible so I made it clear that if that's how it had to be, it was fine by me – but we would get relegated. They said: "That doesn't matter. It's all about the survival of the club."

A year later, we went down to the basement section for the first time in the club's history. We drew our last four matches of the season. If we could have just managed to turn one of those into a victory, we would have survived. I got real aggravation from supporters. Perhaps understandably, they wanted me sacked – but they didn't know the half of it. The directors did, and they stayed incredibly strong. They insisted I'd run the club properly and they wanted me to stay. I wasn't sure if I wanted to do so.

Pam and I had bought a house at Loughton, a lovely area close to Epping Forest, but it was a really difficult time for her. I was working 16 hours a day, which meant she was left to fend for herself. Not surprisingly, she struggled to settle. My daughters didn't like their new school and it used to screw me up when Pam told stories about how she would stand at the school gate, desperately hoping someone would speak to her. I know it's an occupational hazard for families tied into the football business but I do live with a guilty conscience about the sacrifices my wife and children had to make as I moved them around the country. My daughters never blamed me for affecting their education but I know that all the upheaval did significantly influence their lives.

I'd tasted the high life to a large extent during my spells as a player at Newcastle and Forest. My new situation could hardly have been more contrasting. We literally didn't have two pennies to rub together. Every week was a struggle to stay alive. Yet strangely, although I was under intense pressure, I enjoyed it. The challenge was massive but every time we won a game or even picked up a point, the satisfaction of knowing what had gone into achieving that was immense.

I worked hard at getting to know and understand the London

football scene. Several days a week I managed to get in two games in a day because reserve-team matches in the Football Combination took place in the afternoons and evenings. I developed a brilliant network of contacts. The frustration was that when I spotted someone who I really fancied could do a job for us, invariably we couldn't afford to sign them. Part of me said what's the point of going to all these games – but I lived in hope that our financial fortunes might change. I was filing away information for the future, about people like Stan Collymore and Kevin Campbell, and eventually got my rewards.

We'd found our level in the Fourth Division and at last began to win more games than we lost. Although we were seven points adrift of promotion, it was a great effort to finish fifth in the 1985-86 season. I had to get my 'kicks' wherever I could. Paul Shinners and Kevin Hales provided two of them. Shinners was a Londoner, a big, powerful striker who I'd spotted playing for Gillingham. He only made one League start for them but I thought he had something so I signed him on a free transfer. What an impact he made! He scored 19 goals for us that season, then 13 more the following year before injury forced him out of the game. As for Hales, I'd had my eye on him for some time and when Chelsea released him after he'd suffered a bad knee injury, I thought he'd be out of our reach. I gave it a try anyway and I couldn't believe it when he accepted my offer. I told him we could only afford £200 a week with no signing-on fee and he went for it. What a diamond! He was a great lad and a very good midfield player who turned out more than 400 times for Orient. He was still there when I left and was a fantastic servant to that club.

We were starting to make some headway on the field but in financial terms, we continued to stagger from one crisis to another. Every day I turned up for work hoping we would get a lifeline and every now and again, something happened to give me a boost and keep us alive for another week. A classic example was the situation with Keith Houchen. He was destined, of course, to score a famous FA Cup Final goal for Coventry City but it was a totally different scene when Ken

Knighton bought him from Hartlepool. He never settled in London. Like us, he discovered that the only way he could afford a house was to buy one miles outside of town. Because of that, he never really got close to the other lads. Out of the blue we got a £15,000 offer for him from York City and my orders were to snap their hands off. But then I got involved in a tug-of-war between Keith and Brian Winston, who was still on the Orient Board. Keith said he wouldn't go unless he got a pay-off, Brian said he couldn't have it. When I went back and told him, Keith said he would take less than he'd initially asked for. Brian still wouldn't budge. I said: "You keep telling me we're desperate for money but you could let this deal slip through your fingers." In the end, the deal was done – and Keith got nothing. Incidentally, I always thought it was one of Brian's great strengths that you could have a blazing row with him one day and it was all forgotten the next. That theory was tested a number of times as we hovered on the brink and nerves were constantly frayed.

The financial situation was dictating everything. Even when I knew a decision was wrong, I just had to nod along with it. Decisions were taken based not on their merits but on what the cost implications would be. For example, we had a couple of promising lads coming to the end of their time as YTS trainees and although I was determined we would offer a professional deal to Kevin Nugent, I also wanted to sign Warren Barton. He'd already been rejected by Watford because they thought he was too small and although his size was an issue, which made him a border-line case, he had a fair bit going for him. I told the Board we ought to stick with him for another year. They said: "No chance. We can't afford them both … it's Nugent or Barton." I stand by my decision to go for Nugent, who served Orient brilliantly for seven years before moving to Plymouth for £200,000. As for Barton, he proved everyone wrong as he went off to play for Maidstone United and then, several years down the line, became English football's costliest defender when he moved from Wimbledon to Newcastle for £4million.

It was around that time that I got a call inviting me to go for an interview. Southend United were looking for a new manager and I was to meet with the chairman Vic Jobson, vice-chairman John Adams and the one and only Bobby Moore, who was their Director of Football. We hadn't been talking for long when Jobson asked me for my thoughts on discipline. I said it was vital and although I didn't like to be petty, the players always had to know the rules and abide by them. He informed me that they operated with a disciplinary committee, which included the three of them, and that set alarm bells ringing. The very best thing about my job at Orient was that I was left to get on with it, with little or no interference. I sensed it would be very different at Southend. I didn't like the tone of that meeting and decided the job wasn't for me.

I thought I'd take my chances with Orient but what a terrible decision that appeared to be when I turned up for a Player of the Year function at the end of that 1985-86 season. Winston pulled me aside and told me we were going out of business. All that time and effort that I'd put in had been for nothing. But then, incredibly, our saviour arrived on the scene. With no fuss or formality, Tony Wood slipped a cheque for £10,000 into the hands of the chairman. Neville Ovenden's eye-sight wasn't the best and at first, he thought it was for £1,000. He was close to tears when we put him right and that was hardly surprising. Just imagine being the man at the helm when your football club, which means so much to the community and the people involved, goes out of business. I'd had a taste of that as a youngster when I used to go and watch Gateshead play at home. It was horrible to see them die.

None of us had even heard of Tony. He was an East Ender who'd done well for himself working in the City before moving to Africa, where he made a fortune from coffee production in Rwanda. He was a born and bred Orient fan but only got to games very occasionally because he didn't spend much time in this country. He'd shown his hand as a man who could breath new life into Leyton Orient. I was dispatched a few days later to meet him and ask if he might be prepared to take over the club. What I certainly didn't expect was for him to throw it back into my lap. He said he might be prepared to do that but only if I agreed to stay on and run the club. He was shrewd, Tony. He could sense that I'd had enough. All those long days and the stress of scrimping and saving were wearing me down and it was a very thankless task. But I delved a bit deeper into his thinking and eventually he won me round.

His ambitions seemed very realistic when I asked him where he wanted to take the club. He wanted to see Orient re-established at tier two level and to re-build the youth scheme, so that it started to produce a regular flow of players. I liked the sound of that and was even happier with Tony's response when I told him it would cost him £100,000 a year for five years to bring that to fruition. "That's ok," he said in matter of fact fashion. "The interest on my Swiss bank account will cover that." Someone had just flicked a switch as far as I was concerned. My instant reaction was that it would put an end to all those embarrassing moments, like when I always had to take a cheque with me to away matches and settle the hotel bill as we checked out because our credit rating was so poor.

Tony insisted the deal was that I would become managing-director, run the club day-to-day but still keep control of the football operation. In return, he would pump in the cash and although I wouldn't actually see much of him, he'd be available to me on the phone any time I wanted him. I kept thinking there must be a catch here – "What's in it for him?" There never was a catch. He was just a thoroughly nice man, a brilliant chairman and we had a great relationship. Although he was definitely no-one's fool, Tony never had an ego and always preferred to stay in the background. He used to wander into the ground when he was over from Rwanda and turn his hand to any odd job that needed doing. He even used to work in the Club Shop – and he loved it.

The goalposts had moved for me in one respect but life wasn't going to get any easier because from then on, I'd effectively be doing two jobs. You gain strength from winning matches, though, and it was starting to feel like a proper football club again as we mounted a spirited challenge for promotion in 1986-87. That was the year when the Promotion Play-offs were introduced, as was automatic relegation out of the League, and we found ourselves caught up in some real drama on the final day of the season.

It might seem difficult to believe in Burnley's current situation but we travelled north to play them knowing that a win would not only take us into the Play-offs, it would relegate the famous old Lancashire club to the Conference. How could that be? It wasn't that long since their team of star-studded internationals were challenging for the League title and appearing in FA Cup Finals. It was a massive story. The eyes of the nation were on us and very few people wanted us to win. We knew that anyway but it was highlighted a few hours before kick off when Billy Songhurst went to Turf Moor to lay out the players' kit. He was clearly shaken when he got back to the hotel. He told me a policeman had pulled him aside and said: "Tell your gaffer that if you win, there's no way we will be able to guarantee your safety." I told him firmly that he must keep that completely between the two of us. One of the issues was that the dressing rooms at Burnley were behind a goal, so we wouldn't be able to just nip straight down the tunnel at the end of the game. It was certainly unsettling but we'd worked incredibly hard after a poor start to the season to get ourselves into a position where we could win promotion. We were not going to just lay down for anyone.

It seemed as if the entire population of Burnley wanted to be there. The attendance was given as 15,781 but it was surely many more than that. They even had to delay the kick-off by 15 minutes to try and get them all in. The hostility towards us eased a bit when they went in front before half time and then scored again. But Alan Comfort pulled one back five minutes later and the tension was incredible. A draw was no good to either of us. We had to go for goals and when I leapt out of our box at one point to urge our players forward, Billy, still feeling very twitchy, was quick to tell me to sit back down. Burnley survived. It finished 2-1 and although I was bitterly disappointed – not least for the near-1,000 fans who had followed us to Lancashire – there was light at the end of the tunnel.

We narrowly missed out again the following year – two more points would have guaranteed us a Play-off spot – and that was the season when I went head-to-head with 'Cloughie' after we were drawn to meet Forest at Brisbane Road in the fourth round of the FA Cup. It was certainly good for Orient because the tie pulled in a big crowd and the prospect of Clough v Clark attracted lots of publicity. At one point, though, I wasn't sure if the match would go ahead. 'Cloughie' hated arriving early and consequently, it was often touch and go whether they would be there for the kick off. This was one of those occasions. He had totally disregarded the fact that you can spend an hour going no-where in the East End traffic. They finally arrived 25 minutes before kick off and I was hoping that just might throw them out of their stride. No chance. We gave a very good account of ourselves but lost 2-1.

It turned out to be third time lucky in 1988-89 in our quest for promotion, and no one was more delighted than me when Orient secured their first success for 19 years. Mind you, the signs were not good when we won only one of our first seven games. I could have been gone by Christmas. I actually offered to resign after we suffered an embarrassing FA Cup defeat against Enfield and promotion was the last thing on our minds at that stage. But the directors refused to accept my offer and a series of significant changes helped us to build up a terrific head of steam. One was that we introduced Paul Heald to the team and the young goalkeeper performed remarkably well. Another was that talented midfielder Steve Castle returned to action after missing four months through injury.

The other big deal was that I managed to sign Kevin Campbell. It was a major blow to us when local lad Keith Harvey got injured because he'd been doing well. Billy told me Harvey was going to be out for a lengthy spell so I had to do something quickly. I'd heard on the grapevine that Campbell had signed a new contract with Arsenal and got straight on the phone to see if they might let him out on loan. George Graham was a canny operator and although Campbell had reached the stage of his development where he needed to be playing League football, the manager blocked it until he agreed to sign a new deal. As soon as he did so, George let him join us for three months and what an impact he had. He was a smashing lad – none of this "I'm a First Division player" bull-shit – and the move was good for his career and brilliant for us. When Harvey recovered, we used the two of them together up front and they were a right handful for defenders. We ended up winning 11 of our last 16 games to sneak into eighth place and were heading for the Play-offs.

Unfortunately Campbell wasn't around to help us finish it off because he had to go back to Arsenal when his loan expired. We nearly didn't have our best player, either. Alan Comfort was a talented left-winger who also scored goals and he had a special place in my heart because he was the first player I ever bought. I paid £10,000 to Cambridge United to take him to Brisbane Road. It was a great piece of business for the club when he eventually moved to Middlesbrough for £175,000 … but that's another story. Alan scored 19 League goals that season. He was massively important but the problem was that when we were struggling in mid-season, he went and organised his wedding for the middle of May.

It was a situation that called for desperate measures and I managed to pull a 'fast-one' that even 'Cloughie' would have been proud to claim. The Play-off semi-finals were no problem for Alan. He was available for both legs against Scarborough, which were bound to be 'tasty'. One of their lads had suffered a broken leg in the League game and I ended up chasing their manager Neil Warnock up the tunnel because he got me so angry. Fortunately a big Geordie policeman intervened and calmed me down. Anyway, Neil, had gone to Notts

County by the time we met them again and the Play-offs were two very tight games, which we won 1-0 on aggregate.

The final wasn't staged at Wembley in those days. It was over two legs – home and away – and having done a job on Wrexham to get a goalless draw at the Racecourse Ground, it looked as though we would be without Comfort for the return. He didn't want to postpone his wedding, which was taking place in Ireland and had been arranged for months. I sympathised with his predicament but devised a little scheme that Alan was happy to go along with – and by some miracle, we pulled it off. Wearing my managing-director's 'hat', I persuaded our Safety Committee, the Football League and the local Police that we really ought to kick off at 12noon to avoid the risk of crowd trouble. Then I got a Sunday newspaper interested in having exclusive rights to Alan's story and they paid for a helicopter to pick him up straight after the game and whisk him off to Ireland. It was a fairytale situation for all concerned and the newspaper got good value for their money. Harvey gave us the lead and although Wrexham equalised, Mark Cooper clinched our 2-1 win. One of the things that sticks in my mind about that game was that, with five minutes to go, a shot from a Wrexham player bobbled up and hit our goalkeeper smack on the nose. The ball could have gone anywhere. The margins between success and otherwise are so slender.

Incidentally, Comfort became a vicar when injury forced him to retire early from the game and it was a lovely twist that when he found himself working back in the East End of London, he became Orient's chaplain.

So, we'd finally made it back to the third tier of the Football League and that signalled a period of change for me, and for the club. Everything was positive. Attendances were up, the finances were in order, bills were getting paid and our work with the youth scheme was starting to reap rewards. We re-established ourselves comfortably enough in the third tier, finishing 14th in the 1989-90, and when I was offered the chance in March to bring something fresh to the table, I went for it.

Justin Fashanu had just returned from America, where he'd undergone an operation to fix his damaged knee. He was looking for a club. He'd signed up with an agent called Ambrose Mendy, who had an office in the East End, and he called me to ask if I'd be interested in taking Justin on a month's trial. It was a really interesting one. Even though I'd tried to talk Peter Taylor out of signing him for Forest, I knew that Fashanu fit and firing would be a sensation at our level. If things worked out well, he'd bring enough extra people in through the gate to cover the cost of his wages. In the end, he was only with us for two months, played five games without scoring a goal, and wasn't quite up to what we wanted. His fitness was decent but basically, he just couldn't do it any more. When I called him in and told him it wasn't working, he admitted he was expecting it.

I felt sorry for 'Fash'. He was clearly a very troubled soul and Billy Songhurst and I spent a lot of time talking to him, trying to be helpful. He hadn't come out at that time as being gay and although we knew the score and so did our players, he was terrified about how people – and the media in particular – would react if he made it public. Interestingly, it never appeared to be a problem with our players. Quite the opposite, in fact, because he had a good influence in our dressing room while he was with us. But the predicament he was wrestling with was quite obviously messing with his life. I was very sad a few years later when I heard he'd committed suicide.

I brought in Peter Eustace midway through the 1990-91 season as first-team coach and at the end of it, after we'd finished 13th, I told Tony Wood it was time for me to back away. The demands of running the club were growing all the time and although I would remain fairly hands-on with football affairs, Peter became the team manager. It worked out well. The only slight conflict was that he wanted to bring in more experienced players and I wouldn't sanction that. Although the financial situation was infinitely better, we still had to tread carefully and I was aware that the owner was having problems. The war that had broken out in Rwanda was significantly hurting his business and he was a worried man.

Tony had pumped his money into Orient as an interest-free loan, knowing full well that there was every chance that he would never see it again. All the while his business was thriving that wasn't an issue but now we needed to try and return the favour to the man who had kept the football club alive. Other clubs were keen on buying our star players. I told Tony that if we sold one or two, he needed to start clawing back his money or his loan would become too big.

Nugent went to Plymouth for £200,000, Steve Castle made the same move for £225,000, Comfort went to Middlesbrough for £175,000 and Sheffield Wednesday won the race to sign the talented Chris Bart-Williams for £275,000. The fans weren't happy to see them go, especially as it affected our promotion chances, but those deals were right for Orient at that time. We had some good players in our dressing room and generating that cash enabled us to do things that would help to grow the club.

We only missed out on a Play-off place on goal-difference in 1992-93 and despite that disappointment, I knew we were in a good place. I'd come to love my role as managing-director. I enjoyed all the corridors of power stuff and that was now my new life. I'd given up hope of achieving my ambition to become a top-level manager.

The problem was, though, that in the football business, you never know for sure what could be just around the corner.

TOP A big day in my life. One of three appearances I made on stage at the world famous Hundred Club in Oxford Street. All the stars have played there! Saying farewell to Chris Bart-Williams with Peter Eustace as he heads for Sheffield Wednesday.

PLAYER - **MANAGER** - CHAIRMAN

FA Cup 4th round special

Clark has Cloughie on red alert!

By Richard Lewis

LEYTON ORIENT boss Frank Clark takes his side into tomorrow's (Saturday's) FA Cup fourth round clash with Nottingham Forest declaring: "We can be the 'shock' side of this year's competition."

Managing director Mr Clark, comes face-to-face with Brian Clough, the man who made him big in his playing days, confident of causing the football sensation of the season.

Mr Clark said: "We've had three bad results and are ready to bounce back in a big way. It's over right. Last season we reached the semi-finals of the FA Cup. We have no pressure to prove things and are in a great frame of mind for the match.

"The aggravation that has been prevalent having faced top class sides and having so many first division teams in recent seasons, it's been much easier for me to get the players geared up.

"Cloughie plays a big part, too. It's his 50th year at Brisbane Road, we're back now we await success.

"We have an idea of what to expect and after a couple of seasons of not experiencing glory against the top teams, then maybe our turn has come round again.

"FA Cup romance is the FA Cup and there is no more justified than in this tie. As a

cant; praise all round.

"He's one for the future." was the general opinion from Brisbane Road. How that's been proved right. Last season Foster, the 6ft 4in centre half, and he's taken the first division by storm.

But Foster will never forget the way Mr Clark had faith in him — even when the O's hit rock bottom.

He said: "When we were relegated from the second division, Frank got rid of a lot of the young players. But he had faith in me, kept me on and I'll be grateful always for that.

Faith

"I owe him everything I have now. The way he rehabilitated me to Nottingham Forest and allowed me to go there.

"He had faith in me all

LEYTON Orient managing director Frank Clark admits promotion from the fourth division is the club's number one aim. Yet he added: "This fourth round tie is something so special. It's a great boost for the team, the supporters and the whole town in general.

"Having faced first division teams in the competition over the past three seasons, we could hardly have imagined a draw such as this. It's captured the imagination of the whole footballing country."

Chapter 16
SIXTH IN LINE FOR CLOUGH'S THRONE
1993-94

It's just as well I've never been easily offended or I would have told the Nottingham Forest chairman exactly where to stick his manager's job. "Do me a big favour," Fred Reacher said when he rang. "Five people have already turned me down so will you take it on?"

I knew Fred well from my previous stints at the City Ground. I knew what he was all about and although no one could possibly dress it up as a vote of confidence that he'd asked me to become Brian Clough's successor – it was more an act of desperation – there was a much bigger picture to be viewed. Absolutely everything pointed to the fact that the new manager would be on a hiding to nothing. Trying to step into the shoes of one of the all-time great football managers was a formidable enough task on its own but on top of that, the team had just been relegated, and four international players seemed determined to leave. I'm sure that a combination of that lot will have been uppermost in the minds of the five people who had already turned Fred down.

I needed some time to think as well when the offer came. I was reluctant to walk away from Leyton Orient after years of working incredibly hard to turn the club around. Just as I'd come to terms with the fact that I was never going to get a top management job, one had landed in my lap. There was a lot to consider and I must admit that one of the factors that swung it for me was that it was an opportunity to move Pam and the family back to where they wanted to be.

Orient's owner, Tony Wood, wasn't happy when I told him I was leaving. But I'd given the club 12 years of total commitment – often reaching far beyond the call of duty – and my conscience was completely clear. Forest made them a generous compensation payment to buy out the remainder of my contract and when I took the team to Orient for a pre-season game, I insisted we waive our share of the gate receipts. Had it been any other club except Newcastle, I might well have stayed at Brisbane Road. But Forest were very dear to my heart. The chance to revive their flagging fortunes was one that I just couldn't pass up.

I told Fred I'd take the job and made arrangements to travel up and meet him. Forest were playing Notts County that evening in the County Cup Final and it was Brian Clough's official farewell. It was bound to be an emotion-charged evening and although part of me really wanted to share it with him, I didn't want to do anything to take the gloss off the occasion. I was stopping overnight at Fred's house and when he went to the game, I stayed put. I had plenty to think about in preparation for the following day's announcement that I was the new manager.

The next day, 'Cloughie' was taking all the players and staff on one last jamboree to Cala Millor but Fred had a quiet word with Alan Hill when to arrived at the ground. He said that he wanted him to pull out of the trip. As Alan tells the tale, he went to the boss and said that the chairman wanted him to stay behind and help the new manager.

"New manager?" said Brian. "Who's that?"

"It's Frank," said Alan.

"Frank who?" was the reply. "Our Frank?"

Apparently there was a lengthy pause after Alan confirmed it was me. Then Brian said: "Good... you must stay behind and help him."

The best thing about the time I'd spent back at Forest some 12 years earlier, when I was reserve-team coach for a few months, was that I got to know Alan well. I stayed in the hotel that he and his wife Janice owned and we enjoyed each other's company. I knew he was completely and utterly trustworthy and I wanted him to be my assistant. Injury had ruined his playing career at a very early stage but he was a football man through and through. His contribution towards the Forest success story had been considerable. Although his official title was Head of Youth Recruitment, that didn't start to tell the tale. He was Cloughie's confidante, involved in all aspects of the City Ground football operation, and he was incredibly well connected. As a person, he was also the complete opposite to me. I saw that as a good thing. I've always tended to be a bit deep. I like to think things through before making a decision. Alan is much more impetuous – you just have to look at his forehead to know what he's thinking.

Anyway, I'd made my first key decision by appointing him as my right-hand man. Now I had to get on with ticking some more boxes and making myself at home in my new office. Of course it was daunting to find myself sitting in the chair Brian had occupied throughout 18 years of unbroken success. People tend to forget that Peter Taylor was only with him for six of those years yet until the last season, Forest had never been out of the top half of the table and had collected seven major trophies. I went in, shut the door and allowed myself two minutes to reflect on all that must have gone on in that office. All that plotting and planning that he and Taylor did and the massive decisions they'd taken. It was in there that they'd negotiated the first £1million transfer in British football history, worked out a way to win the League Championship and two European Cups, and turned a modest Second Division club with no financial means into one of the giants of Europe. If I thought about it for too long, it would frighten the life out of me. I snapped out of it after two minutes.

There was far too much to do to spend time looking backwards.

It was good to be back in a friendly environment and I obviously knew a lot of the people at Forest. By the same token, you couldn't fail to notice the feeling of apprehension and uncertainty around the place. The 'Bungs Inquiry' was going on at the time. A World in Action team of investigators had based themselves in Nottingham and they were 'door-stepping' members of staff. That was a horrible thing for them to contend with and so was the fact that Forest had just lost their top-flight status. There are always casualties when that happens.

Somehow I had to find a way of bringing some stability to the place and convincing players and staff alike that relegation was not going to be the end of the world. That was far easier said than done. I was very aware that I wasn't everyone's choice for the job and having been out of front-line management for several years, would I be up to the task? To be honest, people were right to question me because I was questioning myself. But I also knew that I'd worked hard to learn my trade with Sunderland and Orient and I really wanted to have a crack at Forest.

Incidentally, just in case I didn't fully understand the size of the challenge, Fred Reacher spelled things out to me on Day 1. "I don't want to hear any comments about consolidation," he said. "I expect you to take us straight back up to the Premier League. And by the way, there's no money to spend."

The biggest favour 'Cloughie' did me at that time was to keep right out of my way. He'd gone on record as saying many years earlier that I should be the man to eventually succeed him and also said some nice things about me in the media when my appointment was confirmed. But he knew I needed some space to stamp my own identity on the situation – and the top priority was to deal with the lads who were looking to leave. Until we'd done that, we couldn't move on. The signs were not good in terms of persuading them to stay but I had to try.

I knew that Brian had been desperately trying to get Roy Keane to agree a new deal but he had a clause in his contract saying that if

Forest were relegated, he'd be able to leave for £3.5million. When one of the first calls I took was from Alex Ferguson, I instantly knew the score. "Now then Frank," he said. "Congratulations on getting the job... about this clause in Roy Keane's contract." Roy had been given an extra week off because he'd had international commitments but as soon as he reported back for pre-season, I had him in for a chat. I said I don't suppose there's any point in me trying to persuade you to stay. He just shook his head and said: "Nope." I told him he could continue to train with us until the deal was sorted, but not with the first-team. It was all very amicable and that's why it came as a surprise when he apparently wrote in his book that I'd made life difficult for him. That's certainly not how I remember it. Manchester United chairman Martin Edwards came down to Nottingham, took Fred and me out to dinner, and the deal went through very smoothly. I'd lost an outstanding midfield player, potentially the most influential in the country, but at least Fred told me I could have the £3.5million to spend.

Nigel Clough was also a massive loss but I was never going to win that one either. Things had gone on at Board level over Brian leaving that had left a sour taste. From a personal point of view that was a shame. I'd have loved to work with Nigel but he went to Liverpool for £2.5million.

Next on the list was Gary Charles, a talented young full back who had been the victim of a horror tackle by Paul Gascoigne two years earlier in the FA Cup Final. Non-football issues were weighing him down. He'd been in trouble with the police for drink-related problems and insisted very convincingly when he came to see me that he needed to get away from Nottingham to make a fresh start. I accepted that, shook hands with him and wished him all the best. What I didn't expect was that he would turn up a couple of weeks later just down the road at Derby County!

So, I was 3-0 down before my new career at Forest had hardly begun. But there was still a chance that I could claw one back... the one that I really wanted. The big thing I had going for me as negotiations opened with Stuart Pearce was that I sensed immediately that he didn't really want to leave. You don't come across exceptional people too often in life and when you do, it's essential to recognise their true value. I only knew 'Pearcey' by reputation but Alan knew him well. He confirmed everything I'd thought. Not only was he a very fine player but also, as a leader of men you'll struggle to find better. It was abundantly clear that if Fred Reacher was to get his wish of an immediate return to the top flight, we had to find a way to keep him on board.

'Pearcy' had fallen out with the manager the previous year and had missed a lot of games through injury. He wasn't in a particularly good place. But his biggest concern was that playing in the Championship might end his international career. I called Graham Taylor, the England manager at that time, and he said there was no way he would leave him out if Stuart was playing well. Another box ticked but actually getting to the point where he put his signature onto a new contract proved to be incredibly difficult. In fact, had I known it was going to be so difficult I might well have taken a different stance. I had so many other things to sort out that I told the chairman I didn't have time for lengthy rounds of contract negotiations. He said there was no one else at the club who could handle them ... I'd just have to get on with it. In the end, we got the deal done. It was a massive boost to everyone and it didn't take long for me to gauge how important it was to have 'Pearcey' on our side.

I'd decided when I took the job that I wouldn't bring anyone with me. I wanted to give the existing coaching staff the chance to convince me that we could work together – but things changed. I asked the coaches to put forward their plans for pre-season and basically, it was just more of the same. I could understand that Forest's methods were tried and trusted but the club had just been relegated. Something clearly wasn't right and a fresh approach was required. I'd used a chap called Pete Edwards on a part-time basis at Leyton Orient and he'd impressed me with his fitness training ideas. I knew it would be a massive gamble to get him involved at Forest but decided I'd go for it. Pete was a bolshie bugger, who could be really tactless. I had to balance whether the good would outweigh the bad. He was totally different to anyone else we had on the staff. I called the coaches together to tell them what I was going to do. I explained that he would really get up their noses and they'd all think he was after their jobs but that I felt he was what we needed to freshen things up.

The next challenge was how the players would react to a new regime when they reported back from their summer break. I didn't have to worry about that for long because 'Pearcey' took over. I could sense the players weren't convinced about what was happening but they were waiting to see how the captain reacted. He did brilliantly for me in that regard. Pete would say: "Right boys, today we're going to be doing this and that." Whether he agreed with it or not, Stuart would just go and do it – and the other players all followed.

The clock was ticking and I needed to spend some of the Roy Keane cash on strengthening the squad. When I asked Alan Hill if any transfer targets had been earmarked, two of the names he mentioned fitted exactly with my thinking – Colin Cooper and Stan Collymore. I'd seen a lot of Cooper playing for Millwall and he was my sort of player. He was a strong character with excellent defensive qualities. I wanted him in our team. We agreed a fee of £1.5million with Millwall and met up the following day at a London hotel to complete the deal. It was all very straightforward compared to most transfers but it was massive for me. I'd only ever spent £10,000 on a player, when I bought Alan Comfort from Cambridge United, and when it was done I said to Alan: "I need a drink!" That impetuous streak instantly took over as he responded by saying: "Right. Now let's get straight on the phone to Vic Jobson and do a deal for Collymore."

I knew all about Stan. I'd watched him play many times in the reserves at Crystal Palace and although he was never outstanding, I could see he had something. I'd discussed him with John Griffin, the Palace scout who had discovered him playing for Stafford Rangers, and

I would certainly have tried to sign him had Orient had any money. Stan struggled to adapt at Palace, where the likes of Ian Wright and Mark Bright ruled the dressing room, but he immediately started to blossom when Colin Murphy took him to Southend for £150,000. Our top priority was to sign a goal-scorer. Pierre van Hooijdonk was top of Alan's list. He was rapidly building a reputation for himself in Holland, rattling in the goals for NAC Breda, but I preferred Collymore. It would be a risk because he was still largely unproven at Championship level but my gut feeling was that we should go for him.

Just as Alan had suggested, we got straight on the phone to Jobson. We agreed a fee of £2million, plus add-ons, and arranged to meet Stan in Croydon on the day he got back from holiday. That actually turned into something of a pantomime farce. Ambrose Mendy, who I'd dealt with when I signed Fashanu, was trying to become Stan's agent and Alan and I found ourselves in a situation where we were chasing Stan and his girlfriend around the streets of Croydon – trying to get to him first. Thankfully we managed to do that and when we discovered Colin Murphy was helping Stan, acting as his advisor, the deal was completed far more easily than it might have been.

Stan was a great lad – but a handful every day. He insisted he wanted to live with his mother in Cannock and although there was nothing in his contract to say he couldn't live in the West Midlands, it meant that he didn't socialise with the other players. That was an issue in my eyes because it left him a bit isolated. But it didn't change the fact that he was a terrific player. He had everything and should have been a regular in the England team for years. It doesn't always follow when you're 6ft 3in tall that you will be good in the air but he was. He was immensely powerful with great balance, a tremendous athlete with unbelievable natural ability. Of all the players I worked with as a player or manager, Stan would have to be the best in terms of pure ability. He was a problem all the time but was worth every minute of the aggravation.

If he knew we were planning a hard training day, he normally had an excuse for not taking part. He rang one day to say that he wouldn't be in because he had to go to his grandmother's funeral. Alan decided to call his bluff and sent flowers to his mum. Just as we'd expected, she called us to say thanks and ask what she had done to deserve them. "But Stan told us your mum had just died," said Alan. Needless to say, she hadn't. On another occasion, we decided to go overnight for a game at West Brom and Stan stayed out until 2 o'clock in the morning. I was furious and let it be known he would be heavily fined and suspended. Liam O'Kane and 'Pearcey' came to me and said: "Don't do that... he'll win us the game." We won 2-0 that day, he scored them both and one of them was as good a goal as I've ever seen in my life. It was vintage Stan as he picked the ball up in his own half, turned and worked his way through their entire defence before coolly slotting it home.

It was a sharp reminder to me that some players have to be handled differently. The key is to do what has to be done to bring out the best in them but it has to happen in a way that doesn't rock the boat. I didn't want the players thinking there was one rule for Stan and one for the rest – even if there was to some extent. I used to treat Pearce, Cooper and Steve Chettle, who were all good senior professionals, as my War Cabinet. I called them in to discuss it. I explained that we all knew Collymore was getting away with certain things and I needed to know they were OK with it. They could live with it, they said, because they understood his value to the team.

Mind you, things didn't just happen overnight with Stan when he moved into the City Ground. Ironically, our first game of the season was away to Southend and although we kept it quiet until the last minute that he'd miss it because he had a virus, people got very excited about the prospect of him returning to Roots Hall. More significantly, he didn't score his first goal until the final game of September. By that stage, people were questioning whether it was £2million well spent – and they were certainly questioning whether I was the man for the job. We won only three of our first 12 League games. In today's world, I cannot imagine I'd have survived. There was a lot going on, of course, as people adjusted to life after Brian Clough, plus a much-changed team, and on the surface at least the Board were very supportive. But the fans, who'd been spoiled for the best part of 18 years, were much less tolerant and a lot of them chose to take it out on our goalkeeper. For some reason, they didn't take to Mark Crossley. They certainly did nothing to help him and although he insisted that being regularly booed was not affecting him, I felt it went beyond that. It was creating a negative atmosphere within the ground at a time when we desperately needed the fans on our side. I decided I had to act and brought in Tommy Wright from Newcastle.

Things just weren't right. There were a lot of smiling faces around when we beat Grimsby 5-3 but that scoreline flattered us. We had no discipline in our play. People were just 'bombing' forward and I was told it was a carry over from the previous season when players would just go out and play, without thinking about what had to be done to win the game. One of Cloughie's great strengths was his obsession for passing the ball forward and running forward with it. That had gone out of our play. Too many people didn't want to take any responsibility. They just wanted to knock it sideways and backwards and we had to do a lot of work in training to restore good habits.

Things were just not clicking into place and Alan and I decided we needed to thrash it out with the players. We hired the upstairs room at The Griffin, a pub in the nearby village of Plumtree, ordered fish & chips all round... and then the gloves were off. Everyone was encouraged to speak their mind, help us get to the bottom of what was going wrong and it turned into a massive clear-the-air session. We didn't hold back. Things that needed to be said were said and although it could have gone one of two ways, it was conducted in a very adult fashion.

We got huge benefits from that session and when I also invested £450,000 in a Norwegian midfielder called Lars Bohinen, we were finally on our way. A contact of Alan's said Lars wanted to come to

England and suggested we ought to take a look at him. When we flew out to see him play, he made a big impression on us. We could see how slotting him into the centre of midfield would enable us to move some round pegs into round holes in other areas of the team. Unfortunately, it took until the end of October to get the deal done for Bohinen and by then, we were stuck in the bottom six.

I'd always played with one central holding midfielder at Leyton Orient and had it in mind when I arrived at Forest that Neil Webb would be ideal for that job. You need to be very disciplined to do it successfully and although I knew Neil had lost some mobility as a result of two knee operations, I thought his experience would see him through. It didn't work out that way but when Bohinen arrived, we were able to create a lovely balance in midfield. David Phillips, who we'd signed from Norwich in the summer, took to the anchor role superbly, and switching Steve Stone to the right really brought out the best in him.

We went to Birmingham and won 3-0 on the day Bohinen made his debut. That was the start of a 13-game unbeaten run that saw us surge up the table. In fact, we only lost twice more for the rest of the season and it was an amazing contrast compared to that early period. By the time we went to Derby for a midweek match towards the end of April we were really flying and the performance of Collymore than night had to be seen to be believed. We'd made a tactical change by that stage, introducing Scott Gemmill in midfield and leaving Stan to operate on his own up front. It worked brilliantly. Stan was no good at defending if we lost possession so we wrote him off. We told him to just stay upfield and that night, he ran the Derby back-four ragged. We won the game 2-0 and he was simply magnificent.

It meant that if we could go to Peterborough and win the following Saturday, it would guarantee we'd bounce straight back to the Premier League as runners-up to Crystal Palace. Fifteen minutes into that game, we were 2-0 down. But two goals from Stan and the bravest of diving headers from Pearce completed the perfect comeback.

The job was done. The players deserved enormous credit for the way they'd turned around our season and although I was delighted for the supporters, unfortunately a number of them didn't do themselves any credit that day. They went way over the top with their celebrations, were involved in some disgraceful scenes, and the Police even got me to go on the PA system and appeal for calm. I couldn't believe it when I picked up Monday's Nottingham Evening Post and they castigated me for being a killjoy. They clearly didn't see the women and children screaming in fear as our fans ran riot.

As for our directors, I was grateful to them for sticking by me when it would have been easy to panic. I got a substantial pay-rise, a new contract and the best car I've ever driven. I was especially pleased for Fred Reacher – even though he was less than convincing as he told me he always knew I'd get them promoted!

PLAYER - **MANAGER** - CHAIRMAN

FOREST EYE ORIENT BOSS

CLARK ABLE

Frank tipped to move

By HUGH JAMIESON

FRANK CLARK, the man once named by Brian Clough as his successor, could be heading back to Nottingham Forest.

Clough's decision to quit at the end of the season has opened up the way for Clark, 49, the former Newcastle and Forest defender.

Clark is now managing director of Leyton Orient, who are on the fringe of the Second Division promotion race. He played a key role in Forest's promotion and title-winning side in the three years after Clough arrived at the City Ground.

Clark managed Orient for eight years before handing over the coaching role to Peter Eustace two years ago.

And with the Forest board discussing the situation next Tuesday, an insider said: "A lot of younger managers have been bandied about, but Clark will be high on the list.

"He's got all the experience needed for what will obviously be a very tough act to follow. And he could bring in his own coach."

CLARK was a key figure during some of Forest's finest hours – and departing boss Brian Clough has always rated him highly.

CLOUGH: A Clark fan appreciate his feelings but his head is ruling his heart.

Lee's agony

● CRYSTAL Palace defender Lee Sinnott is to have an operation on the shoulder he dislocated while playing for the reserves.

Palace manager Steve Coppell said: "Lee will need an op similar to the one Bryan Robson had after the 1986 World Cup."

● JASON Cundy will see a specialist today about a nagging back problem. The injury-hit Tottenham central defender has played only twice since January.

DOES HIS HEAD CAVE IN?? ⑱ FIND OUT — SEE IT - YOU WON'T BELIEVE IT!!

TOP The new Forest manager meets the media with chairman Fred Reacher and vice-chairman Irving Korn.
Pointing Robert Rosario and Steve Chettle towards promotion.
Pictures: Nottingham Post/Nottingham Local Studies Collection

PLAYER - **MANAGER** - CHAIRMAN

TOP Welcoming our new signing Stan Collymore to the City Ground. One of the best day's work I ever did.
Giving my blessing to Barry Fry as I launch my new Forest career at Southend United. *Pictures: Nottingham Post*

THE CLARK ERA IS UNDER WAY

Clough is my inspiration — new boss

FRANK CLARK today launched a new era at Nottingham Forest with a promise to Brian Clough.

Clark's previous links with the club were crucial to his appointment on a two-year contract, according to chairman Fred Reacher.

And Clark walked back into the City Ground today trying to preserve the "wonderful" legacy left behind and insisting he was not worried about the shadow Clough could cast across the City Ground.

THIS IS YOUR LIFE

Date of Birth: 9-9-43.
Place of Birth: Highfield.
Previous league clubs: Newcastle (1963-75) 457 games, 1 goal. Forest (1975-79) 157 games, 1 goal.
Managerial record: Sunderland (assistant manager 1979-81). Forest (reserve coach) 1981. Orient (assistant manager, manager and managing director) 1981-93.
Playing honours: FA Amateur Cup winners' medal (Crook Town), Inter City Fairs Cup winners' medal, League Championship winners' medal, European Cup winners' medal, League Cup winners' medal, Charity Shield

Chapter 17
MIAMI MISSION SETS UP DREAM COMBINATION
1994-95

I went to the Board before the dust had started to settle on our promotion triumph to ask how much I could spend to give us the best possible chance of making an impact in the Premier League. Why was I not surprised when my question was met with an uncomfortable silence? Forest at that time was the only club in the country run by a committee. The 200 or so who held a modest shareholding elected nine good men and true to form the committee and none of them had a commitment to inject any worthwhile cash. In fairness, why would they when they could have been kicked off the Board at any moment? It made the feats of Brian Clough all the more remarkable when you think about how the club operated at that time but I couldn't fight against that. My only concern was how I could move things on. We'd put together a capable squad that I fully expected to survive at the higher level – but you cannot be content with that.

You have to keep pressing ahead and that was part of my thinking when I decided to freshen up the backroom team in the summer of 1994. I was never really convinced that Archie Gemmill and the physio Graham Lyas were 'with' me and when we took the lads to

Tenerife at the end of the promotion campaign and those two said they didn't want to go, I felt it confirmed my feelings. Richard Money came in from Aston Villa to run the reserves and John Haselden, a real football man who had previous experience as a player and coach, joined us as physio. I was happy about that but I just felt it would be a big mistake to start the season without a single new signing. It would send out the wrong message to the players and supporters.

Fred Reacher was a really good chairman from my point of view. He collared me after that Board meeting when I'd been told there was no money available and said: "Don't take that as gospel ... there might be a little bit of leeway."

I'd had a call a few days earlier from Pino Pagliari, an Italian restaurant owner in Manchester who was trying to get into football. He got himself tangled up in allegations about illegal payments years later but at that time, he was proving to be a good contact. He'd organised a pre-season trip to Italy for us the previous year, which had already been arranged when I arrived, and he came with us to make sure we were well looked after. In the course of that phone call he asked if I was looking for any players. I mentioned that I could do with a left-sided midfielder. He said: "Someone like Brian Roy?" I laughed it off at first because I guessed he would be well out of our price range – especially when my total budget was zero! But Roy was with Foggia, who had just been relegated from Serie A, and Pino said I'd get him for £2.5million.

Jimmy Greenhalgh, my mentor from Newcastle days, had watched a lot of Premier League football over the years and was firmly of the belief that when you take a team to that level, you have to go for quality in the transfer market, rather than quantity. Jimmy's approach was that if you have £1million to spend, blow the lot on one player – but make sure you get it right.

The Roy situation was certainly an interesting one. I took it to Fred and told him I needed £2.5million. He said I should keep it completely between the two of us but go for it. See where it leads.

Foggia were happy for me to speak to Roy if we agreed to pay their asking price but that was easier said than done because he was locked away with the Dutch squad in America, taking part in the World Cup. When I shared it with Pino, he said Roy's agent was the son of the Dutch FA chairman and he would find him. It looked promising when he came back to me because he said the Dutch manager had agreed to let Roy leave the camp to speak to me.

I immediately got myself on a flight to Miami, where they were based, and when Pino met me as I landed, he said he had good news and bad. The bad news was that the manager had changed his mind about letting Roy out of the camp. The good was that providing I kept a low profile, I could travel to watch the game that night on the coach laid on for Dutch officials and players' wives. I managed to 'suss' out which of them was Roy's wife and engineered a situation where I could sit beside her. When I skirted around the idea of a move to England, she was clearly receptive but as an aspiring actress, the main thing she wanted to know was how long it takes to get from Nottingham to London. I must admit that I was a little bit liberal with the truth on that one! I can't remember which team Holland played that night but Roy didn't do very well. Had it been my first look at him, I would have walked away. But I knew he was a quality performer who would be excellent value at £2.5million. By the time I returned home, we'd agreed that he would come to Nottingham for talks as soon as the World Cup was over.

The only slight problem was that I still had no idea whether the Board would sanction the deal. I kept wondering how Brian Clough would have handled that situation. I came to the conclusion that he'd have made it happen. He'd have begged, stolen and borrowed to generate the cash, probably threatened a time or two to resign, and eventually bulldozed it through. I was convinced the deal would be a case of speculating to accumulate and we had to get it done. Unfortunately, any chance of amicably winning over the Board went right out of the window when Pino leaked the story to a newspaper.

"Roy heading for Forest" screamed the headline on the day of our next Board meeting, which just happened to be the same day that Roy was flying in for talks. You can just imagine the scene as we gathered in the Boardroom. Even though everything I'd done had been with the chairman's blessing, I'd totally ignored the fact that they told me there was no money to spend. The reaction was hostile to put it mildly. Had I not been in a position of some strength, having just won promotion, there's every chance I would have been shown the door.

Negotiations were long and pretty heated. When the hands went up for the initial vote, only Fred and I were in favour of going ahead with the deal. We weren't prepared to leave it there and ended up going round and round the table with a series of votes. The directors kept saying we couldn't afford to sign the Dutchman while I insisted we couldn't afford not to. In the end, we wore them down.

As I remember it, Brian and his wife were easy to deal with. My long trek to Miami turned out to be very worthwhile because I'd been able to paint a picture that they liked. They really fancied the idea of sampling life in this country and the impact that signing a World Cup star made was just what I was hoping for. The players got a massive lift from it as they reported back for pre-season and season-ticket sales went through the roof. The directors were able to rest easy – and Fred Reacher deserved a lot of credit for going out on a limb. I liked Brian. He was a pleasant, chirpy character who quickly became a popular figure with the other players. The fact that he spoke impeccable English made the settling-in process so much easier. He did have a touch of arrogance about him but I never thought that was a particularly bad thing in a footballer because self-belief is so important.

I was really excited about taking on the Premier League and now that deal had been clinched, it held no fears for me. Forest were back in the big time and my priority was to find the best way to fit in the new-boy without disrupting the team that had performed so strongly in the second half of the previous season. All along, I'd seen Roy figuring on the left-side of midfield but two things happened in pre-season that forced me to change my mind. The first was that Ian Woan, our established left-sider, had clearly said to himself: "He ain't going to take my place." He was a talented lad with a superb left foot but I always felt during a game that I needed more from him. He always seemed to stay within his comfort zone. Suddenly he started to give me more – on a regular basis – and I didn't see any way I could leave him out. The other thing was that Roy didn't really want to play wide-left. Although he wasn't a prolific scorer, he preferred to play further forward so we decided to push him up alongside Stan.

It worked a treat and the two of them hit it off brilliantly. Stan didn't need anything to make him a better player but he did respond to the competition. There was no way that he was going to share the limelight with anyone. Roy was quick and elegant, beautifully well balanced and with a really sharp footballing brain. When you matched that up with Collymore's pace, power and shooting ability, we had a strike-partnership that was the envy of every manager in the country.

We hit the ground running as Roy scored the goal that gave us a win at Ipswich on the opening day and it wasn't until the end of October, 11 games into the season, that we lost for the first time. I was delighted to win the 'Manager of the Month' award for September – but a lot more delighted to be the manager of this team. I don't like trying to make comparisons but it certainly had the feel of my time as a player at the City Ground when we won the League Championship in our first season in the top flight. Mark Crossley had come back really well after his difficult spell to establish himself as a fine goalkeeper and was part of an exceptionally solid back-five. We had skill, strength and vision in midfield and our attacking options were incredible.

Sadly, we ruled ourselves out of a serious Championship challenge when we picked up just two points from six games after suffering our first defeat against Blackburn. But I was so proud of the way the lads responded to that difficult spell. We completed the season with a 13-game unbeaten run and produced a brilliant brand of football. At one stage we strung together five straight wins in which we scored 19 goals. Seven of those came at Sheffield Wednesday as we became the first team in Premier League history to score seven times in an away game. Collymore had fallen out with two or three players at that stage and wasn't talking to them. As I said to them all in the dressing room afterwards: "Just imagine how many goals we might have scored if you lot all got on well together!"

It was the perfect response to all those who feared Forest would never be able to cope without the great Brian Clough – but I couldn't please all of the people all of the time. For some reason, I always seemed to get a rough ride at the Annual Meetings. I'd had a fair bit of experience of those at Leyton Orient but they were a different class at Forest as people queued up to have a snipe. I couldn't believe it at my first AGM when a shareholder demanded to know why the manager and his coaching staff were swanning around in flash BMW cars. I said: "Don't blame me – blame the commercial manager Dave Pullan, who did the deal before I got here." I'm pleased he did! I was in the stocks again a year later because I'd organised to get the coaches into a pension scheme. The Football League ran an excellent scheme and I was flabbergasted when I took over to discover they weren't in it. I took that to the Board, who immediately said they would rectify the situation, but not all the shareholders were in agreement. One of them stood up at the meeting and asked: "Why are we allowing the manager to do this?" I should have said absolutely nothing but couldn't help myself. It didn't do me any favours when I said that I didn't realise I was working for a company who believed in sending boys up chimneys.

We eventually qualified for the UEFA Cup by finishing the season in third place, behind Blackburn and Manchester United, and I won the League Managers' Association's 'Manager of the Year' award. I've never been a massive fan of rewarding individuals for their part in a team game but I was delighted – especially as it meant I'd collected the highest number of votes from my peers. I honestly hadn't seen it coming and made the worst speech of my life when I went on stage at the LMA Dinner to collect the award.

I was by no means the only one to gain recognition and it was a great thing for Nottingham Forest when Stuart Pearce, Colin Cooper, Stan Collymore and Steve Stone all got picked for England. Despite 'Pearcey' being concerned that dropping down a division might cost him his international place, he was still going strong and who will ever forget that fantastic moment when he scored in the penalty shoot-out against Spain in Euro '96?

It pleased me immensely to see Cooper and Stone included in the squad. Bearing in mind that Steve had broken a leg three times earlier in his career, it really was a fairytale for him to pull on an England shirt. He thoroughly deserved it. He'd been a revelation since we'd decided to move him to the right-side of midfield. There's a definite step up in class to international level and I have to admit that Colin rather got found out. He was probably two inches too short for the ideal central defender, and a yard short of pace. But you can only work with the God-given tools you have and he was a fantastic player for me. I was so pleased that I made him my first signing for Forest.

I didn't see how Stan's international claims could be ignored any longer. He'd scored 19 League goals during the season when we won promotion and followed that up with 22 in the Premier League yet clearly, he wasn't everyone's cup of tea. Terry Venables picked him in the squad for a three-team tournament at Wembley at the end of the season. Brazil and Japan were also involved in what was seen as a trial-run for Euro '96. They'd only been together for a few days when Terry rang me.

"What is it with Stan?" he wanted to know.

"What's he been up to now?" I asked.

"It's not that he's done anything wrong," said Terry. "It's just that he's acting as if he doesn't want to be here."

My advice was to stick with it because he'd find that the good things would definitely outweigh the bad – but maybe he didn't have as much patience as me.

Stan only won three England caps and one of those was as a last minute substitute against Brazil. With his talent, he should have won so many more.

There were plenty of situations that could have led to us falling out but unless his actions really affected others, it was best to let things ride. For example, we organised a trip to the pony and trap racing during a pre-season trip to Sweden and the lads were on the coach and ready to go when we realised Stan wasn't on board. Alan was dispatched to find him and came back to say Stan was refusing to come because he had strong principles concerning cruelty to animals. I wanted him to be involved in what promised to be a good bonding session but it wasn't worth having a row about. Many years later Alan turned up in the audience at 'An Evening with Stan Collymore' and when it got to the Q&A part of the schedule, he raised his hand.

"Could you tell me," he asked... "What was the real reason why you didn't join us for the pony and trap racing trip in Sweden."

Stan remembered it well. "She was 6ft tall, blond and beautiful," he said.

It's always the way when you have a good season that people start chasing your best players and it was inevitable at some stage that we would have an issue over Collymore. Not too many clubs could have afforded him but I knew I'd have a problem when we beat Manchester United at Old Trafford and he scored a wonder goal. Sure enough, Alex Ferguson started ringing the following week and I ignored his calls for ages. Stan was Stan. He never seemed totally content with life but he was doing the business for us on a very regular basis and I desperately wanted to keep him. I wanted him to be part of our plans when we took on Europe the following year and to help us mount a proper Championship challenge. But the longer the season went on, the less likely it seemed that we would keep him.

We'd missed a trick after promotion because we should have got him in immediately and tied him down on a new deal. Yet again, the tight finances at Forest got in the way of that happening. He'd signed for three years when he arrived from Southend and people thought: "We'll worry about a new contract in another year or so." By the time it got to the talking stage, it was too late. His head had been turned.

He'd become a genuine star. Everyone wanted a slice of him and as he didn't have an agent, I suggested he really could do with someone to look after his affairs. I'd had some dealings in the past with Paul Stretford and was impressed at the way he handled his clients. I put the two of them together and I have to say that in Paul's case, I don't think I ever did anyone a bigger favour. He must have doubled the size of his mansion on the strength of that!

Nothing we said or did could persuade Stan to stay. When the season finished we went on tour to Australia. We stopped off in Singapore along the way and at the end of that leg, the international lads had to fly back. Even though Stan wasn't always the most popular with some of our players, they all tried to talk him out of leaving. I had my say as well. I told him: "We've got European football to look forward to next season and I've built the team around you. We're all set up to work to your strengths." It was to no avail. Liverpool made an offer of £8.5million and he became English football's most costly player.

Incidentally, that tour of Australia was a fantastic experience for all of us and my personal highlight had to be a night we spent in Brisbane. I was less than pleased to discover when we arrived that in order to help promote one of our matches, I had to appear at a function. The venue turned out to be a concert hall that was packed. Several hundred people were in the audience and a local media personality had been signed up to interview me. I remember thinking what the hell am I going to say to keep these people interested for a whole evening? Alan Hill, as he so often did, had read the script. He had a quiet word with the organiser and asked if they had a guitar handy. When they said they did, he told them if I started to dry up, just sneak on stage and hand it to me. It was completely spur of the moment when this bloke suddenly strolled on with the guitar – but I was in my element. I'd got nothing prepared but put on a show for the next hour or so and the reception the audience gave me was incredible. They even demanded an encore! Maybe I missed my way in life.

Fred Reacher had told Collymore before he went to Anfield for talks not to sign before speaking to us again and we would match whatever they offered. He never came back to us. He still had 12 months to run on his contract. We could have dug our heels in but there would have been no point. If a player gets it into their head that they want to leave – especially if they are a key man – you are better off getting them out of the place before they start affecting the others. And being blunt about it, it's almost inevitable that their transfer valuation will drop as well so you have to cash in while you can.

Southend were due a chunk of the money and Stan would have been entitled to 5 per cent. However, if he left Forest at his own request, he wouldn't get any of that £425,000. We didn't have a transfer-request in writing but everyone knew the score. He'd made all the running. He'd been dropping out stories to the newspapers for weeks about his desire to move and we were not prepared to hand over that money without a fight. We took it to a Football League Tribunal at Lytham St Annes and it was Fred Reacher, Alan Hill and me lined up against some big-hitters, including the PFA chief executive Gordon Taylor. After an hour of so, things were not going well. But I had an ace up my sleeve or, to be more accurate, in my top pocket. I hadn't told anyone in advance but I'd managed to secure a tape of a radio interview in which Stan made it abundantly clear that he felt his time at Forest was done and he was looking forward to making a fresh start. You could have heard a pin drop as it was being played and needless to say, the business of the day was concluded very quickly after it finished.

Fred took us out for fish & chips and champagne on Blackpool seafront and we had a great time. But I had very mixed feelings. I would much rather have still had Stan to work with and no matter how much of a positive spin we tried to put on it, I knew he would be virtually irreplaceable.

I don't think Stan held the outcome of that Tribunal against me too much and we've always managed a laugh and a joke between us whenever our paths have crossed. I always tell him he should have got 100 England caps and he shrugs his shoulders with indifference. He was a wonderful player and although it certainly wouldn't be true to say that his career was wasted, he definitely under-achieved.

Collecting a Manager of the Month Award as we took the Premier League by storm in 1994-95.

Chapter 18
TIPPED FOR ENGLAND... BUT IT ALL FELL APART
1995-96

Fans love a good chant. It's always been part and parcel of creating the special atmosphere of a live football match. Some are more original and acceptable than others, they're often very witty, and my all-time favourite has to be when Nottingham Forest fans sang: "There's only one team in Europe." It made the players and I feel really proud. We'd qualified to take part in the UEFA Cup in 1995-96 and by the time we got to March, we were the only surviving English team with an interest in any of the various competitions. It was a great effort to work our way through to the quarter-finals, especially when I think back to all we had to contend with at the start of the season.

Losing Stan Collymore to Liverpool was always going to have major repercussions but I certainly didn't expect the pile up of problems it triggered off. It turned into a case of not just finding a suitable replacement but anyone who could replace him. A week before the new season was due to kick off we didn't have a single experienced striker available.

I have to accept my share of responsibility for that. Brian Roy had been injured in the final game of the previous season and instead of telling him he must stay behind for treatment, I allowed him to go home to Holland. It had seemed like nothing more than a routine knock but when he returned for pre-season, it was still troubling him. On top of that, Jason Lee and our new signing Kevin Campbell also had problems. Within 24 hours of Liverpool's down-payment for Stan landing in our bank I spent £2.8million of it on signing Campbell from Arsenal. I should have been a lot less hasty. I'd had him as a youngster at Leyton Orient and he impressed me hugely as a player and a person. He was always high on my wanted list and I was really excited at the prospect of him joining us. So excited, in fact, that I did something very out of character. I don't think you could accuse me of getting above myself too often during the course of my career because that wasn't in my nature. I do, though, have to hold up my hands over Campbell. We'd agreed the deal with Arsenal but when Kevin came to Nottingham for his medical, our club doctor Lyn Jarrett advised me not to sign him. I knew he'd undergone a back operation and the doctor felt that although he'd eventually make a full recovery, it would be taking a risk to complete the deal at this stage. 'Clever Clogs' thought he knew better, didn't he? Kevin assured me he was fine and I took a gamble that badly misfired. He suffered one injury after another in that first season, and was a shadow of the player who had helped Orient to win promotion. As for Lee, he'd had to pull out of a pre-season trip because his wife had complications after having a baby. One way or another, we had problems.

But what the hell was I worrying about? We went to Southampton on the opening day of the season, played incredibly well to win 4-3 and Roy, Campbell and Lee all figured in some form or another. By the time we got to November we were third in the table, undefeated in 12 League games and already starting to make waves in Europe.

It was a lovely moment for Campbell when he opened his goals account back at Highbury – we drew 1-1 with Arsenal – but I knew that as a unit, we weren't scoring enough goals. At some stage our lack of strike power would catch up with us. Something had to be done to change it. I still had some money put aside for a rainy day after I'd paid £2.5million of the Collymore cash to Sheffield Wednesday for Chris Bart-Williams, a versatile player who'd also come up through the ranks with me at Orient, but we needed to use the balance as a matter of some urgency. Great in theory but signing strikers who can guarantee to get goals in the Premier League is no easy matter.

After I'd made a few fruitless inquiries the word was out that we had money to spend. That got the phone ringing and one of many calls I took was from Pino Pagliari. He was alerting me to the fact that Andrea Silenzi was available and knowing how helpful he'd been in setting up the deal to sign Roy, I took careful note. There was plenty to consider. Although we'd signed Roy from Foggia, no Italian player at that stage had ever made the move to English football. There was no precedent in terms of how difficult they would find it to adapt to our way of doing things. Silenzi, though, was a current member of Italy's international squad. He was big, powerful and experienced. At the age of 29, he should be in his prime. He'd spent a fair bit of his career in the lower divisions in Italy but had scored more than 30 goals for Napoli and Torino to win a place in the international squad. Of course it was a gamble to sign him. Every transfer always is and although I wasn't able to go across to see him play, we did as much homework as we could. I spoke to Don Howe because I was aware he knew all about Silenzi and he recommended him. I knew he wasn't a prolific scorer but the videos I watched suggested he had all the target-man attributes I felt we were lacking. He was mobile and had a great build for a striker. We desperately needed to get someone in and although it went against my naturally cautious nature, I decided to move it on.

I flew out to Torino to negotiate with their President – and what an experience that was. When I went into his office he was sitting behind the biggest desk I'd ever seen in my life and had four mobile phones in front of him. I didn't dare ask what the function was for each of those. I was treated to a fabulous lunch and everything was fine until we broached the subject of money. The fee of £1.8million had already been agreed but suddenly there was talk of extras for this and that. I just got to my feet and said "Right. I'm off" in very determined fashion. The President could see I wasn't falling for that one and we got the deal done.

There's no getting away from it. That deal turned out to be a disaster for all concerned and the buck has to stop with me. I can use up a few pages talking about if only this and if only that but there would be no point in doing so. The fact is that Silenzi never managed to settle in this country, never did himself justice as a player and his record of two cup goals in 20 senior appearances was a massive disappointment. I have to balance that by saying he was a smashing lad who certainly didn't want to fail. And had his wife – who had just had a baby – found it easier to settle, things might have been very different. We did all we could to accommodate him and when I changed the shape of the team to play with three up top, hoping it would bring us more goals, he had a good understanding of his role. We sat him down on numerous occasions to try and find a way of bringing out the best in him. It wasn't to be. There's only so much talking you can do.

Silenzi did play a minor part as we continued to pull up trees in the early part of the campaign. When we won four games out of five, and drew the other one, it hoisted us into third place in the table. Bearing in mind that we'd finished the previous season with an unbeaten run of 13 matches, it meant that by the time we travelled to Blackburn we hadn't tasted defeat in 25 League games. By then, two significant things had happened. Lars Bohinen had left us and Jason Lee, who'd started to develop into a more than useful striker, had lost his way.

We'd signed Bohinen two years earlier for £450,000 and he'd been a brilliant buy for us. He'd helped us win promotion, was a stylish midfield mainstay in the team that finished third in the Premier League the following year and I still felt there was plenty more to come from him. We'd actually started talking about a new contract but I backed off when he came up with a long list of clauses he wanted inserted into the deal. I couldn't possibly agree to most of them because it wouldn't have been fair to the other lads who had given me blood, sweat and tears. That was the signal for his agent get busy and when Blackburn came in with an offer of £700,000, we had no option but to let him go because I'd agreed a buy-out clause when he signed. We were a struggling second tier outfit when he arrived and were basically asking Lars to take a step down at an important stage of his career. That was a big concern to him so in order to help us get the deal over the line, I agreed to allow him an easy exit if things didn't work out. I was shocked at first when Blackburn came on because I'd completely forgotten I'd agreed to provide Lars with a 'side' letter, confirming the buy-out clause. What I didn't realise at the time was that 'side' letters were illegal because you were not allowed to provide financial inducements that didn't appear in the contract. I got into trouble for that and the club was fined. But Fred Reacher was fine with me – he knew he had to be. I'd been very naïve but yet again, it was a consequence of me having to handle complicated contract issues for players when I really wasn't fully qualified to do so.

Losing Bohinen was a huge blow and even though he was joining the Premier League champions, I did feel let down. Brian Clough always said you should never be surprised when footballers let you down but I was very disappointed. I'd given Lars that buy-out clause as a favour, just in case things didn't work out for him at Forest. I certainly didn't expect it to be used against us in the way that it was. He had been good for us – but we'd also been very good for him. It left a sour taste. However, I do regret allowing my feelings to show in the Press conference afterwards, when someone asked: "Why do you think he wanted to go?" I pulled some loose change out my pocket and tossed it on the table, indicating 30 pieces of silver. I shouldn't have done that.

The Jason Lee situation was interesting. We'd signed him for £200,000 as a squad player from Southend in the latter stages of our promotion season and he was filling that role very effectively.

Physically, he was a real handful for defenders, brilliant at chasing lost causes, and had the handy knack of going on as a substitute and making an impact. To be honest, I never saw him being a regular starter in our attack but importantly, his all-round game was steadily improving. Everything was fine until Frank Skinner and David Baddiel turned him into a figure of fun on their TV show. I laughed along with the rest of the country when it first started and it didn't bother me in the slightest that the joke was on me as well as Jason. The sketches were very funny – and clever – and Jason had left himself wide open to criticism by having his silly 'pineapple' haircut. But there are limits and in my opinion, Skinner and Baddiel went beyond them. They were merciless in the way they treated him, week after week, and even the strongest of characters couldn't fail to be affected by it. Lee had scored six goals for us at a very tidy strike rate in the early part of the 1995-96 season but once the mocking started, he was never the same again. He only scored two more goals that season and not only did he slip right out of the picture at Forest, his career went into a sharp decline. Whatever people might think about the glamorous and lucrative life of professional footballers, some of them get dealt a very poor hand. Jason didn't deserve to be nationally humiliated in that way and the 'mud' stuck to him for the rest of his time in football.

Sooner or later, I suppose, we had to taste defeat and when that time came at Ewood Park in November, we didn't mess around. We lost 7-0. Just about everything that could go wrong, did. Colin Cooper strained his back during the warm-up, Steve Chettle got sent off and Alan Shearer got out of bed on the wrong side from our point of view. Chettle and Cooper were a fantastic pairing in the centre of our defence. They were a match for any strikers in the country – except for Shearer. He always caused them problems. He scored a hat-trick that day and just to rub salt into some very open wounds, Bohinen also scored twice. Sometimes you just have to take it on the chin. Our fans sang "Always look on the bright side of life" and it was crucial that we did. I forcefully told the players afterwards that we had to instantly wipe that defeat from our memories. They'd done fantastically well for me up to that point and there was plenty more to look forward to – not least the fact that we were playing Lyon in the UEFA Cup three days later.

Isn't it amazing how often football produces coincidences you wouldn't believe possible? My farewell appearance as a player had been in the European Cup Final against Malmö and my first European venture as a manager, 16 years on, was against... Malmö! Everyone wanted to get me to roll back the years but I needed to focus on what would be a really tough assignment. I knew they'd be incredibly well organised because that was their trademark and it turned into a cagey affair. We lost the first-leg 2-1 in Sweden but Alan Hill and I were convinced that Ian Woan's away goal would be crucial. We couldn't see them scoring against us at the City Ground. We were right and when Brian Roy scored, we won 1-0 to go through on away goals.

One of the big lessons we learned from the early rounds was that teams are very reluctant to play in an expansive fashion in two-legged ties. Malmo went on to win their League Championship that season, as did Auxerre and Bayern Munich who we met in later rounds. They were fine teams and were very adaptable. But they treated European ties very differently to domestic matches and we needed to adopt the same cat-and-mouse approach.

All the reports we had about Auxerre were that they were a very good team and when we went to France for the first leg, we took some 'stick' over our choice of line-up. On reflection I suppose it was a brave decision on our part. Our information was that they played with a rigid system that included an out-and-out sweeper. We wondered if it just might cause them a problem if they only had one striker to deal with. We got to hear they'd concentrated much of their work during the build-up on dealing with Roy so we countered that by leaving him out. Brian was fine with it when we explained our thinking and it worked a treat. We were backs-to-the-wall for much of the time and Auxerre can maybe count themselves unfortunate that Mark Crossley had been inspired. Someone had shown us a copy of the local newspaper and when a massive headline was interpreted into English, it read: "Big Fat Goalie". The story underneath, we were told, said Auxerre would have no problems going through if they kept the 'keeper busy. Crossley had actually been superb in all of our UEFA Cup games and when we showed him the newspaper, we knew how he'd respond. No one was going to beat him that night and when Steve Stone converted one of our rare chances, it was enough to give us a 1-0 win. My abiding memory of that trip was the reaction of our directors at the final whistle. They were leaning over the top of the tunnel as we left the field, struggling to control their excitement. There were more cat-and-mouse games to come in the home leg. We re-instated Roy and went 4-4-2. They again had most of the game but couldn't break us down. When it was still goalless with 20 minutes left, I was thinking maybe we should pull Roy off and shut up shop. But even though Auxerre had to score to remain in the competition, they still didn't change formation. We decided to stay as we were and the goalless draw was good enough.

Next up were Lyon and when they came to the City Ground, it highlighted our striker crisis. We had to name two raw youngsters – Bobby Howe and Paul McGregor – among the substitutes and I threw them on with 15 minutes to go. Our fans didn't like it but Silenzi and Roy were making no impression at all against their well-organised defence. We were desperate to find something to cling onto in the second leg and I thought it was a gamble worth taking to swop international experience for enthusiasm and naivety. More often than not, it wouldn't have worked. This time it did. When Stuart Pearce had a late penalty saved, McGregor reacted quickest to steer in the rebound for the only goal of the tie. We were through to the quarter-finals and a clash with Bayern Munich – but there was a three-months gap before that came around. By the time we travelled to Munich for the first leg on March 5, Bayern had enjoyed a mid-winter break and had played just eight times in the intervening period. We had played 20 matches in comparison. That had always been an issue for English teams in Europe – not least when Forest were winning and then retaining the European Cup. I'd been down this road before as a player and did my best to keep the lads fresh and fit. It really was asking a lot with such a small first-team squad. Although scoring goals was a constant problem, the contributions of Woan and Stone were a big part in keeping us competitive in the League and we fought our way through to the sixth round of the FA Cup. It didn't help in the grand scheme of things that we had to contend with replays in all three rounds leading up to that stage. But we ploughed through them all and just as we were fancying our chances of a trip to Wembley, it was a massive disappointment to lose 1-0 at home to Aston Villa. In fact, we went out of both cup competitions in the space of a week. Whatever people might say about excuses, I'm absolutely convinced that fatigue had a big influence on those results.

Alan and I flew to Hamburg in advance of the first meeting with Bayern to watch them in action and when we boarded the flight, sitting next to us were members of Status Quo. Hard to believe, I know, but they had been booked to provide the half-time entertainment at the match! Needless to say, with my great love of music, I was absolutely in my element and as we parted, the group's manager said that if ever we wanted tickets to one of their concerts, give him a call. Incidentally, I don't think I've ever been colder in my life than I was that night. How they managed to play guitars I'll never know. Trying to spot weaknesses in the Bayern set-up was no easy matter. They were formidable. The best we could come up with was that they gave you a chance at the far post. Chettle underlined that by scoring with a header in the first leg and although a 2-1 defeat was not a bad result in the away leg, it could have been better. I'd always been obsessed with the shape of the team and the tempo of our play and we'd been tremendous with that throughout the UEFA Cup run. I didn't feel we were quite on top of the job that night and knowing we'd reached a stage where fine margins could be vital, I feared we could be made to pay for it. The story of the night really concerned Pearce. He'd taken a knock on the shin in the previous game but when he said he was fit, as usual his name was first down on the team-sheet. Then, an hour before kick off, our club doctor, Lynn Jarrett, pulled me aside and said I needed to take a look at 'Pearcey's' shin. It was badly swollen, probably infected, and the doc said that he felt he shouldn't play. You have to listen to the experts in that situation but it's not easy to argue when 'Pearcey' puts on his most determined face. He insisted he was going to play and under the circumstances, his performance that night was nothing short of magnificent.

I got trapped a little bit between the proverbial rock and hard place when Bayern arrived in Nottingham for the return leg. I was very aware that people were looking for England's last survivors in Europe to keep the flag flying but also that we were facing a different class of opposition. Bayern were masters at soaking up pressure and hitting teams on the break. We had to decide whether to keep it tight and hope to cash in on our away goal or set out to attack. We opted to use Chris Bart-Williams as a second holding midfielder alongside David Phillips but the goalposts had shifted by half time. We were 2-0 down, which meant 4-1 on aggregate. Now the choice was to go for broke or try to keep the scoreline respectable? I could sense the feeling of the players and said: "Sod it. We've come this far … let's go out and give it a go." We changed to a more attacking formation and played right into Bayern's hands. They tore us apart in the second half and won 5-1. It was a disappointing end to a glorious campaign but I thought the crowd were very fair to us that night. They could see we'd given everything and had been beaten by an exceptionally good team.

People hate going out of cup competitions, especially when the exits in both cases are at the quarter-final stage, and I had a big job to do. Somehow I had to try and rally the troops. The challenge was a step too far because they had very little left to give me. We had a good Easter, beating Tottenham and Leeds, and closed the season with a 3-0 win over Queen's Park Rangers but in between that we struggled.

And we also got tangled up in the famous war of words between Alex Ferguson and Kevin Keegan as Manchester United and Newcastle battled it out for the League title.

We were due to play them both in less than a week at the vital stage of the run-in and when Alex got to know Newcastle were coming to the City Ground at the end of the season for Pearce's testimonial match, it was great ammunition for him to start his mind games. I got a call from a journalist to say United are suggesting your lads might take their foot off the pedal because Newcastle are doing you a favour. There was no way I was getting involved in that and I made it very clear to the players that I didn't want to see them spouting their mouths off on the subject. We played badly at Old Trafford and got smashed 5-0, then held Newcastle to a 1-1 draw. But United finished four points clear at the top anyway.

I'll always have a special affection for Newcastle and although my approach to that situation was never anything less than totally professional, I'd have loved to see them land the title. It was clearly a massive disappointment to Keegan but he handled it a few days later with real class. He brought his entire first-team squad down for the testimonial, even the injured lads, and 15 minutes from the end he and Terry McDermott stripped off their tracksuits and joined in. The crowd loved it and started chanting for me to do the same. Much as I wished I could, that really wouldn't have been sensible.

We'd finished 9th in League and reached the quarter-finals of two cup competitions. Taken in isolation, it was a very good effort and had we finished 9th in our first season back in the top flight, I'm sure everyone connected to Forest would have been delighted. Instead, it was seen as slipping backwards after we'd finished third the previous year. Setting high standards can be difficult to live with.

Incidentally, during the course of the 1995-96 season I found myself in the frame for the England job. Graham Taylor was leading the call for me to be named as the man to succeed Terry Venables after Euro '96 and was very generous in his comments about me. Seeing the screaming headlines on the back pages of the national newspapers was great for my street 'cred' but I'd been around too long to get taken in by that. Time would tell whether there was anything in it or not – but circumstances change incredibly quickly in football.

Simmering beneath the surface at Forest was a move to change the antiquated way in which the club was run and during the months ahead I got unwittingly involved in that. For years, we'd been the only club in the country run by a committee and quite rightly in my opinion, they decided the time had come to look at a different way of financing the business. When I took over as Forest manager they operated on an unsecured overdraft at the bank and that was comfortably covered by the value of the players. If we needed money, we just sold one. But the Bosman Ruling changed all that. All of a sudden, international stars could simply walk out when their contracts expired and that possibility caused the bank to get very twitchy.

It was right and proper to change the constitution and search for major investment. The problem was that people were treading water while we waited for a new overlord to come forward – and that took an eternity. It was perfectly understandable that committee members were not prepared to stick their necks out, knowing they could be removed overnight, but that was no help to me. Of course it was a difficult situation but from my point of view we were a ship without a rudder. Here's an example of how it affected me. I'd signed a year's extension to my contract at the end of the season and told Alan Hill I would speak to the Board about bringing him and the coaches in line with me. I took that proposal to the next meeting and it was accepted. Then Alan came to me weeks later and asked whether I'd ever done anything about our conversation. When I took it up with Paul White, our club secretary, he said the Board had blocked it because of the possibility of a takeover. That really damaged my credibility with the staff. They knew it wasn't my fault but it still put a big strain on relationships.

The Board had made it clear at the end of the season that they were not prepared to sanction any significant summer transfer activity but then things suddenly turned full circle. Fred Reacher told me they were very worried about a slump in season-ticket sales and it would be helpful if I could sign a couple of players, to try and give them a boost. I hadn't seen that coming and we weren't fully prepared for it. No wheels had been put in motion to identify suitable transfer targets and open negotiations. It was typical of Forest at that time. No serious forward planning was being carried out and there was a distinct lack of logical thinking. Things were being done on a whim and key issues were landing on my desk that would inevitably have long-term consequences.

The City Ground was one of the venues that summer for Euro '96 group matches and when Croatia played a couple of games there, I was really impressed with one of their central defenders. Nikola Jerkan looked a million dollars. He controlled everything, strolling out from the back to set up attacks. If I was going to do something that would influence season-ticket sales, I had to act quickly and when I checked, his pedigree was impressive. Apart from winning 30-odd caps for

Croatia, he was starring for Real Oviedo in Spain and a couple of years earlier had been voted Best Defender in La Liga. We agreed to sign him for £1million and also paid £1.5million to bring Dean Saunders home from his spell in Turkey with Galatasaray.

We made an incredible start to the season as Kevin Campbell scored a hat-trick and we beat Coventry 3-0 at Highfield Road. Ron Atkinson was their manager and he came to me straight after the game and said: "I'm going to have a big bet on you to win the Championship." I sincerely hope for his sake that he didn't because it was to be my last League win as Forest manager. I stayed on for another four months and although we drew almost as many games as we lost, the pressure steadily built up. It eventually got to the point where I couldn't take it any more. It was making me ill.

It wasn't easy living with my decisions as Jerkan flattered to deceive and Saunders failed to justify his price tag but the problems went far deeper than that. Various potential investors, some serious and some not, were making the newspaper headlines and the takeover seemed to be the only thing on the agenda, inside and out of the club. I even had a meeting in London with Irving Scholar, who was part of the consortium who eventually took over. He indicated that my job would be secure if they moved in. In the meantime, it was clear that problems were mounting up and that was highlighted when Irving Korn came to see me. He'd taken over as chairman at the AGM in October when Fred completed his three-year term in that role and he told me he'd had the bank on the phone. I would have to sell a player as a matter of some urgency.

I said: "OK. I'll organise to send a circular around to other clubs to notify them that the likes of Stuart Pearce, Colin Cooper and Ian Woan were available."

That threw him into a complete panic. "You can't do that," he said. "The supporters won't tolerate it." It didn't seem to have occurred to him that clubs would only be interested in our best players.

It couldn't carry on. Although we weren't getting battered, we couldn't win a match for love nor money and I realised the day Liverpool beat us 4-2 at Anfield, eight days before Christmas, my time was up. For the first time in my life I didn't feel able to handle the pressure. I wasn't sleeping and had lost faith in the methods that had always served me well. The final straw was when I came as close as I'd ever done to hitting a player. Saunders could be an annoying little sod who always had plenty to say for himself and when he argued in the dressing room at Anfield about what I'd asked him to do, I struggled to restrain myself. I went back out for the second half knowing that if it had reached that stage, my only option was to walk away. The night before we did that, Alan and I took our wives to the NEC as we accepted our invitation to see Status Quo in concert. They were fantastic – but I had other things on my mind.

Brian Clough always told me that if you're thinking about resigning, go to bed and sleep on it. Then, if you're still feeling the same way the following morning, go back to bed again. There weren't too many pieces of advice he offered that I chose to ignore but that was one of them. I cared too much about Nottingham Forest to see them struggling in that way. I felt I had to ship out while there was still time to turn things around. I told the chairman he could either sack me or I would resign. He said he didn't want me to go and seemed very sincere about it. In the end, I walked away when I still had 18 months to run on my lucrative contract.

My advice to the chairman was that he should give the job to Pearce in the short-term because he had a better chance than anyone of getting an instant reaction from the players. Although they won the next game against Arsenal, they couldn't dig their way out of trouble. The day I left was one of the saddest of my life. 'Cloughie' had once told me I'd never make a decent manager because I was far too soft. I couldn't see it at the time. Maybe he was right after all.

FRIDAY, DECEMBER 20, 1996 * * MS

SPORT 4

FOOTBALL / Leading consortium withdraw takeover bid for Premiership strugglers

Pearce pauses to reflect on Forest's offer

By Christopher Davies and Mihir Bose

STUART PEARCE hopes to be part of the new Nottingham Forest management following the resignation of Frank Clark yesterday.

Forest captain has for 24 hours to consider the board's offer to be caretaker-manager at City Ground.

It is believed Pearce is given assurances that he will remain part of the playing or management set-up in the club's new era, who should be in post in February, appoint a permanent manager.

Clark supported the elevation of Pearce, 34, who has 76 England caps and is the popular choice of supporters. "It's a wise move and I'm sure the club will get a lift from it," he said.

A problem for the existing board is the pending court case of the club — further complicated yesterday when one of the rival consortiums headed by Monte Carlo-based businessman Phil Lewis, withdrew his bid.

The Lewis consortium had backing of the majority of Forest shareholders and was set to beat a rival bid composed of local businessmen.

However yesterday morning, within hours of Clark's decision to go, Lewis rang his fellow consortium members — writer and businessman Phillip Soar and former Tottenham chairman Irving Scholar — to tell them he had decided to withdraw his offer for the club.

Clark, no doubt realising that with Forest bottom of the Premiership and a new board about to be put in place, decided the best option was to resign even though both rival consortiums had given him their backing.

"I'm resigning in the hope that it will give the team a short-term lift," said Clark, the fifth Premiership managerial change this season.

Forest's 4-2 defeat at Liverpool on Tuesday, which left them three points adrift at the bottom of the table and without a win in 16 games — a Premier League record — persuaded Clark it was time to leave the club he has served as player and manager.

"You could say the Liverpool game was the final straw," he said. "I saw certain warning signs in that display. I didn't want to hang around until they [the players] lost faith in me. That would have been a disaster for the club.

"Also, I didn't want to stay until they [the new owners] came in. There could be another five or six games played by then and it might have been too late. It's vital now that the team gets a couple of wins. If they do, it will transform the picture."

Clark may not be out of management for very long. Stephen Boler, the new Manchester City powerbroker after his £10.8 million cash injection, would like Clark as manager at Maine Road.

However, Francis Lee, the chairman, is on holiday until Jan 4, as are two other directors, so nothing is likely to be decided in the immediate future.

The Football League's six-man board will be replaced by an independently chaired nine-man body. It was decided at an emergency general meeting yesterday.

The three First Division representatives are likely to be David Sheepshanks, of Ipswich, Ron Noades (Crystal Palace) and Oldham's Ian Stott. There will be contests for the positions among the Second and Third Division clubs. The new board will officially come into being by Jan 9.

Birmingham striker Mike Newell has joined West Ham on a month's loan, with a view to a permanent move. He could make his debut at Chelsea tomorrow.

Face of defeat ... Frank Clark at the City Ground yesterday his resignation as manager of Nottingham Forest

Problems from boardroom to dressing

FTSE much-lauded dipping employment figures embed a single and very sad yesterday.

The departure of Frank Clark at Nottingham Forest is far from a footnote in the history of managerial fortunes. It shows how clubs can be palsied by anxious financiers waiting to hear Clark's resignation is the uncertainty afflicting City Ground.

concern. Caspian moved into Leeds. Newcastle, West Bromwich, Birmingham, Sheffield United, Sunderland, and Southampton are also wooing the pinstripe fraternity. Football is putting the City into the City Ground.

While the rival, doubtless well-intentioned syndicates have been jockeying for position, Forest have stagnated. Mid-season takeovers are madness for all concerned.

The dressing room senses the

COMMENT

HENRY WINTER

revive the side (in attack) or cover injuries (right midfield). So Forest struggle. The new owners may be acquiring a team destined for the First Division.

The likelihood that other clubs will pursue Clark reflects the

properly. Andrea Silenzi and Kevin Campbell are not Premiership material.

Clark is. The first few months of '96 saw this decent man lauded as the only manager left in Europe, his team showing organisation and resilience in reaching the UEFA Cup quarter-finals. Clark, honest and respected, gets people to play for him.

One of them, Stuart Pearce, is now expected to become player-

committed the back-more conti

Clark, c.v. Manch than Fore ested. But and Alex F with City. If Clark Maine Roa ing vacanc Howard

Chapter 19
POISONED CHALICE? IT DIDN'T HAVE TO BE
1996-98

I was very grateful to Alex Ferguson for the nice comments he made when I arrived at Manchester City. He told the media in December 1996 that City had appointed a good manager and he fully expected me to revive their fortunes. He also said he didn't think it would be too long before local derbies were back on the agenda. The prospect of sharing the Manchester football platform with Alex was undoubtedly part of the appeal when I got the chance to go to Maine Road. I'm sure he felt a strong rivalry between United and City was essential – not just for Manchester but for English football in general – and I was being tasked with bringing that about.

Crossing swords with him on a regular basis would have been very special and even though I admit to having concerns that the call from City had come far too soon, how could I possibly turn them down? Everywhere I went people told me the job was a poisoned chalice and knowing what a delicate state I was in after my final few months at Forest, I should have rejected their approach. I'd always prided myself on making sensible decisions yet here I was, thinking I could do what countless others couldn't. The minimum requirement to take on such a daunting challenge was to have total faith in my own ability yet just at that precise moment, I was probably less confident than I'd ever been. What I really needed was a decent break from the game – something I'd never had. I should have re-charged the batteries and taken stock, rather than leaping straight into my next job.

It was less than a fortnight since I'd resigned from Forest. I was still feeling raw but I had to get a grip. I needed to remind myself that in just over three years at the City Ground, I'd guided them to promotion and a third place finish in the Premier League. And then we'd reached the quarter-finals of the UEFA Cup. It was little more than 18 months since LMA members had voted me 'Manager of the Year – probably the highest individual accolade a manager can achieve in this country – and the City job was a marvellous opportunity to get my career back on track. It was a genuine chance to build something special.

Plenty of people had told me I was a fool to step straight into Brian Clough's shoes when I went back to Forest. That had worked out well enough. Surely, I thought, it cannot be any more of a challenge at Maine Road. City had been relegated from the top flight the season before, just as Forest had when I went there, so why shouldn't I turn them around in the same way? It didn't take me long to discover that this was a whole new ball game.

I already knew the City chairman Francis Lee quite well because we'd played against each other many times and were team-mates for one day when we played for the Football League against the Irish League. When he called to ask if I'd be interested in the manager's job, I was certainly keen to look at it. He painted a very good picture. Unfortunately, it turned out to be a false one – but I want to give him the benefit of the doubt. I don't think he meant to mislead me in a nasty way. In fact, I do believe he wanted what he told me to be the truth. The word on the street for some time had been that City were a club in turmoil, run by directors who were constantly warring with each other, and their record of hiring and firing managers was incredible. Alan Ball had departed early in the season and Steve Coppell lasted just six games and 33 days before resigning because he claimed the job was too stressful. Asa Hartford and Phil Neal had also had fairly lengthy spells as caretaker manager. I was effectively their fifth manager in five months! Lee's version of events was that the problems were all in the past and everyone was desperate to make a fresh start. The directors, he said, were now united behind him and with their fantastic training ground and fan base, all that was needed was the right manager to get them going. I was flattered that he thought I could be that right manager and in fairness, he did back it up by offering me a deal for three and a half years that was worth far more than I was on at Forest.

I didn't have a problem with Lee – at least not until results started going badly. I quite liked the idea of working with a chairman who was a vastly experienced football man and he had clearly enjoyed a lot of success in business. My gut feeling was that we would work well together and I couldn't help but be excited about the prospect of managing a club with such enormous potential.

I wasn't naïve enough to think that it wouldn't be tough but when he told me I could bring in my own backroom team and remove anyone that I didn't want, I thought that was a good start. I wanted Alan Hill as my assistant, along with Richard Money as coach and Pete Edwards to work as fitness coach. I'd already been informed that Phil Neal would be leaving and told the chairman that I wanted that dealing with before I arrived. I also said that I'd like to keep the other staff on until I'd formed my opinions about them. It was all-good … but then two things happened on my very first morning that set the alarm bells ringing.

I was told that David Bernstein, the vice-chairman, would pick me up from my hotel and take me to the training ground. The "fantastic" training ground turned out to be a council facility that was shared with the general public. It had a huge car park and when we arrived I couldn't understand why Bernstein had driven us to a point as far away as possible from the main complex. Then it all made sense.

Despite what I'd agreed, the Neal issue had not been dealt with before I arrived. We had to wait until he'd cleared his desk and said his goodbyes to the players and staff. We sat there for what seemed like an eternity. That got me off on the wrong foot and then I discovered that Tony Book, a true legend of Manchester City and a very popular guy, had been sacked from his role as kit man. Apparently I was being blamed for it. I'd specifically said that I didn't want any of the staff to leave until I'd had chance to form an opinion about them and as one of my first jobs, I felt the need to find Tony and make that clear to him. It was a rubbish way to start my new assignment, and there was plenty more of that to follow.

I couldn't believe some of the things I found. The football operation at Manchester City, one of the biggest clubs in the country, was being run like a Fourth Division outfit. The whole culture needed to change and I found myself trapped between trying to do that and improving a team that was next to bottom in the Championship and had lost six of their previous seven League matches. Let me give you a few examples. To start with, I inherited more than 40 professionals, who were all on decent contracts. It was hardly surprising that City were heavily in debt. They had one of the largest wage bills in the land and yet at least a third of those players had no chance of ever making a first-team appearance. How could I possibly hope to keep that many players happy? Just accommodating them in the changing rooms was an issue every day and trying to work them in a constructive fashion was an enormous challenge. In fairness to the players, the majority always turned up wanting to work. I felt very sorry for those who were wasting their careers away. I said all the usual things when I addressed them on the first morning about clean-slates and everyone getting chance to impress. I'm sure they'd heard it all before and they realised there was no way that could realistically happen – not with more than 40 of them involved.

The players were entitled to feel unhappy about the way they were being treated. Basic things that were taken for granted at other clubs were not in place. They didn't have any personalised training kit, for example. It was all washed and tossed into a skip and the first players to arrive in the morning picked out the best of it. As for the training ground, the chairman surely didn't believe what he told me at our initial meeting. There weren't enough pitches to work on and the best of them had to be used sparingly because matches were played on them. Although they were fenced off, the general public could stand on the other side of it and watch us working. Sometimes, upwards of 100 people would turn up and the players took some fearful abuse. It was a terrible environment for building confidence and bringing out the best in them. Because it was a shared facility, the restaurant area in the main complex was also open to the general public so the lads got very little privacy. All in all, it was totally unsuitable.

Another thing I couldn't believe when I arrived was the team bus that ferried us to away matches. It was far too small and cramped and had no basic facilities like a toilet or any means of preparing and heating food. How could that be at a club on the scale of Manchester City? After using it for the first time I demanded a meeting with the managing-director of the coach company we used. He was a lovely man who was shocked by my reaction. He insisted no one had ever complained in the past but understood what I was saying. I sent him to Nottingham Forest to look at their team bus and after he'd been, he immediately ordered a new one and hired an upgrade to use until it arrived. All it took was a simple conversation and the players appreciated the fact that we were doing something to try and improve their 'lot',

There wasn't exactly a them-and-us situation running through the club but from the minute I walked through the door I felt there was a real lack of togetherness. I've often claimed that City at that time was a commercial organisation masquerading as a football club. Maybe that's a bit strong but the commercial set-up was brilliant – fantastically well-run and successful. It just seemed to me that in comparison, the football operation was the poor relation. I accept that the onus was on us to haul ourselves up to the same level – on and off the field – but it would have been so much easier to do that had everyone pulled together. Having said that, I did put a block on one of the joint ventures. City had lots of supporters groups dotted around Greater Manchester and the players were expected to regularly work with the commercial department to attend functions. I was fully in favour of that but was horrified to discover these often took place on Thursday and even Friday evenings. It's always been a golden rule that footballers don't have nights out within a couple of days of a game and I immediately put a stop to that. Players are a strange bunch and you have to make sure they have no excuses for playing badly. That was another box ticked.

Slowly but surely the atmosphere improved, and maybe that was helped by us organising a Christmas party... in February! Alan Hill was staggered to discover that the players hadn't had a Christmas 'do' in living memory. He insisted that had to change and signed up a Beatles tribute band that we knew in Nottingham. A bit late in the day but everyone in the club attended – with partners – and had a great time.

City fans gave me a fantastic welcome to Maine Road. There were nearly 30,000 of them for my first game – at home to Crystal Palace – and we managed to steady the ship after a lengthy run of defeats. We drew that game, and the next one at Huddersfield, and although I was really worried about a tricky FA Cup tie at lower division Brentford, I saw plenty of encouraging signs that day. We were second-best for much of the game but showed a lot of character to dig out a 1-0 win – thanks to a second half goal by Nicky Summerbee. A run of four straight wins during February went a long way towards dispelling relegation fears and there were definite signs of progress. In fact, we only lost two of my first 17 League games in charge and were taking on the look of a side capable of challenging for promotion. We finished the season in a respectable 14th position and the reception the fans gave the players after we'd completed the campaign with a 3-2 win over Reading was incredible. If I didn't already understand the full extent of City's potential, that certainly brought it home to me. Unfortunately, a lot of the adulation was aimed in the direction of Georgi Kinkladze – and that was a problem to me.

It wasn't just the fans who worshipped the Georgian star. The chairman did too and he could do no wrong in the eyes of most people. But although there's no doubt that he had special talent with his exceptional dribbling skills and knack of scoring spectacular goals, we felt he was in the wrong place at the wrong time. We'd spent our first four months trying to work out exactly what his role was. He wasn't really a midfield player, he certainly wasn't a striker and we eventually came to the conclusion that he was a luxury we couldn't afford if we were to mount a serious challenge for promotion the following year. We'd only scored 59 League goals during the 1996-97 season – nothing like enough. Kinkladze, who we'd used up front alongside Uwe Rosler, had scored just 12 of those and six had come from the penalty spot. Talented as he was, we felt he was standing in the way of progress and the only answer was to try and move him on. We knew there would be all sorts of repercussions but felt that if we stated our case well enough, people would understand. As I stood on the pitch as the players went out to acknowledge the crowd on that final day of the season, I realised we couldn't do it. It would have taken someone a lot braver than me to have made that happen. You could say that I 'chickened' out and you would be right. The fans would not have tolerated it. Somehow we had to find a way of playing that would give Kinkladze the best possible chance of influencing games. In the end, we tied ourselves in knots trying to do that.

Our only hope of achieving it was to make him see that he needed to act more responsibly. If anyone was going to be late for training you could put your money on him and it was very revealing that he had a habit of dumping his car on double-yellow lines anywhere in Manchester. I found out that when the parking fines were delivered to the club, they would pay them. I had him in and told him that wasn't going to happen any more. I said: "We think you're a special player and want to build the team around you. But that's only going to work if you accept more responsibility for your actions as a player and a person." He had a way of looking at you sideways and you never quite knew if he was taking it in or not. I guess when people spend all day every being told how wonderful they are, it's not easy to accept that they have to change their ways. We decided we had to use him in a role behind the centre-forward and write him off when we didn't have the ball. Had he been surrounded by six of seven internationals that would probably have worked well. With the group we had available, he remained a luxury we couldn't afford.

We needed to go down a different route to try and generate more goals if we were serious about getting promotion and during the summer of 1997, I invested a club record £3million on Lee Bradbury. Alan and Richard Money had also been to watch him play for Portsmouth but it was my decision to sign him. The buck stops with me, if that's the way to put it, but although I'm very aware of how City fans view that deal, things could have been so different with him.

Before I talk more about Bradbury, it's important to say that I was happy with where we were that summer. The players had responded really well to our ideas and there was plenty to be pleased about in our performances in the second half of the season. We'd made significant progress in cleaning up the overall football operation. The players had a lot less to complain about and that was reflected in a much better spirit across the club. Having said that, I was still very aware that we had still only scratched the surface.

The chairman was not happy with the way the youth scheme was functioning and told me I had to take an in-depth look at it. I argued that I had enough on my plate, dealing with 40-plus players, but he said it had to be done. Alan was an expert at such matters so I passed it on to him. It didn't take him long to report back that just about everything about the set-up was wrong. Most important, there was a real lack of quality among the youngsters. We agreed that a new broom was needed to bring about a complete change and identified Jimmy Cassell as the man to do it. Jimmy had done a lot of good work in a similar role just up the road at Oldham. He knew the area and was well connected. When we sounded him out, he was very interested in joining us. He wasn't on a massive wage but by way of coincidence it amounted to almost exactly what was being paid to our two youth coaches added together. When we took it to Francis Lee, he said we could only appoint him if we got the other two youth coaches off the wage bill to balance the books. One of those was Colin Bell and I said: "We can't sack him. He's an absolute legend at this club." City fans have since hailed him as their Greatest Ever Player. He even has a stand named after him at the City of Manchester Stadium. I had no problem personally with Colin. He was on 'peanuts', and we should have found a role for him to avoid all the flak that inevitably followed. Realistically, there was nothing in it for me. There was no chance of me still being around to get the benefits of an improved youth scheme but it was absolutely the right move for the club. Long after I'd gone, Cassell was instrumental in setting up the Academy that developed loads of good young players.

Reverting back to the Bradbury situation, signing him was a defining moment in my time at Manchester City. Had it worked out as planned, I'm confident we would have won promotion in 1997-98. It didn't... and I was out of work by the end of February. Some you win, some you lose in our precarious occupation, yet I'll always maintain that it wasn't a bad decision to sign Bradbury. I wasn't the only one who thought that either. I well remember sitting next to the chairman in the Directors' Box at Turf Moor when we played Burnley in a pre-season game and our new signing really looked the part. "Well done," said Lee. "You've found us a player."

Bradbury was a late starter in the professional game, having served in the army for some time. He was 20 years of age when he started with Portsmouth and two years on when he joined us, he was still relatively raw. But we felt he had all the attributes that you look for in a centre-forward – and loads of potential. A strapping six-footer, he was as brave as they come, was a real handful for defenders and had already gained England Under-21 recognition. He wasn't a natural goal-scorer but that was something we could work on. We could see him developing a good partnership with Uwe Rosler and if Kinkladze found some consistency behind them, and served up plenty of ammunition, they could become a formidable attacking force. I could see a situation where Bradbury would eventually take over from Kinkladze as the 'main man' at City but the price-tag weighed heavily. Instead of taking the place by storm, he made a slow start to the new season. So did many of the others, and it turned into one long struggle.

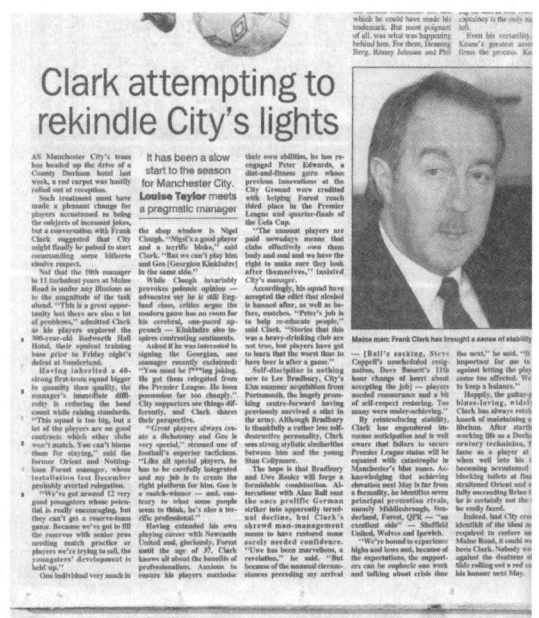

Bradbury didn't open his goals account until mid-September, when we lost 2-1 at Norwich, but was on target again the following week when we smashed Swindon 6-0. At last, we thought, we're up and running. Not so. He cracked a vertebra at Ipswich in the very next game and was out for the next four months. It was a disaster for him personally – and for me – because it meant that when he did return, he virtually had to make a fresh start. That was asking too much, especially the state we were in by that stage. Within days of Bradbury damaging his back, we also lost Rosler through injury and then Kinkladze was involved in a nasty car crash. It meant that all three components of the 'formidable attacking force' we hoped would take the Championship by storm had gone missing. We had to throw in a series of untried youngsters and hope they would come up trumps. It had worked for me in the past. This time it didn't. We only managed one goal in a six-game spell and that sapped the strength and confidence out of us. The difficulty in that situation was that instead of being inspired by the fantastic backing of 30,000 passionate fans, that support became a massive burden to the players. Some could hardly move for fear of making a mistake and the expectations became impossible to live with. You need really big characters to deal with that amount of pressure and we didn't have many of those. Visiting managers very quickly read the script. They knew that if they could keep us quiet for the first 20 minutes, the crowd would start to lose patience and put the players under fearful pressure. Once that happened, we had no chance of doing ourselves justice.

I hadn't quite realised it at the time but part of the reason for our encouraging form during my first few months at Maine Road was that the players were able to perform with relative freedom. Results had been so poor during the first half of the campaign that there were no expectations piling pressure on them. Once the new season began, the atmosphere was totally different. Season-tickets sales had been good on the back of our decent run, we'd strengthened the squad and had an impressive pre-season. That lot added together caused the expectations to soar. Under the circumstances, it was absolutely essential for us to make a really good start. If we could do that, the fantastic support would intimidate opponents and help us to turn Maine Road into a fortress. It just didn't happen and as the mood changed, certain players wilted. I got the brunt of supporters' frustrations, which was completely understandable. I was experienced enough to live with it but what I found really difficult to accept was the directors and shareholders playing their own little game behind the scenes. I had no idea who half of them were, which wasn't necessarily a problem because I shouldn't need to come into contact with them. But then I'd find myself in a situation where someone I'd never heard of was dictating policy to me. I hadn't been at City very long when I was summoned to a meeting at The Mere Golf Club with Stephen Boler, who was a major shareholder. When I got there, he told me that although the chairman had suggested when I arrived that I'd have a generous budget for buying players, that money would only be available in dribs and drabs over a period of time. In itself, that was absolutely no problem to me. What was a problem was that they couldn't all get their act together and agree one policy. Too many people were pulling in different directions and that was right at the heart of City's problems.

Half the time I got to know what was going on at Maine Road by reading about it in the newspapers. Under normal circumstances, a struggling Championship club would have warranted very few column inches but the national papers all had staff writers based in Manchester. They needed to justify their existence so they were always digging around for scoops and someone within the club was only too pleased to feed them. I made it my business to identify the person responsible for leaking information that only our key people could have known. I never did find them.

My main concern was winning football matches but I kept getting dragged into situations that should have been way down my priority list. There was so much that needed my attention and I can see now that I was guilty of allowing other things to get in the way. The biggest of many regrets that I have about my time at City is that I didn't spend more time on the training ground. I didn't need to be leading the coaching each day – I was happy enough with the job Money was doing – but I should have got closer to the players. There's always a thin dividing line where that's concerned because it can work against you if you get too cozy. I went too far the other way.

City were in a class of their own when it came to tittle-tattle. Former players and managers were always knocking around and in itself that was great. The problem was that most of them had strong opinions they were anxious to share yet they did nothing to help us. A few well-chosen words of encouragement would have helped to boost the players' confidence and maybe swayed public opinion. Very few chose to go down that line. It was standard procedure after home games that when my work was done, I'd take myself off to the Boardroom for a drink with the chairman and he was never slow to give me his views. In fairness, he was my boss. That entitled him to have his say and he had a habit of starting with: "You probably don't want my opinion but I did play centre-forward for England." It usually ended up with me saying that if he wanted to pick the team, all he had to do was sack me. Those after-match sessions in my first season were a pleasant enough way of winding down but when results turned, they became increasingly difficult. It reached the stage after one particularly depressing home defeat where I couldn't face it and told Alan Hill he would have to put in an appearance. Apparently when he got to the Boardroom Malcolm Allison was holding court about everything that was wrong. Allison had been Joe Mercer's right-hand man during City's glorious period in the Sixties and Seventies and later returned for two stints as manager. If I remember rightly, those periods could hardly be described as successful yet he remained a big figure at City and people certainly listened to him. Alan listened as well for a few minutes while Allison let fly about us and the players but then couldn't take it any more. He forcefully told them that if only they would get behind the manager and players and support them, instead of being totally destructive, we just might be able to turn things around. I'd never seen Alan so angry as when he came back to my office.

It was an incredibly difficult environment to work in and nothing was really going to change until the problems at the top were sorted out. Francis Lee was quoted as saying when he was appointed as chairman that he was going to make City "the happiest club in the land". How wrong he was.

In theory it was an excellent move just before I arrived to raise money for new players by selling shares in the club. The scheme was very successful as new investors came forward but in reality, what happened was that the balance of power shifted significantly. Stephen Boler, John Wardle and David Makin became major shareholders and as Lee's holding was modest in comparison, it made his position very difficult. His influence had been significantly reduced. At the beginning of my second season, we had just arrived at the Any Other Business item of the Board meeting agenda when it was announced that Dennis Tueart was going to be working at the club. When I looked across the table at the chairman he was studying his shoes so I asked: "What's Dennis Tueart going to do?" I was told he would be looking after the interests of the new shareholders. Lee still said nothing. It was all way above my station, brought about by the suspicion and mistrust that was rife in the Boardroom, but it was bound to have an impact at our level.

I'd known Dennis a long time. Our paths crossed regularly when we were players in the North East and I had no problem with him. Mind you, he probably had a problem with me if he thought back to the time when we clashed in a testimonial match straight after he'd helped Sunderland win the FA Cup. They were full of themselves, as you'd expect, and he sounded off to the newspapers about what they were going to do to us in that game. He didn't look so clever when I timed a challenge brilliantly to dump him in The Paddock at St James' Park and the crowd loved it when he cleared off over to the other flank – and David Craig stuck him into The Popular Side.

Anyway, life moves on and the first thing he did in his new role was to sound off to the Press about all that was wrong at Maine Road. I fixed up a meeting with him as quickly as possible and when he asked what he could do to help, I told him the most important thing was to stop stirring things up in the media. People said that he was a threat to me but I didn't see it that way. He was openly acting as the eyes and ears of the new shareholders but it didn't bother me that he was asking searching questions. I had nothing to hide. I thought he did a number of good things in that early period but it was always going to be an issue that he didn't represent the whole of the Board.

It seemed inevitable that sooner or later there would have to be some 'blood-letting' and it was no great surprise when I got tangled up in that. Things really came to a head when David Makin called a local radio phone-in as an act of frustration and sounded off about me –

but more especially the chairman. It was a staggeringly unprofessional thing to do and illustrated just how acrimonious things had become. One of the accusations Makin levelled against Lee was that he was acting like a dictator. I thought that was wrong. To start with, no one person could be held responsibly for all that was wrong at Maine Road and had he been a dictator, it might even have been a good thing. A strong, all-powerful chairman wouldn't have tolerated the lack of unity that was eating away at the club.

I knew in the February of my second season that I couldn't possibly survive when we suffered an embarrassing home defeat against Bury, our poor relations from just up the road. Someone would have to carry the can for that. But even then, the various factions still couldn't find a way to sing from the same song-sheet. One group issued a statement saying that I'd been given a stern warning that results would have to improve. I only found out about that when a journalist called me, asking for a comment. I said that I didn't need telling that results had to improve – but no one had actually done so. At the same time, another of the groups within the Board gave me the go-ahead to sign a player on loan, which suggested they thought I should be given more time to improve things. It was all so typical of the 14 months of chaos I had to endure and even the last rites were not delivered properly. When I got back from a midweek trip to Sunderland, where I'd been to watch Reading because we were about to play them, there was a message on my answer-machine. It was from John Richardson, a Daily Mail journalist and a friend, who was tipping me off that his paper was running a story that I was about to be sacked. When I turned on the local radio the following morning, the lead story was that I was out and Joe Royle was replacing me. About 15 minutes later the phone rang and the chairman asked me to pop in to see him on my way to the ground. "I wonder what that's about," I said.

The conversation was probably more difficult for him than it was for me. The fact is that the end came as a relief. I just couldn't see any way that things would change for the better in such a toxic environment. I was better off out of it. Lee was anxious to make the point that it was nothing personal and he hoped we could still be friends. Fine. I hadn't quite been through 14 months of hell because there had been some good times during that first season. And if I'd helped to make Joe Royle's task a little bit easier with some of the 'cleaning up' work I'd done, so much the better.

I got the benefit of a clause the Football League insisted all clubs should put into their manager's contracts, saying we'd be entitled to 12 months pay if we were sacked within our contract. Well, I almost did. I got a call from the club's solicitor – a nice man who I liked – and he said Francis Lee had authorised payment of 80 per cent of my entitlement. "What happened to the other 20 per cent?" I asked. He said that according to the chairman, I'd been ordered by the Board to sell players and hadn't done it so they were reducing the payment. It was complete rubbish and I insisted I wanted to see where that appeared in the minutes of any Board meeting – or some sort of evidence to substantiate the claim. They couldn't find any, of course, and the whole thing dragged on for a while. In the end, I wrote off a fairly significant chunk of cash. I was badly bruised and just couldn't be bothered with it any more. The experience had worn me down.

The other staff I took with me to Maine Road were also shown the door and I was especially sorry for Alan because he'd recently moved house to Prestbury, so he could be closer to his work. Life's not all bad, though. It freed him up for a much-needed hip replacement operation and when he came round from the anesthetic and switched on his phone, he'd had about 50 calls from people offering him jobs!

The Chairman

Nottingham Forest (October 2011- July 2012)

Decision to appoint Clark is a great one

I HAD heard a few whispers before hand so to hear the official news that Frank Clark had been appointed chairman at Nottingham Forest was music to my ears.

My former playing colleague is a tremendous appointment to the role, a much-needed addition at what is proving to be a difficult time.

As all Steve Cotterill, he has wasted no time in helping the club choose a manager who I believe will work well under the financial constraints expected to be put in place.

But firstly, let's talk about Clark.

If anything, the club should have sought his help long before, instead of using David Pleat as an adviser.

But, with Clark taking over as the chairman, it brings some football experience to the board, something that has been drastically missing.

He might originate from the north-east but Clark holds the club close at heart.

He is still a regular at games, lives nicely and has even acted as a player and manager in his day.

After all, he helped win the European Cup as a player and then led the club to promotion into the Premier League, then a third-place finish and a won-

On top of that he has spent a decade working for the League Managers Association and is now vice-president.

When it comes to today's game, he is totally up-to-date with everything and has his finger on the pulse.

So, for Forest, they need to tap into his knowledge, listen to him, learn from his ways.

Obviously, unlike Nigel Doughty as chairman, it is not Clark's money that is being pumped in.

He will head up committees, oversee meetings and make recommendations. At the end of the day, it is Forest's future, not his, at Forest.

But let me say one thing. When he makes recommendations, listen.

Forest have all the problems cited by former managers

a man in Clark who knows all of his ins and out. He will go into dealings with so many contract wrangles, arguments over signing-on fees, compensation pay-outs, wages.

But when it comes to sorting such problems out in the future, his experience will be golden for the likes of chief executive Mark Arthur to act upon.

Clark knows more than a few things about the game, he has more than a few friends, people put together and that is why his appointment excites me. I'm very happy about it.

We all have different personalities, there were many different ones in that Forest squad that won the European Cup.

Clark is a true gentleman. That is the best way to describe him and you can't fault him. He says when we used to have a couple of drinks down him and then he would get his guitar out and play it.

Frank is a very reserved man - as we will go waiting in there, he will listen and then make his points.

I can't stress how much of a good choice this is for the club in terms of helping steer Forest forward. But I can't stress enough how much the people

HE'S BACK: Frank Clark has played for, managed and is now chairman of Nottingham Forest.

Clark is there to help – let him the lead the way in all areas because everything he says will be for the good of the club and best out of decades of experience as a player, manager and on the LMA.

He has been a success in all those positions and I see no reason why he cannot be a success as a chairman, too.

I wish him all the best. As for Cotterill, it could prove to be a shrewd move, only time will tell.

It has been made clear, with

them to the League Two title, budget will be tight.

If anything, the new manager will be expected to get the best out of the small has at his disposal, with a lot of tinkering here and there.

Cotterill has lots of Championship experience from his Burnley days and more recently Portsmouth, where he enough money to have a team there but that experience will stand him in good stead for the challenge ahead.

He knows these parts, after

decide working for the League Managers Association and is

I can't stress enough how much the people on the board at the City Ground have to listen to him (Frank Clark)

Kenny Burns

them to the League Two title, budget will be tight.

But (thankfully he has inherited a talented group and it is down to them to produce the goods when they cross the white line) on having it tough hasn't happened so far this season.

Clark's appointment as chairman is a genuine hope the are as Cotterill in the man-

Kenny Burns' column in the Nottingham Post

Chapter 20
IN THE HOT-SEAT WITH NO PLACE TO HIDE
1998-2018

I was still only 56. In management terms I should have been in my prime but the Maine Road experience convinced me I didn't want to do it any more. I'd been at it in one form or another for more than 18 years and although you never know for sure what tomorrow might bring, I'd had enough. At the very least it was going to take an extremely appealing job to make me re-consider. Although the phone didn't ring too often, I wasn't bothered.

The one call that interested me came from Middlesbrough. I've always had great respect for their chairman Steve Gibson and chief executive Keith Lamb. They run an excellent football club and I'm sure I would have enjoyed working with them. But the offer was to become their Academy Director. That didn't make sense. Although I'd filled virtually every available staff job in football, that wasn't one of them. When I dug a bit deeper they admitted what they really wanted was for me to "keep an eye" on Bryan Robson. He and Viv Anderson, who I knew well, of course, from our days together at Forest, were Middlesbrough's management team and the feeling was that Robson needed reigning in from time to time. Gibson and Lamb thought I was the man to do that, using my experience to have a good influence on him, and I really fancied it. But I argued it would be impossible to carry out what they wanted from a position of Academy Director. They needed to make me Director of Football so that I had sufficient authority to work with the management at the right level. For whatever reason, they didn't feel able to go the extra mile and the whole thing fell through.

I was very disappointed because I'd thought for a long time that Director of Football was the ready-made role for me. I'd pretty much done it at Leyton Orient for a number of years when I was managing-director but still hands on with the football operation. I could see the value of having someone in that position. The game was changing and it had become just as important for managers to manage upwards as it was downwards. The job wasn't just about what happened on the pitch and in the dressing room any more. It seemed really logical to me that the answer was to have someone more experienced to work alongside the team manager, dealing with the directors and the business side of things, but it took a long time for the idea to catch on. Managers didn't like having to be answerable to someone other than the chairman and clubs were very reluctant to go down that line. In fact, at that time David Pleat at Tottenham was the only Director of Football as far as I was aware.

Missing out wasn't the end of the world because it gave me an opportunity to devote my energies to working with the League Managers' Association. I'd been involved from the start of the LMA, way back in 1991, and believed very strongly in what it stood for. Prior to that, all staff at football clubs – managers, coaches, secretaries and commercial managers – were members of the Football League Executive Staff Association. The problem was that it was very unwieldy and people inevitably had different agendas. I particularly remember Graham Taylor being a strong mover in wanting to form our own section and it was agreed at the Association's 1991 EGM that managers, coaches and physios would in future come under the

LMA banner. Taylor was made president at our initial meeting with Howard Wilkinson as chairman, John Camkin as chief executive and Olaf Dixon as secretary. I served on the committee alongside George Graham, Brian Little, John Lyall, Steve Coppell and Alex Ferguson.

Later that year, 71 managers attended our first conference in Birmingham and things rapidly moved on. We secured funding from Barclays Bank, ITV Sport and later The Premier League and the following year, formal discussions began with the FA regarding the primary aims of the LMA. These included registration of manager's contracts, the formation of a tribunal to settle disputes, a code of conduct enforceable through the tribunal, and training courses for future managers. To cut a long story short, it has since grown into a multi-million pound operation that offers outstanding support to managers young and old with an excellent programme of education and welfare schemes. Although Richard Bevan and his team keep coming up with new ideas, including the LMA Institute of Leadership and High Performance, that incorporates a Diploma in Football Management, it does seem to me that they now have every angle covered. Especially at the top level, the manager's role has changed out of all recognition. Top clubs now employ fitness experts, psychologists, masseurs, analysts and so on. The list is endless and someone has to manage them all, otherwise it will be chaos. Consequently, it's essential for modern managers to have a good knowledge of all aspects and the LMA provide a means to that.

I've been vice-chairman for much of the time since the LMA was founded and even had a spell as chief executive in the early days when I was at Orient. They paid me a pittance for my efforts – Orient also received a modest payment for my time – but I couldn't carry on with that when I got the Forest job. Steve Coppell succeeded me, then Gordon Milne and Jim Smith, before John Barnwell moved in to do an excellent job for many years. The package being offered to managers was growing all the time and I became a mentor on a course being offered through Warwick University. I really enjoyed that and it was easy to see the value that managers were getting from it.

The whole thing was such a far cry from my early days when I went to Sunderland as assistant-manager. I'd prepared for the challenge as best as I could, getting my Prelim Badge and attending coaching and management courses. I'd always had a thirst for knowledge and a desire to be the best I could but in those days, basically you had to learn on the job. I loved rubbing shoulders with legendary football figures on the courses. Most shared their knowledge quite happily and not only did I have a great time, I also made lots of good contacts. For example, it was on a coaching course that I met Ken Knighton for the first time and he got me into management at Sunderland.

My LMA role kept me very involved in the game. I represented them on various committees, like the NSPCC charity and Kick it Out Advisory Board, and I still work with the Football Association and Football League, sitting on their various tribunals that settle disciplinary and transfer disputes.

I also had a spell scouting for England during my 'interim' period, which was great. The job took me to matches at all levels and to various countries and I felt I was making a contribution. Scouting for England had tended to be done by friends of the manager and when Howard Wilkinson became the FA's Technical Director, he was astonished to discover there was no library of information about players and teams. He wanted a team of independent scouts, not a group that came and went every time the manager changed, and I thought there was obvious logic to that. Not everyone agreed. When Howard finished with the FA and Sir Trevor Brooking took over, he soon dispensed with our services. I remember going to a Forest reserves match and 'Cloughie' came across when he spotted me. "Hello Frank, how are you?" he said. "I hear you've lost your England job. That Brooking knows even less about football than you do!" I never managed to work out whether that was a compliment or not.

Even so life was comfortable and I was enjoying it. I wasn't missing 'sharp-end' management in the slightest and I certainly wasn't looking to become chairman of a club that was in real danger of going out of business. But I've never been very good at saying no when it involves something close to my heart. I spent the majority of Saturday afternoons watching the East Midlands clubs – Forest, Leicester, Derby and Notts County – and they all made me incredibly welcome. I remember very well the day I went to watch Forest – they were playing at home to Birmingham – and a mass demonstration had been organised that was mainly aimed at the chairman, Nigel Doughty. A large group of fans were chanting "Doughty Out" when I approached the City Ground and I wound down my car window and said: "You lads need to be careful what you wish for". That was in October 2011 and Forest were really struggling. They were awful that day. They were fourth from bottom in the Championship and if ever I saw a team destined for relegation, this was it. Steve McClaren fell on his sword. He immediately resigned and walked away after the game.

A couple of days later, I got a call from Doughty. He'd had enough of the abuse from supporters. He wanted to back away and asked me if I'd be prepared to return to Forest as a consultant. I was delighted. The timing was hardly ideal with the club in such turmoil but especially as it was Forest, I'd been waiting for that call for a long time. Before I'd had chance to take it forward he rang again and said there had been a change of plan. He wanted me to come back as Executive Chairman.

Nigel was a very private man, hugely successful in business. A venture capitalist, he was co-founder of the largest private equity firm in Europe. It made him extremely wealthy and much of that – just short of £100million – he pumped into Forest. It was an incredibly generous act from a man who was born just up the road in Newark and although the money was invested as a loan, he knew full well that he'd never get it back. He certainly didn't deserve all the 'stick' that frustrated fans were giving him and I thought I could do something to help. To start with, I didn't think his money had been invested wisely and I was sure I could have a good influence in that regard. The club were losing £1million a month which Nigel was covering. He was prepared to continue doing that but wanted to get right out of the firing line. He said I'd have executive powers to do anything I wanted as chairman. The one stipulation was that additional spending would have to stop. I wouldn't be able to bring people in unless we covered the costs by selling players.

We didn't make the best of starts to our new relationship because I almost got tangled up in an incredibly embarrassing situation. Knowing we urgently needed a new manager, and assuming making an appointment would be my responsibility, I interviewed a high profile candidate I knew very well and offered him the job. He turned me down. Just as well because it turned out the vacancy had already been filled. I got a call from chief executive Mark Arthur to go to his house on my second day as chairman and meet the new manager. It was Steve Cotterill, who had resigned as Portsmouth's boss and a significant compensation package had been agreed. With Doughty stepping back, Arthur and the finance director John Pelling were now running the club and the three of us clearly had to improve our communications and team ethic. The club was in trouble and it was crucial that we worked well together. We agreed it made sense that each of us should concentrate our main efforts on our respective areas of expertise.

I'm a big believer in transparency and hid nothing from Cotterill. I laid it on the line that there would be no money to spend on players unless we could do some trading and although he could bring in an assistant, he'd have to inherit McClaren's well-paid staff. Steve had a reputation for being difficult to handle but I knew he was a good coach. Judging by what I saw a few days later, he'd have every chance to prove his reputation was justified. He sat immediately behind me at Coventry as we produced a dreadful performance. It wouldn't have surprised me in the slightest if he'd suddenly leaned forward and said he'd changed his mind.

In the short-term there was very little we could do. We had to find a way to generate some cash to spend. When I was looking through the contracts I discovered that Wes Morgan would be free to leave at the end of the season. It was a crazy situation that he wasn't earning anywhere near as much as some of the other players. When I talked to Wes about a new deal he said it was too late. He'd apparently been trying to get an improved contract for two years without getting anywhere and had decided he would let his existing one run down and then leave on a free. I'm very reluctant to be critical of Nigel Doughty. Any man who commits £80million-plus of his own money to a project deserves the utmost respect but I couldn't understand the Forest policy of allowing contracts to run down.

The same situation applied with promising youngsters emerging from the Academy and although one in particular was creating a lot of interest, no one was banging my door down and saying we should tie him up on a professional deal. Patrick Bamford had scored four times in an 8-0 win over Wigan in the FA Youth Cup and I was going to be very interested to see how he performed when we were drawn against Southampton in the next round. They had a big reputation for producing their own players and on the night, they had a real swagger about them. But our lads won 4-2 – and Bamford scored the lot. We were not permitted to give him a new contract until he was 18 but we could set things in motion. I decided we had to do that as a matter of urgency but when I called his agent, I was told he was already being tracked by a number of Premier League clubs and there was no chance of us getting him on a new deal. I was furious. I said that if I got to hear that Bamford had been to one Premier League club, in breach of the regulations, I'd have them up in front the FA before he knew it.

I got a call soon afterwards from Chelsea. I told them we didn't want to sell but admitted we were desperate for cash so we might listen if the offer was good enough. They were willing to pay £500,000 up front with another £500,000 to follow. I turned them down. The next thing I knew, Bamford's agent was on the phone, asking if there had been any interest from Premier League clubs. That was a surprise! A week later, Chelsea offered £1million up front and knowing that the boy's father was adamant he would not sign for us, I had to take the offer seriously. We gave him permission to talk to Chelsea but I said don't sign for them until you talk to us again. He never did come back to me and it was easy to see why. We'd already made him the best offer Forest had ever made to an 18-year-old but the contract he got at Chelsea was amazing. Almost immediately, Leicester City inquired about signing Morgan in the January transfer window and were prepared to give us £1million up front. That was a great deal for us because he would have left for nothing at the end of the season.

It meant we had managed to generate £2million for Cotterill to spend on players. He brought in five on loan – Greg Cunningham from Manchester City, Adlene Guedioura from Wolves, Danny Higginbotham from Stoke, Scott Wootton from Manchester United and George Elokobi from Wolves – and they made all the difference. We eventually finished 19th. Steve was happy and we'd managed to set aside some of that transfer cash to strengthen the squad going forward.

By then, though, we'd been plunged into crisis. Nigel Doughty had collapsed and died in the February while running on the treadmill at home. He was only 54 and it was a massive shock to everyone who knew him. It also had major repercussions for Forest because as I soon discovered, it put us in very real danger of going out of business. I hadn't signed up for that. John Pelling had a system set up for receiving and using the £1million that Nigel pumped in at the start of each month to cover the running costs. As far as we were concerned, there was a firm commitment to continue doing that. It turned out, that wasn't the case. The people running Nigel Doughty's estate informed us that the monthly payments would cease. I was lost for words when I heard that. There was no way we could survive without their backing. How had I allowed myself to get into this situation? I could have settled for a quiet life and lived comfortably in my retirement. Instead, I was right in the firing line and I didn't have the answers. I genuinely feared my legacy was going to be that I was the man at the helm when Nottingham Forest went out of business.

We tried to avoid spelling out to supporters how critical the situation was because that wouldn't have been helpful. But there was a growing awareness that we had big problems.

The responsibility was four-square with me, Arthur and Pelling. Somehow, we had to find the answers. Inevitably, I suppose, it led to tensions between us. It was literally a case of surviving day by day but when the figures just don't stack up, that's not easy to do. Pelling was not only a brilliant finance director he was also the straightest man I've ever come across in football. He made it clear that there was no way he would be party to Forest trading fraudulently by spending money we didn't have. We were absolutely on a knife-edge and on several occasions it seemed the only options we had would be to liquidate the club or call in the administrators.

We had regular visits from the solicitor for the Doughty estate, who was charged with looking after their interests. He was key to the whole thing. Nigel's family had no interest in football and when you think about it in that context, why would they just keep giving money away with absolutely no return? They'd given their instructions that it had to stop and the onus was on us to prove we could turn things around. That wasn't going to happen overnight – if at all – and we needed them to continue supporting us while we sought a buyer for the club. If they did that, at least they could get some financial return. If they didn't, there was every chance they would get nothing.

Some of the sessions with the solicitor were 'heavy' to put it mildly, which was hardly surprising with so much at stake. Although there was a total block on spending, we always needed him to sign off certain things to give us a chance of moving forward. More than once, we felt as he set off back to London that we'd won the argument because we'd got permission to go ahead with some matter or other. By the time his train pulled into St Pancras, he'd changed his mind. It was incredibly frustrating and stressful. I stuck my neck out on one occasion because I didn't think there was any option. We had three promising young players coming towards the end of their time in the Academy – including Ben Osborn – and I defied orders by giving them two-year contracts. Had we not done that, what message would it have sent to the others? It would have undermined the whole purpose and structure of the Academy.

Despite what some may have thought, there wasn't exactly a queue of people wanting to buy the club. All we could do was strive to stay alive and hope someone would come forward eventually. And there was a much better chance of that happening if we were still in the Championship, rather than down in League 1. I had to do my best to protect Cotterill from all that was happening behind the scenes and keep him going. That wasn't always easy because he was a fiery character who liked his own way but in fairness, he did everything that could have been expected of him in the circumstances. It helped that he appointed Sean O'Driscoll as his assistant. Sean was a good coach but just as important, he was a calming influence on Steve. With three games to go we went to Reading for a night match knowing there was still a danger we could be relegated. We lost 1-0 but ended up celebrating. Pelling had an annoying habit of constantly studying his phone throughout the match but on this occasion, I didn't mind. He was able to tell us results elsewhere were just what we wanted and we were safe.

We couldn't carry on like this. It was imperative that the club was sold during the summer of 2012. Unless that happened, I didn't see any way that the dynasty Brian Clough had created could possibly survive. In July, a deal was completed with the Kuwait-based Al-Hasawi family. In my opinion, it wasn't the best for the club or the Doughty family but we were so desperate that it was almost a case of the first one to put their hand up gets it. I'd told Mark and John at the outset that I didn't want to be too active in the selling process. I felt they were better qualified to handle it than me. I'd leave it to them but as chairman, I needed to stay in the loop. In fairness, they brought the Al-Hasawi family to the table and made it happen. But when it came to the crunch I almost threw a proverbial spanner into the works.

Mark and John told me when we met to ratify the deal that I needed to resign before it could be completed. The last thing in the world I wanted to do was scupper it but I had a contract. I needed assurances it would be honoured before I would resign.

Anyway, they set off to London with the club's solicitor to get the papers signed and a few hours later, while I was sitting in a restaurant in West Bridgford, my mobile rang. Pelling said that the solicitor for the Al-Hasawi family wanted to speak to me. He said if they sent me an email guaranteeing they would honour my contract, would I resign as Executive Chairman? That was all I wanted. I understood that they were a family business and would want their own people running the show.

I was on a family holiday in the Algarve when the takeover was completed. That was unfortunate. By the time I got back, the new regime was already installed and some big decisions had been made. Between them they had very little knowledge of football and certainly knew nothing about the way things worked in this country. Although they might not have thought it, they needed some help and I was keen to provide it. When we met, they suggested they would much rather keep me involved than pay me up. I told them to make me Director of Football. One of their first acts had been to appoint O'Driscoll as manager and although he was an excellent coach, he wasn't a good communicator. There was no way he would be able to cope with the politics and I could have made a difference. They turned me down and said they just wanted me to be an ambassador. Later that day when I was talking on the phone to Billy Songhurst, my old Leyton Orient physio and a good friend, he could tell I was annoyed. "Listen Frank," he said. "You're nearly 70 years old and they want to pay you for turning up at matches. Why can't you be content with that?" He was right, of course, and maybe I was better off out of it because they were very difficult to deal with.

As ambassador, I went to all the matches, often with Mark Arthur and John Pelling, and that was fine. It's a lot easier to have amiable relationships when you aren't battling to stay alive. But they were still very much at the sharp end – initially at least. People were getting hired and fired at an unbelievable rate, especially during the period when Billy Davies returned as manager in February 2013. Long-serving members of staff like Academy director Nick Marshall, media manager Fraser Nicholson and operations manager Brandon Furse, who had all been incredibly loyal throughout the tough times, were shown the door. The list also included Arthur and Pelling – and me. During my spell as chairman, when we were having a bad time, the crowd often took to chanting: "We want our Billy back". That wasn't fair on Cotterill and I came out publicly to give him my full support. Whether that had an influence I've no idea but I was told I was no longer welcome at the City Ground. I got a letter telling me that I was on 'gardening leave'. It prompted an outcry from supporters, for which I was very grateful, and in fairness, the club were quick to settle up my contract.

I wasn't off the scene for too long before a got a call from Fawaz Al-Hasawi. He asked me to go and see him and when I did, he threw out an olive branch. He said they realised they had made a mistake and that they would welcome me back. Of course I was pleased but it was an incredibly difficult time for Forest. The family just didn't seem to have a clear idea about where they wanted to take the club and who they wanted involved. Not long after I was sacked, I'd had a call from one of their representatives who said he needed some help. He asked me to recommend a chief executive and the conversation hadn't gone too far before he was offering me the job. No chance. It had the potential to be the job from hell.

Fawaz took over from his cousin as chairman but the pattern was much the same – a merry-go-round of managers and no prospect of building a team to win promotion. Supporting Forest, as I did, had become a very frustrating business. There was no shortage of activity but everything just seemed to happen on a whim. A classic example was when I got a call from Fawaz asking me to meet him at his beautiful house in Mayfair. He said he wanted me to take over the complete running of the club. I could have any title I chose, I wouldn't have to go into the City Ground every day and I could run things any way I wanted. In the middle of that conversation, he took a call from Paul Taylor of the Nottingham Post, who said he was aware that an American consortium were interested in buying Forest and he'd be running the story the following day. That being the case, how could Fawaz possibly be asking me to take over the running of the club at such an uncertain time? He always had an answer to everything. "Not a problem," he said. He insisted he'd told the Americans all about me, and they were happy with the situation. Two days later, I called his bluff. I rang him to say let's move things forward. I have never spoken to him since.

People will all have their own opinions but I think back to that era as five wasted years for Forest. The only plus I can think of is the development of the Academy and I'll claim some credit for that because one of the best things I did during my time as chairman was to take Gary Brazil to the club. Nick Marshall was an excellent administrator but I felt the quality of coaching was not good enough. I knew all about Gary's work at that level with Fulham and the Premier League and with the new Elite Player Performance Plan being introduced across Academies, we needed to raise our game. Under Gary's guidance the Forest Academy became recognised as one of the best in the country and the rate at which good young players are being produced gives me real hope for the future. The Forest chairman, Nicholas Randall, has got me back involved as an ambassador, working with John McGovern, and I love it. Stability has been restored since ownership passed to Evangelos Marinakis in the summer of 2017 and I'm delighted to say that at long last, Forest feels like a proper football club again.

I live in hope that at some stage they might get somewhere close to repeating the feats we performed during the Clough era in the Seventies and Eighties – just as I do that Newcastle might once again get a taste for winning trophies and give their wonderful fans an opportunity to follow them around Europe. I was so privileged to be with those two great clubs during arguably the finest periods in their history. I've been involved in the game in one form or another for considerably more than 50 years and when I look back to the early days, that's all the more incredible. My career could have been over before it had hardly begun when I broke my leg as a teenager, playing at Liverpool. And to think that for years before that, I kept rejecting the approaches of clubs because I wasn't convinced I wanted to be a professional footballer. I do have regrets – just a few – but overall I achieved all I could have asked for and more. I think of myself as a staggeringly lucky man. I just kept falling into teams that won things.

Black & White And Red All Over

THE KIND PEOPLE WHO HAVE SUPPORTED THIS BOOK

Ian Richardson – Leyton Orient
Luke Dougherty – London
Elliott Stanley – Nottingham
Peter Cope
Alexander Williams – London
Sean Williams – London
Glyn Williams – London
Adrian Hallam
Lesley Hutchinson
Jason Cliff – Grantham
Martin Auckland – Nottingham
Bill Bruce – Wallsend
Jared Robinson – Liverpool
Robbo – Newcastle upon Tyne
Darren Reeve – Newcastle upon Tyne
Colin Driscoll – Forest Hall
David Singleton
Roger Bell – Ryton, Gateshead
Tom Crawford – Wallsend
Paul Ned Tinning – Newcastle upon Tyne
John Phelan – Howden-Le-Wear, Crook

Kevin Bramley
Rob Severn – Quorn
Stan Mitchell – Nottingham
David Barnett – Griston
David Willans – Nottingham
David Marples
Ernest Mills – Stanley, Co Durham
David Mills – Stanley, Co Durham
Colin Macmillan
Andrew Macmillan
David Bunce – Rowlands Gill
Ian Copping – Nottingham
Ian Russell
Ron Brunton – Maidenhead
Graham Telfer – Newcastle upon Tyne
Alan Golightly – Newcastle upon Tyne
Paul Durham – King's Lynn
Barry Errington
Steve Wright – Southwell
Keith Belton – Witton Park
John Payne – Croydon
Stuart Clarkson – Nottingham
Ian R Scott – Newark
George Akins – Nottingham
Nigel Langrick
Dennis Varley – Crook Town
Brian Harvey
Stuart Parkinson
John Bridges – Nottingham
Eddie Smeaton – Newcastle upon Tyne
Peter Charles – London
Lisa Fox – Nottingham
Michael Day
Graham Coleman – Spalding

David Pallister
Peter (Jingo) Jane – Crook, Co Durham
Carl Aldred
David McCrory – Blackhill, Consett
Mark Wood – Gloucester
Rob Shelton – Nottingham
Andy Fosterjohn
Steve J Cunningham
John Truman – Mansfield
Alan Williams – Nottingham
David Shaw – Long Eaton
Robert Gibson – Crook
Lee – Crook
Tony Pearce – Nottingham
Steve Wright – Eastwood
Stan Nelson – Westwood, Nottingham
David Wilson – Nottingham
Mike Maciborskyj – Nottingham
Ivor Gibbs – Burton on Trent
Wilf Dobinson – Crook
Anthony Beecroft – Nottingham
Steven Paul Williams – Nottingham
Fitty
Duncan Neil – Newark
Scott Summerlin – Sandiacre
Andrew – Newcastle upon Tyne
Andy Page – Nottingham
Steve Codling – Birmingham
Paul Rennie
Richard Robinson – Bilsthorpe
Richard Beal – Nottingham
Stuart Beal – Nottingham
Mickey Prica
Neil Masterson

@ForestFanBase – Nottingham
John Parkin – Chicago, IL
John Sheffield
Michael Lane – Derbyshire
Ian Broadley – Newark
Gary Brooks – Nottingham Forest
Reg Parker – Nottingham
Martyn David Stephens – Newcastle upon Tyne
Martyn David Stephens – Newcastle upon Tyne
Nick Herrod – Nottingham/London
Michael Andrew – Newark
Graham Daft – Hucknall
Matt Celentano – born Leyton, now Zurich
Simon Kassell – Underwood
Carl Enever – Nottingham
Roy Clifford – Highams Park
Robert Iain Phillips – Reading
Richard Baggley
Graham Harris – Barnsley
Steve Corry – Nottingham
Nick Crosby – Nottingham
Gary Moore – Goole
Rupert Harker – Nottingham
John Booth – Peacehaven
Scott Ulke – Nottingham
Dean Christopher – Lincoln
Ray Burge – Uttoxeter
Michael Vardy – Teversal
John Douglas – Newcastle upon Tyne
David Low – Beaconsfield
Philip Hardy – Nottingham
Kjetil Hågenvik – Norway
Árni Freyr Helgason – Iceland